Manifesting Miracles 101

The Art of Being in The Flow

Amirah Hall
www.amirahall.com

Printed in USA

ISBN: 978-0-9975552-2-6

Table of Contents

Foreword

Come out of hiding. Basking in the light is the safest place to be ... it just is!"

This book has been in process since my near-death experience (NDE) while traveling in Egypt in 1998. Although I've been on my own spiritual journey now for over thirty-five years, like many other people, I have been seeking answers to and the fulfillment of questions 'what is my purpose?' and 'why am I here?' I am on a journey of developing a deeper understanding of what this life is all about and how I can change the outcome of what it is that I desire.

Prior to my NDE, I had what I thought was a relatively successful sales and marketing career in the design and computer industries, living in Southern California, I felt I had the world by the tail. My career was soaring then suddenly my world was undeniably shaken to the core.

After my spiritually transformative experience, I couldn't get a *'normal job'* to save my soul. After much struggle, anger and emotional pain, I surrendered to the fact that *'my energy was STUCK and I now perceived the world quite different than before'*. I soon discovered my **extra-ordinary ability** to **see beyond the third dimensional reality** and access quantum fields of energy for healing and transformation.

Truths I learned first hand in my Near-Death Experience:

1. **Everything is Energy**. I was invited on a guided journey of the ALL but my guide informed me I could not stay in that beautiful place and I would have to return to my human body on Earth.

2. **The Fabric of All Creation Is LOVE.** *Remember:* **You are LOVE!**

3. **Stuck Energy Creates Dys-Ease.** Our human emotions get stuck in our energy fields and create **dys**-function, **dys**-ease and death—*that is death of good health, harmony, fulfillment, clarity, purpose, spiritual guidance, finances, careers and relationships*.

4. **I Am Wholly Responsible For Everything I Manifest.** Thoughts, feelings and expressions create our experiences and I am responsible for the outcomes.

5. **Regular Meditation Builds A Healthy Body, Mind, Spirit.** Balance and harmony of the Body, Mind and Spirit are keys to well-being.

Having experienced first-hand something that had not been even labeled yet, Quantum Physics, I withdrew from the world not knowing what to do with my newly discovered information as I learned over time to apply exactly what I share with you in this book.

In spite of this phenomenal experience, after my NDE, my life was suddenly a whole different story. With every passing day, ordinary living became harder and more painful for me. Desperately trying to connect with my heart and what was important to me -- I only came up empty handed. All of a sudden I had no idea what would make me happy, never mind what I was passionate about.

With no clue as to where I should turn or what I should do, I stopped everything!

Actually, I was forced to. Feeling wedged between a rock and a hard place, I desperately tried to understand what was happening to me. I had no idea that an inner and outer transformation was occurring. I strained, digging deep, trying to connect with what was beyond my comprehension at that time.

Besides having an out-of-this-world (literally) experience I couldn't function in the work-a-day-world anymore. With all of what was happening, I shut out my friends, family, my hobbies and anything remotely meaningful. Then, I was terminated from my job. I was mad as hell at God and anyone who would listen. Frustration, depression and anger oozed out of me. Let's just say I was *'miserable to the core'*!

I paced the floors, pounded pillows, sobbed and meditated. All the while, I was feeling myself falling apart at the seams.

How was it possible to connect with the Divine, yet feel so dislodged from living? My life felt so JAMMED UP, it was as if nothing was working for me. *How can that be?* This can't be right! *Wouldn't you normally assume that after 'seeing the light,' things would automatically flow in a magical way?*

Nonetheless, my life basically sucked! Stuck and suffering for over a year, things didn't start coming together until I discovered how to get into sync with my life force energy within. For me this was THE KEY to changing everything for me.

Returning to my everyday reality after my NDE and trying to integrate what is normally obscure to most humans, my big '**ah-ha** moment' was discovering the root of my problem was that I '**had stuck energy**' made a lot of sense to me.

The next big question was, "**great ... how can I get it un-stuck?**"

The fundamental process of getting '**un-stuck**' is '**clearing the chakras**'. Your chakra system is like your spiritual software and clearing them is like re-booting your computer. This resets your process of '**being in the flow**' and **manifesting**'.

From this point forward however, exploring my spiritual anatomy, also known as the chakra system, my spiritual understanding took on a whole new meaning that continues to change my life on a daily basis. Years before traveling to Egypt, I read the book named The Lost Teachings of Jesus, by Elizabeth Clare Prophet and began wondering if what Jesus of demonstrated, was some of what I began to study, understand and realize about balancing the energy centers and applying the laws of Universe to manifest miracles.

My completely new perspective on life shifted as my clairvoyance (clear seeing), clairaudience (clear hearing), claircognizance (clear knowing) and clairsentience (clear feeling) turned up like a blaring loud speaker. Everyday living was now a sensory overload as I could hear, see and know much more than I could handle at the time.

Honestly, I desperately wanted to shut it all off but didn't know how or what was happening. In time, I learned to adjust the volume so to speak with chakra clearing and balancing. Discovering I had '**stuck**' energy was actually a relief because now I could proceed to '**un-stuck**' myself.

Embarking on a '**chakra clearing journey**' was validated by H. Spencer Lewis in his book, The Mystical Life of Jesus, where he shares that the ancient Priesthood of the Essenes, which Jesus the Nazarene Essene had studied in Egypt, and of which he was a High Priest, featured practices of spiritual purification using energy centers located at seven points along the spinal column. These energy points are popularly known in other traditions as the '**seven chakras**'.

In all spiritual traditions, the purpose of all forms of energy work with the chakras is always to '**clear or cleanse**' them, by '**removing**' clouds or blocks of '**negative energy**', often referred to in early Christianity as '**demons**'. Naturally, the only way to become a High Priest(ess) was necessarily to cleanse one's seven chakras, casting out all negative energies, removing all blocks, to ensure that the Holy Spirit would flow strongly through the Priest(ess).

Additional supporting evidence about the importance of a fully functional chakra system comes from the fact the Apostles had knowledge from the Essenes of how to '***cleanse***' the '***seven chakras***', is found in a prayer which is featured in the Gnostic <u>Acts of Thomas</u>,

> *Come, thou holy name of Christ... Come, compassionate Mother. Come, she that revealeth the hidden mysteries. Come, Mother of the seven houses, that thy rest may be in the seventh house. ... Come, Holy Spirit, and cleanse their reins and their heart, and give them the added seal."*

This invocation proves historical record of an Apostolic practice, specifically to '***cleanse***' the '***seven houses***' to give an '***added seal***' of connection to the Holy Spirit. High Priest(ess) were purified and spiritually elevated by '***casting out seven demons***' from their chakras.

This Gnostic teaching of the Essenes, known and used by Jesus and the Apostles, is also described in Old Testament canonical scripture:

> *Wisdom hath builded her house, she hath hewn [carved] out her seven pillars."*

Proverbs 9:1

The Gnostic scripture ***<u>Pistis Sophia</u>***, features Mary Magdalene teaching the principles of '***cosmic***' spiritual ascent of the soul, through prayerful work with '***seven spheres***' of energy.

It's my '***soul-intention***' to share with you what I feel are '***Jesus sanctified***' practices that enables and propels you into alignment with the Laws of The Universe to Manifest Miracles and discover the grace of '***being in the flow***'.

> *Truly, truly, I say to you, whoever believes in me will also do the works that I do; and greater works than these will he do..."*

John 14:12-14

I believe we are here to create, and engaging the dynamic universal laws of attraction, oneness and detachment, we create miracles. **The** great spiritual masters such as Jesus, Buddha and Lao Tzu did not practice religion, **they mastered themselves in solitude by looking within and meditating**, and as a result they discovered that they were infinite and connected with the universal consciousness. Only later did humanity call this consciousness God. Their core teachings state that we are all spiritual beings, and that we are equal to god, and by practicing such things as forgiveness, kindness, honesty, and introspection we can become the Gods that we already are and create a peaceful heaven here on Earth.

If you are reading this, you are most probably feeling the many shifts and changes occurring around you. You might not know exactly what to do or how to do it, but one thing for sure is that you know you need guidance if you desire lasting transformation.

Instinctively you are adjusting to powerful, accelerating frequencies entering the earth plane that are transforming the world around us. You are being nudged to '**awaken**' and '**ascend**' limiting beliefs and outmoded ideas.

Are you experiencing growing frustration, fear, uncertainty, confusion, depression, un-grounded and physical pain?

You are not alone...!!!

You can change this experience to a live a life you love, being in the flow and Manifesting Miracles. In time, I surrendered more and more to the fact that '**I was different now**' and began to allow my newly discovered **extraordinary abilities of 'seeing and accessing'** what science has now defined as **quantum fields of energy** for healing and transformation. In all honesty, for the longest time I had no clue what I was doing or how the healing occurred. Now, I just accept my abilities along with whatever happens because most of the time '**it makes NO logical sense whatsoever**'.

The truths I learned from my NDE are the foundation of not only what I teach but what I continually strive to understand. I practice these core principles everyday and over the years I have taught thousands of people the **Quantum Energy Tools** (http://bit.ly/29WqnQk) and exercises that have indisputably transformed their lives. It's without question that these techniques work; it's only your willingness to participate that is required. Learning to trust what might not make sense to you in the 3D world, shifting your focus and moving energy is the functional core of creation and manifesting.

Actually, I was inspired to write this book through teaching my **Miracle Mastery Mentoring** program (http://bit.ly/2aitwiO). For this, I want to extend my deepest gratitude to all of my current and former students who have forged their way in mastering their skills of manifesting miracles. In working with them, I have refined and reshaped the practices, format and structure of my program into this book in an effort to reach everyone who wishes to live a fuller and more vibrant life.

Not long ago, I realized there were many people who wanted to work with me but for whatever reason weren't able to access my program. With the wildly successful books such as **_The Secret_**, many people are opening up to the **_Law of Attraction_** and the awareness that their thoughts create. When **_The Secret_** was released, I remember being livid because innately I knew there was so much more to the idea and felt that people were being short changed, bamboozled by one massive marketing campaign.

My intuition and manifesting experiences up to that point, was confirmed by the book Mystic Wisdom of the Masters – The Esoteric Knowledge of Great Adepts. The Supreme Egyptian Adept, Kalika-Khenmetaten, explains there are ten factors that directly impact the potential for specific visualizations and affirmations to produce results.

10 Factors that Directly Impact Manifestation Results

1) The degree one recognizes that Universal Laws consistently creates their personal reality and the collective shared reality of the world based on the contents of consciousness (beliefs, thoughts, images);

2) Underlying core beliefs, conscious or subconscious;

3) Controlling thoughts and inner images;

4) Degree of will power;

5) Opening a space in your life, in a physical and psychological sense, to allow the desired result to flow into your life experience)

6) Available energy;

7) Certainty that the desired result will manifest;

8) Clarity of thought (visualization, affirmations);

9) Consistency of thought (visualization, affirmations);

10) Detachment from result.

The first three factors are foundational requirements and without them the potential of visualizations to manifest are restricted. The fourth factor contains your central intent and if it's half-hearted or unclear, visualizations will most likely fail. The fifth factor means that you must be open to opportunities for what you desire to come into your life. The five remaining factors involve preparation and technique.

But whatever the case may be with The Secret's amazing success, the truth is _**'collectively, humans are consciously and progressively waking up'**_.

The Secret was instrumental in unlocking the proverbial vault of Universal Laws previously hidden from the masses.

Our world is making massive changes around us and our lives are reshaping before our eyes yet so many people are still suffering. Instinctively, we are adjusting to new energy frequencies entering the earth but it's most common that we don't know what's happening, how to handle it, what to do with it or how to move past it.

<u>**Manifesting Miracles 101**</u> and <u>**Miracle Mastery Mentoring**</u> (http://bit. ly/2aitwiO) **give you the guidance and tools to impact your manifestation results in the biggest way.** Now, the time is right and I was inspired to share some of the foundational information and practices of my program in a book so that many more people could be guided in knowledge and exercises that REALLY work. I say this because there's a lot of marketing hype over '***know yourself, trust yourself, love yourself***' and yet the GENUINE '***how to's***' are left obscure.

I believe we are here to create, and by engaging the dynamic universal laws of attraction, oneness and detachment, we can create miracles.

> *If you are experiencing growing frustration, fear, uncertainty, confusion, depression, un-grounded and physical pain, you are not alone....*

After 16 years, I can finally say, I have the awareness, understanding and experience to guide you along your journey using transformative energy practices and exercises that will ignite your passion for living while creating miracles along the way.

I've '***been there, done that***'. I know what it's like to be down-in-the-dumps and what it takes to rise like a phoenix, living my passion and manifesting everything I desire.

> *"Miracles don't happen. You make them happen. They're not wishes or dreams or candles on a cake. They're not impossible. Reality is real. It's totally and completely under my control."*
>
> Julie Anne Peters.

Schedule Your Complimentary Energy Assessment Consultation
http://bit.ly/2ais7ZQ

Acknowledgments

You know how it is. You pick up a book, flip to the dedication, and find that, once again, the author has dedicated a book to someone else and not to you. Not this time.

Because we haven't yet met, have only a glancing acquaintance, are just crazy about each other, haven't seen each other in much too long, are in some way related, will never meet, but will, I trust, despite that, always think fondly of each other!

And, this one's for you!

To all of you who are ready to manifest life changes, in the hope that you may experience the delights of quantum adventures, I'm especially grateful that you picked up this book.

Special Thanks

I would like to express my gratitude to the many **Miracle Mastery Mentoring** students and clients who through their own personal work and journey, this book was inspired.

To my talented editor, Reiny, thank you for your diligence, professionalism and creative infusion; helping me in this book writing process. A special thank you to Eric Ross, Francoise Rapp and Jairam Ransom, author of It All Abides In Love (*http://amzn.to/29NoSZL*), for your support, talking things over, offering comments and the many hours of painstaking proofreading.

I am ever touched by your love and support.

The Introduction

My most crucial 'ah-ha moment' in manifesting what I desire came from learning and understanding that my passion, the fire hose of life force energy, would never come from outside action. I needed to be unleashed from within.

When the invaluable flow of life force energy of the chakras is blocked or stuck, life becomes stagnant and you feel mediocre, flat and empty. I want to help you change that.

I am committed to showing you how to stand fully in your unique creative power.

 I am realistic – I expect miracles."

Wayne W. Dyer

<u>**Manifesting Miracles 101**</u>, gives you practical, effortless and proven ways to experience healing and success as you create the life that you want. Regardless of whether you have failed a thousand times, you will feel more empowered as you reach to your fullest potential. The truth is that the discovery of the hidden secrets of '***energy mastery***' is the only lasting solution. Regardless of what you do as a living, you can apply techniques to improve all areas of your life.

In the chapters that follow, you will learn the '***exact formula and structure***' that I not only used but also taught others for over <u>sixteen years</u> (at the time of this writing), in my <u>Miracle Mastery Mentoring</u> program (http://bit.ly/2aitwi0) to …

• Materialize your dreams.

• Discover the secrets of opening your heart beyond anything you have imagined.

• Find out how to increase your love and appreciation for every aspect of life.

• Receive profound insights on how to create more fulfilling and caring relationships.

• Reawaken your birthright as a true genius.

• Ignite and resurrect your natural spiritual abilities.

• Transcend any fears and illusions surrounding the myth of death.

- And, reconnect with your true mission and purpose for life on Earth.... To be moved, challenged, and changed!

After doing much unusual and non-traditional exploratory work on my chakra system, my life blossomed. My force field began to shine like I never felt before. People began noticing me in <u>big ways</u>. Back then I would have never believed how strong my healing and manifesting abilities would become.

Based on the foundational teachings of my one-year program this book includes:

- 22 chapters of step-by-step guided training.

- Weekly exercise and practices to ensure you integrate and assimilate the changes and information at the physical, mental, emotional and spiritual levels.

- Content exclusive to the <u>Miracle Mastery Mentoring</u> program (http://bit.ly/2aitwiO).

- Unique stories, insights and information compiled from various sources and years of first-hand experience.

Realizing this information was extracted from my **Miracle Mastery Mentoring** program (http://bit.ly/2aitwiO), please consider that you are on a journey of discovering a hidden treasure within. ***It's not meant to happen overnight— nor will it.***

On any journey, starting first with a map, you then proceed to the route. Along the way, you might stop for a snack and fill up with gas. Then, you might rest or rent a hotel room for the night. So it is with this work.

> *Don't expect to eat the whole buffet in one bite.*
> *Starving to death and then shoveling down a whole plate of food in a frenzy only gives you indigestion and gas.*

Reading a chapter a week and practicing according to the recommended guidelines at the end of each chapter is a healthy pace to follow by giving yourself time between reading each chapter, you give the body a chance to adjust to the energy shifts you are instigating.

I know you're in A VERY BIG HURRY to MANIFEST some very important stuff, but pacing yourself will ultimately be the wisest decision. It makes me think of the song, ***You Can't Hurry Love.***

You can't hurry love. You just have to wait. Just trust in a good time. No matter how long it takes... You can't hurry love."

The Supremes

Doing more doesn't get there faster. In fact, keeping pace and staying with it definitely will make all the difference to what and when you manifest. Just follow along. Do the practices to the best of your ability then LET GO. Let go of '**willing it**' to go forward or faster. Remember that to successfully crawl, walk and then run, you must allow yourself to grow, learn and adjust between each stage.

Your natural process of manifestation is unique to you and how that is realized is exclusive to you. But, what I can promise you is that before long your manifesting magic will sneak up on you when you least expect it. I encourage you to have fun with it and be amused with what you notice in your life that begins to look '**different**'.

"There are only two ways to live your life. One is as though nothing is a miracle. The other is as though everything is a miracle."

Albert Einstein.

Congratulations on choosing to begin this most amazing journey of
<u>Manifesting Miracles 101- The Art of Being In The Flow.</u>

Chapter

(1)

Searching For Abundance

This world has conditioned most of us to view everyday activities in a dim and flickering light. Instead of focusing on everything we are blessed to have, it's easy to focus on the things we don't have. It's easy to view menial tasks as obligations instead of daily blessings we constantly take for granted.

> *Are you 'unhappy' with everything that life has been dishing out?*

You have the choice to do something different with your life and make some quantum changes. Because you chose to be here, it means that you are READY for a quantum leap in creating the abundant, miraculous and magical life you want.

Searching For Abundance

Manifesting Miracles 101: The Art of Being in The Flow is all about connecting with your deepest desires and becoming a fuller, more vibrant expression of yourself. I'm your guide, and I'm here to help you manifest everything in your heart.

Much like you, I wanted success and to live a life filled with passion! In search of abundance, I discovered the world of metaphysics. Studying this field taught me that success and wealth are not limited to money, but that they meant abundance in all things-- friends, support, confidence, resources, information, solutions, adventure, freedom, opportunities, ideas, joy, harmony and YES, money too.

The path took me on a journey, winding through pockets of abundance and success as I learned more about the Universal Principles. It wasn't until my Near Death Experience (NDE) while traveling in Egypt that I began to understand what scientists refer to as Quantum Energy. Ever since then, I have been continually learning and practicing the energy principles that are creating my life.

Thoughts Create

What I understood from my NDE is that all my thoughts (conscious and unconscious) and emotions in my life had unconsciously been creating the path for my life. Beyond that, I realized that I was an infinite being of light. I absolutely knew from that point on, that I have had many past lives and will have many more lives in the future. Life is infinite.

Prior to my NDE, I learned and was consciously applying principles of many of the Laws of the Universe, but I wasn't aware of what I '*wasn't aware of'*. It's as if I was an iceberg and the only part of me that I knew existed was the 10% floating above the water. The was rest of me submerged. Hidden, but real nonetheless.

Although I couldn't see it or feel it, energies were creating for me things I wanted and things I didn't want. Since my near-death experience, I've been learning more and more about that submerged part of me and the rest of the Universe.

Everything is Energy

What I also learned in my NDE was that 'everything is energy'. Energy is moving and creating all the time, whether you are aware of it or not. Back in 1998, prior to any access to what science now tells us about quantum energy, there were no words for me to define what I then learned, but the experience has branded in my mind the foundational lesson in energetic attraction.

The science of Quantum Physics now shows us that everything is energy. At the most basic level, you are energy. In order for things to change in your life, you have to change your energy. In changing the way your energy flows and operates, you create something different.

Since '*everything is energy'* you will begin changing how you attract, what you attract and when you attract. Everything that you manifest will then appear different as you change and shift from the inside out.

> *Everything is energy and that's all there is to it. Match the frequency of the reality you want and you cannot help but get that reality. It can be no other way. This is not philosophy. This is physics."*

Darryl Anka

Amirah Hall

That's what's so exciting about being here right now. You are beginning to break through unconscious beliefs, ideas and energies that are holding you captive. Changing your vibration will change what you attract and manifest in your life. Breaking out of that 5-sense *'perception prison-cell'* frees you from limiting and restricting vibes, aligning you with your natural intuitive and self-healing abilities.

Colors Have Different Frequencies

If you're like most people, you're dependent on a belief system that relies on your own five senses (see, hear, smell, touch, or taste). But there's so much more to life than this.

With your eyes, you see different colors. In high school science, we learned that different colors are light with different 'wave lengths' or 'frequencies'. For instance, green light has a different frequency than red light or yellow light. Your eyes pick up these different wavelengths and your brain interprets them into a 'picture or image' containing different colors of light. That's how you see.

Sounds Have Different Frequencies

The same is true with different sounds; they have different frequencies. Your ears pick up the frequencies, and your brain decodes them into sounds. That's how you hear, touch, smell and taste. Overall, things just aren't what they appear to be. In fact, what appears solid -- isn't! In fact, your reality may not be as solid as you think.

Mainstream science estimates that only 4% of the energy in the universe is visible to humans. Without exaggeration, we could literally be an infinite number of frequencies beyond our awareness that exist. Now, that's overwhelming to comprehend! Your eyes cannot see infrared or ultraviolet light yet everyone knows that they exist. Your ears cannot hear 'ultrasound' yet everyone knows it exists. Dogs, bats, deer and elephants hear ultrasounds. It's there—it exists!

We Live in a Vast and Infinite Universe

 Limitless undying love which shines around me like a million suns it calls me on and on across the universe."

John Lennon

The more you realize that there's more to life than what you can see, hear, touch, taste and smell with your five senses, the more you realize the immense possibilities that are available.

- Imagine how your life would be if you interacted with the other 96% of 'invisible' energy.

- What could you achieve?

- How would you feel?

- Are you beginning to realize how your perception through only your five senses can limit you?

- Can you see that you can achieve so much more?

Imagine that you have a master key opening your 5-sense ***perception prison*** unleashing the power hidden within.

Creating Goals You Desire

In Manifesting Miracles 101, our ultimate mission is to create the goals you desire. For YOU (your body, mind emotions and spirit) to come into alignment. When those four parts of you are expanded and the parts of you beyond your physical conscious awareness come together – that's when the magic occurs. That's when our natural profound magical abilities emerge and we begin creating miracles in our life.

I truly believe that when you start to realize you can have anything you want when you are in alignment with YOU and the flow of the Universe – that's where we create miracles.

There's so much more available for you than you even realize at this moment. And, that's what I'm here to do—to help you experience all that you ARE by revealing the hidden 90% of your iceberg.

On your journey with me through Manifesting Miracles 101, you will be guided through a series of practices, quantum energy clearings and exercises that bring you more into alignment with the core essence of who you truly are. I promise you, it will be beyond anything you could imagine today. Your changes will astound you.

I have worked with thousands of clients just like you over the past two decades, they surpassed their goals and I guarantee you will too. Before you know it, you will be achieving goals that weren't on your list and dreams bigger than you imagined. I promise!

Going Beyond Your 5-Senses into a New Life

Since extra-sensory perception (ESP) is awareness of the world beyond the senses, it would be inappropriate to term this Sixth Sense 'extrasensory'."

Stephen Richards

In working with Manifesting Miracles 101, clients' lives change dramatically in just a few months because they begin working with universal principles and vibrations that are always working. These are the divine natural laws of the universe. When you start working with them <u>CORRECTLY</u>, everything else in your life starts working correctly too. Whether you are aware of them or not, they affect everyone, everywhere, always.

It's just like the Law of Gravity. You are not aware that gravity is always working. Likewise there are other forces of nature working including the Law of Attraction, Law of Compensation, Law of Reciprocation and others that are always working whether you are aware of them or not.

"What we call luck is the inner man externalized. We make things happen to us."

Robertson Davies

There's No Such Thing As Bad Luck

There's no such thing as BAD LUCK! It's just becoming aware of these Laws and how they are working in your life. Once you get into the flow of things, all the Laws begin supporting you.

When life is filled with adversity, accidents or is seemingly out of control, you need only to become aware of how to connect with the universal principles to create something different altogether. And here's why...

These principles are predictable and controllable. You just have to know about them and apply them to create what you want. It's that simple.

When you want light – you just turn on the switch. You don't have to know about the principle of electricity—you know it's there, you turn on the switch and you have light. When you want the light off, you just turn off the switch.

You cannot see infrared and ultraviolet light but that doesn't mean it doesn't exist. It's the same with these principles. Knowing how to use them, you can put them to work to navigate your life's path. And you can do it starting today!

These hidden Laws affect your entire life. They determine what happens or doesn't happen to you. What you get or don't get. They determine every person or situation you 'attract' into your life!

Universal Laws are Infinite and Always Exist

A big part of <u>Manifesting Miracles 101</u> is based upon you becoming aware of these hidden principles. Then you can start '*pulling the strings in your life*'.

You are the one who dictates and interacts with these Universal Laws and decides what it brings you. First you need to clearly state what you want then just '***allow***' your desires to come to you. It's when you are '***in the flow***' of these Universal Principles and take action when needed that your life becomes magical.

The reason that your life might appear off track or feel like you're on a losing streak and/or 'unlucky' is one of three reasons:

1. **You're not aware of the Universal Laws working and directing your life.**

2. **You're NOT aware of one or more of these Universal Laws, and you focus on just one of them, while consciously or unconsciously ignoring the importance of others.**

   For example, many people focus merely on the Law of Attraction, while there are extremely important other principles to be taken into account if you want to make things work for you! In other words, you have to let go of things or focus on releasing what you have completed. Unless you are willing to release, you cannot attract other things to you.

3. **You're working with one or more of these Universal Laws incorrectly.**

   Maybe you did know about these Universal Laws. Maybe you know just one or only some of them. But in spite of being aware of them, you still haven't been able to create and manifest the results you want in life.

If that describes you, let me tell you what that means:

Knowing about one or some of the Universal Laws isn't enough. You must know exactly about how to apply these Universal Laws, and how to apply them in conjunction with each other!

You'll be happy to know that the universal law that created miracles hasn't been repealed."

Dr. Wayne Dyer

Not knowing about these laws and the correct ways of applying them can cause some serious disruptions in your life. Instead of living your life on purpose, you seem to be running around at random, without a clear direction, and without any conscious control over whatever the heck is happening.

In Manifesting Miracles 101, you will learn about powerful information that allows you to create whatever you want – at will! Imagine having a Universal free pass that sets you free from struggle and allow you to create the life you have always dreamed of.

Although the Universal Laws have always been present, never before in history has timing been more ideal for you to reclaim your power that has always been deep within you. By becoming more aware of the Universal Laws and consciously applying them, you can create a life of happiness and joy.

Applying them correctly, you create success. You create joy and fulfillment and abundance – guaranteed.

I often hear my clients say,

 How did that happen? It IS really a miracle!!!"

Every area of your life will transform including your career, business, family life, personal relationships, finances and your health! Every aspect of your life is affected by energy you emit, the energy that's flowing (or not) and it's constant motion.

 There is only one true love affair; the one with yourself. All others are expressions of it."

Hemal Radia

You can delve into the Universal Laws or you can correctly apply them in simple, practical and straightforward ways. There's so much more than The Law of Attraction. Attempting to understand the interplay of the multiple universal principles at work can become increasingly complex and difficult to completely understand.

From my experience on this path, you need to completely grasp the '**big picture**' to ensure success

Are You Ready For Success?

Embracing the hidden laws of the universe is the first step. Being part of the Manifesting Miracles 101, you receive exact information and a process that guides you in making the changes you desire almost effortlessly.

Basic But Powerful

In this chapter, we discuss several basic tools that are most important on the journey together. I can't reiterate enough, how important and powerful these basic tools are. You will use them over and over and although they are rather simplistic, their power will astound you.

Creating Undisturbed Space To Practice

In doing this work, you want to create a space where you can practice undisturbed. Unplug your phones. Hang a DO NOT DISTURB sign on your door. Or listen quietly inside your car if you don't have space at home or work.

You might want to light a candle or incense to set the mood and create this sanctuary space for yourself. Although, that's not necessary, I do encourage you to have a notebook beside you where you can jot down some notes, questions or reminders.

Set A Convenient Time For Your Schedule

Try and establish a set time of day that you can do your practice. The body has memory and will remember the energy you set for your process.

Other than that – there are no rules! Do your best to practice the **Quantum Energy Tools** (http://bit.ly/29WqnQk) at the best of your ability and give yourself validation for doing just that.

What's most important in taking your first step, is that you make the body feel safe and comfortable. Sitting straight in a chair with your feet flat on the floor helps the body and mind stay alert to the practice. There's no question if you lay down – you <u>will</u> fall asleep!

Therefore make every effort to always practice sitting upright.

Practicing Quantum Energy Tools

Using the Quantum Energy Tools (Also: See Resources Page) on a daily basis is the basic foundation for clearing and resetting your energy for manifesting miracles. These tools are as powerful whether they are practiced individually or in sequence. One thing I can't emphasize enough is, '*the more you practice, the bigger the benefit*'.

Begin your regular practice with these basic **Quantum Energy Tools** (http://bit.ly/29WqnQk) for clearing, releasing and revitalizing yourself.

Begin by sitting upright in a chair, with your feet on the floor. With your eyes closed, notice what you notice. Bringing your awareness to the body, what do you notice?

Just imagine you are aware of the space, your bubble around you and begin tucking your energetic space in around your body approximately 3 feet around you.

Grounding Quantum Energy Tool #1
Guided Meditation
(http://bit.ly/23CIjde)

In order to take your steps, your body wants to feel safe. The body wants to know that whatever changes you're making, it's not going to fall apart. It's been holding on to all the information you have accumulated to this point.

Grounding yourself and bringing your awareness to your body is the first step. Since 'grounding' is a new tool to you, you might set an alarm or reminder for yourself to check throughout the day and see if you have a grounding cord.

To practice grounding, visualize a laser beam, tree trunk or cable connecting the body to the center of the earth. You may have grounded yourself in the past by going into nature, eating or exercising. In making the body feel safe, you can easily let the busy-ness of the day fall away down your grounding cord.

Attach a grounding cord to the base of your spine and hook it securely to the center of the planet.

> *What does your grounding cord look like today? .... waterfall, a train track, tree trunk, laser beam or a super slide? Allow yourself to play with the imagery.*

Give yourself permission to widen the grounding to the edge of your energy bubble and begin releasing down your grounding cord. Engage the ever-present gravitational pull of the planet, and release energy from your day down the grounding cord.

- *Release activities, work, play, projects, people, worry, fears, doubt, pain, expectations, people, family members, colleagues, your boss, husband, wife, kids and pets.*

- *Release unfinished business, things to do, your calendar, messages on the phone, computer work, vacations and travel plans.*

- *Let go of any situations, problems of other people, parties, events goals and dreams. Just for now, releasing any energy that is not in present time. Letting go of anything that keeps you out of this present moment.*

- *Imagine releasing family, friends, co-workers and your boss.*

- *Imagine pain, stiffness and tightness falling away down the grounding cord.*

Notice energies flowing away, down the spine and off the body. Ask yourself, where am I holding tension right now? Notice this without judgment. Give yourself permission to let it flow away down the grounding cord.

There's no hurry, right or wrong. Let go of busy-ness of the day, family problems, relationships and money challenges. Let it all release.

Focus on where you want to go, not on what you fear."

Anthony Robbins

Bring Aura Close To Body

Imagine taking the edge of your aura in closer and closer into the body. Imagine squeezing or compressing a sponge, bring the aura close to the body. When it's snug around the body, notice how that feels to your body. Notice the stillness. Notice the calm. Does your body feel safer?

With your awareness on the edge of your aura, let it bounce back to a normal space 3-4 feet around the body. Notice the relief and any subtleties. Can you feel the difference? Do you feel lighter?

Golden Net

The Golden Net tool is another way of collecting and releasing foreign energy from your energy space.

Now imagine a golden net below your feet. Imagine it slowly coming up through the body, dragging it up though the feet, legs, hips and torso. Collect energy

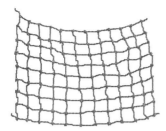

from your organs, your body systems. Using this quantum energy tool, collect foreign energies you are ready to release. Bring the net above the head and toss the golden net with the energies into a black hole and let it dissolve.

Notice how your body feels. ***Are you ready to take your next step and have more clarity?***

Clearing Center of Head Quantum Energy Tool #2
Guided Meditation
(http://bit.ly/1W4FE65)

This **Quantum Energy Tool** releases and resets energy inside your mind creating clarity and vision. Clearing the Center of Head gives you freedom of thoughts and beliefs.

> *Have you ever had someone or something you could NOT get off your mind?*

There's a good chance they had their energy stuck there. Sometimes we go over and over something, and we can't get it out of our mind. This is a great exercise to do when you can't stop obsessing about worries or problems. The worry gets bigger and bigger as we go over and over it. We can't seem to find the solution because this space is cluttered up with stacks of old information or projects.

> *Bringing your awareness, up to the center of head, and imagine sitting inside the center of your head. Take a look around inside and notice anyone you can't get your mind off, worries, problems and anything just taking up space... with amusement. Imagine using a vacuum cleaner tool or a magic wand to clean out the cob-webs, collect up projects, to do lists, sticky notes, worries, people wanting communication, your boss, husband/wife kids... move everything and everybody out.*
>
> *Imagine this magic wand or vacuum all filled up and toss it inside a black hole and let it dissolve. Reset and replenish the energy of the center of your head by bringing in Golden Suns.*

Replenishing Quantum Energy Tool #3
Guided Meditation
(http://bit.ly/1p54KVb)

This energy tool reclaims and replenishes your aura now that you have cleared much foreign energy from your energy space.

Imagining a beautiful, bright, illuminated golden sun about 3 feet above your head. Imagine that golden sun pouring into the center of your head. Its beautiful bright light fills the left and right side of your brain. That golden light feels like warm liquid gold and it fills in the entire head --- ears, eyes, nose, eyes, lips, cheeks, jaw and teeth.

Visualize the golden light filling in the neck, shoulders, arms into your creative channels where it helps you create and manifest. Imagine gold light filling your chest, heart, torso, tummy and all the vital organs with golden light. Visualize the golden light filling in sex organs, hips, pelvis, thighs, calves, ankles, feet and toes.

Visualize and feel golden space around the body, filling every cell of the body. Imagine it expanding filling the room you are in, the building you are in, expanding filling the entire city, expanding again filling the entire state, expanding filling the entire country, expanding more filling the entire globe.

> *As you heal yourself you heal others around you.*
> *Expand this frequency of purity that is connected to the infinite source of all.*
> *Feel the power, the infinite.*
> *Feel the abundance, truth and peace.*
> *You are the light. You are the power. You are the source.*
> *You are a creator.*
> *You are born in the likeness and image of our divine source - the creator.*
> *Your job in this physical body is to create—*
> *And CREATE you will.*

Practice these **Quantum Energy Tools** (http://bit.ly/29WqnQk) regularly, as they are valuable beyond their simplicity. It's my hope that you embrace them every day as I do making every day brighter and brighter, clearer and more vital. Bringing yourself more into the present moment, you align with the power of all creation and manifestation--Being in the NOW.

> **Congratulations on this giant step forward on your path of discovering YOU.**

The point of life is happiness"

The Dalai Lama

"I can't express my thanks to Amirah; I have made incredible changes in my life by following her guidance and practicing with the Quantum Energy Tools in her programs. What feels like SECRET keys has opened me to a whole new ME. For the first time in my life—I feel like it's the REAL me! This program really gets you into the 'flow of life', it's even hard to believe how EFFORTLESS manifesting things have become for me. I'm not exaggerating one bit either. Thanks to Amirah's wonderful support and guidance, I feel amazing and my goals are manifesting before my eyes. It's truly the best investment I've ever made in myself."

Angela Montgomery

Chapter 1 - Practice Guidelines

Practice the following tools this week:

1. Grounding – Quantum Energy Tool #1
2. Clearing Center of Head - Quantum Energy Tool #2
3. Replenishing – Quantum Energy Tool #3

GOALS AND HEALING WORKSHEET

WELLNESS COLOR _____

Physical Goal _____

Mental Goal _____

Emotional Goal _____

Spiritual Goal _____

MISSION STATEMENT

_____

WHAT ARE YOU NOTICING DIFFERENT?

_____

_____

WHAT ENERGIES **SUPPORT** YOU? (Colors, memories, beliefs, thoughts)

_____

_____

OTHER

_____

_____

Chapter

2

The Law of Vibration

> *Believe it or not, the roots of your problems may be sitting quietly in your mind. If you think of your brain as an intricate pattern of wires, you can easily see what a few misplaced wires can do. You need to adjust and retune these wires to gain control over your life."*

Working with the **Quantum Energy Tools** (http://bit.ly/29WqnQk) is an amazing process. Are you paying attention to what is DIFFERENT? Sometimes the changes are subtle and it's helpful to notice what you experience that's 'different' now. Relax, notice how your relationships with others are going and any ways that you are 'feeling' or thinking differently.

Gradually, you will begin to see changes. It's important to track the changes you notice because it validates that 'something is shifting'. At times these changes can be vague and difficult to articulate, but they will happen on their own time; you can't force them.

I want to emphasize again the importance of Grounding. As we progress with the tools, please note that we can use them throughout the day whenever we might need them, and we also use them in the meditative process. They are called **Quantum Energy Tools** (http://bit.ly/29WqnQk) because they are infinitely adaptable and powerful. As we go, we will use them in different ways or applications. A really good way to incorporate them into your daily life is by thinking like you're in kindergarten.

Being In Kindergarten

Can you remember how it felt to be in kindergarten?

Before we enter school, most of us are playful, curious and adventurous. Then we start getting more and more serious about life, with tests, exams expectations, right and wrong, do's and don't's. With time we become programmed to think like everyone around us.

Why fit in when you were born to stand out!"

Dr. Suess

Having a childlike approach with the **Quantum Energy Tools** (http://bit.ly/29WqnQk) will surprise you and allow you to use them in creative and fun ways.

The best part of being childlike is the 'surprise' results you might get.

Play With The Energy Tools

Allow your intuitive genius to use these tools in spontaneous and innovative ways, like Harry Potter's magic wand. There is no right or wrong, or good or bad way to use them. Have fun with them, explore using them in different ways. Along the way, I will share with you examples of using them but I strongly encourage you to just 'make it up' and see what happens.

Think and wonder. Wonder and Think."

Dr. Seuss

Reinvigorate Yourself

We start our lives so happy, clear and positive. Over time, we are all programmed to think like those around us in terms of our social, cultural, religious and traditional values, expectations, and beliefs. When we are born, we begin our journey of learning by 'matching energy'. We match our parents' energy and the energy of everyone around us. We are matching their beliefs, thoughts and fears. Life goes on and we are increasingly '*programmed*' with these energies. Although we might think something is our own thought, chances are it's stemming from our family beliefs or ideas.

We conform to our family's beliefs and thoughts, to our teachers and the world around us, all in an effort to 'fit in' and be accepted. We want to be included and to be a part of our community/family and eventually our careers. We all desire to be accepted and validated for who we are. Over the past 20 years+ of doing this work, students have shared examples of how they are working in a specific field because their family approved of their career choice. I hear similar stories over and over.

I have one student whose father and brother are both lawyers. She expressed how she loves children and began her career as a kindergarten teacher. Over time, she decided to return to school for a law degree because she felt it was a more respected career path in her family's views. Completing her master's degree, she joined the family law practice, and turned into a completely different person once she started working there. She lost herself.

After working together in my <u>Manifesting Miracles 101</u>, her energy began shifting and as she '***unmatched the family energy***' she slowly began to realize that ultimately she was seeking her father's validation and respect within the family. At the core of who she was, she ultimately loved teaching and felt most passionate and alive working with children. In working with **Quantum Energy Tools** (http://bit.ly/29WqnQk) and un-matching the tribe energy, she reconnected to her path of being in joyful and fulfilling work rather than the program of 'if you do this type of work you get respect'.

This is one of many examples of how we get sidetracked unconsciously. Can you think of an example of how you have matched your family energy? How have you matched other cultural energy, let's say at work or with friends?

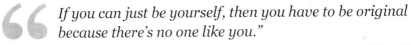

If you can just be yourself, then you have to be original because there's no one like you."

Marc Newson

Universal Law of Vibration

If you want to find the secrets of the universe, think in terms of energy, frequency and vibration."

Nikola Tesla

It has been said that in order for you to get what you want, you have to vibrate to it. How does this vibration work? In order to vibrate to something you must have positive thoughts, or the energy that matches that which you desire. If you don't, you won't get what you are striving for.

When you are in a positive frame of mind and your energy is flowing and receptive, you are more in alignment with the vibration of what you wish to achieve. If you have any slight negativity, worry, or if you are unsure in the slightest degree, this doubting or negative energy can inhibit you from accomplishing your task, unless you stop them immediately and focus on positive thoughts and feelings.

Let's say you are looking to get a million dollars.

You visualize a check for that amount coming to you. The only problem is you doubt slightly if you will get it. What will happen? Nothing. You won't get it because you did not vibrate to it. You did not hold the belief that you would get it and you didn't have a positive attitude about it.

The premise here is that if you aren't sure you want something and you have slight doubts about it, you won't get it because you are not vibrating to it. You are focusing on what you do not want, instead of on what you do want. There is some unconscious belief, thought or energy that attracts what you don't want.

> **The Law of Vibration states that, 'everything in life moves or vibrates'.**

There is nothing that sits idle, even for a second. Everything in life is in a constant state of motion. Look at an atom through a microscope and you will see protons and electrons moving in a circle around a neutron. No matter what it is, it is energy and energy is in constant motion.

Everything that vibrates does so at a certain rate. This rate is known as its frequency. The higher the frequency, the more potent the potential force. Thought is considered to be the highest form of vibration therefore it has the highest frequency. As it is the highest frequency, it is considered as a powerful force in the universe.

Understanding The Law of Vibration

The universe does not know whether the vibration that you're offering is because of something you're observing or something you're remembering or something that you are imagining. It just receives the vibration and answers it with things that match it."

Abraham Hicks

To understand the Law of Attraction correctly, and be in more harmony with it, we must also understand the Law of Vibration.

The meaning of vibration can be considered as a moving backwards and forwards. It also can mean to oscillate, quiver, or swing. Here's a perfect way to think about this concept: If you stick your arm out and keep it perfectly still, you will notice no movement. But what you don't realize is that under that skin of your arm, the electrons that are contained therein are moving on a steady basis. And they are moving at a speed of about 186,300 miles per second.

Although your arm appears '**still**', it is in a '**constant state of motion**'. You can't see this happening because your eyes can't pick up such minute particles of energy that make up the matter of your arm. Now take a second and shake your arm around. Your arm was already vibrating on its own, but you have stepped up the vibration. The vibrating energy of your arm has increased dramatically.

Those who think and feel positively are in a good state of vibration, or are vibrating at a high frequency. Because they are in a good or positive state of vibration, good things will always come to them. Maybe you can recall a time when you met someone and thought to yourself, 'man, they have good vibes'. You like being around that type of energy because it feels good.

These types of people will always attract positive things or personalities. People who think negatively (and that includes our unconscious programming, fears, doubts, and lies we tell ourselves) would be vibrating negative energy or would have 'a low vibrational frequency'.

This is because they are pessimistic and dwell on the bad. Or, it could be that there is a whole lot of buried, unconscious energy that is at a very low frequency. As such, they will vibrate negativity. And because they vibrate negativity, they will attract anything negative in their lives. This means they will attract trouble, anguish, fear, rage, or whatever negative emotion is available.

If you want to control the results you get, you must change, control and select what you vibrate to. This means controlling your thoughts, feelings and energy, because you only vibrate to that which you already are.

Working in Harmony

In electronics, there are electromagnetic fields. If two electromagnetic fields are working together, they are working in harmony or in resonance. When this occurs, the vibrating rate can easily be transferred from one to the other by way of electrons. Let's say you have a glass sitting on a table, and there is a lady singing nearby. She hits a certain high note that cracks the glass. Only that one frequency cracked it because the two frequencies were in resonance. The frequency of the lady's voice was the same as the frequency of the magnetic field surrounding the glass. Do you see my point?

The same thing happens to your thoughts.

When you think of something, and vibrate to it, you are creating a frequency. That frequency goes out into the universe and reaches an object that also vibrates at that same frequency. When this happens, the two are in sync. The electromagnetic waves that your brain creates from your thoughts and feelings vibrate to the exact energy level as the thing or object that you are asking the universe for. By clearing unconscious thought patterns, you increase the energy level of the thoughts of things you desire, and they become more potent.

Invoking the Law of Vibration, you activate the Law of Attraction. Our thoughts, feelings, words, and actions produce energies that in turn attract similar energies. Negative energies attract negative energies, and positive energies attract positive energies. That is the Law of Attraction.

In practicing the Law of Attraction, you must train the Law of Vibration. The two go hand in hand; when you practice one, you also practice the other.

 Let's start with what we can be thankful for, and get our mind into that vibration, and then watch the good that starts to come, because one thought leads to another thought."

Bob Proctor"

The Law of Vibration

Everything in the Universe vibrates and travels in circular patterns. The same principles of vibration in the physical world apply to our thoughts, feelings, desires and wills in the Etheric world. Each sound, thing, and even thought has its own vibrational frequency, unique unto itself.

Anything that exists in our universe, when broken down into and analyzed in its purest and most basic form, consists of pure energy or light which resonates and exists as a vibratory frequency or pattern. All matter, thoughts and feelings have their own vibrational frequency. The thoughts, feelings and actions that we **choose** also have their own particular rates of vibration. These vibrations will set up resonance with whatever has an identical frequency. In other words, your thoughts are inseparably connected to the rest of the universe. **Like Attracts Like**. As you choose good thoughts, more good thoughts will follow and you will be in vibrational harmony with other people who have similar thoughts.

It Begins With Your Thoughts

Everything we do is infused with the energy with which we do it. If we're frantic, life will be frantic. If we're peaceful, life will be peaceful."

Marianne Williamson

For us, thought is where it all begins. As your conscious mind dwells habitually on thoughts of a certain quality, these become firmly imbedded within the subconscious mind. They become the dominant vibration. This dominant vibration sets up a resonance with other similar vibrations and draws them into your life. This is easier to understand if you consider that from the metaphysical view, the whole universe IS MIND. In turn, your vibrations affect everything around you – your environment, the people and animals around you, the inanimate objects, even the seemingly 'empty' space and they, in turn, affect you.

Your Feelings Dictate Your Vibration

Your feeling at the present moment dictates your vibration. It is said that feelings define conscious awareness of vibration. So, your feeling at the moment is your vibration, which sets up things of a comparable nature. Positive feelings = positive circumstances, negative feelings = negative circumstances.

If you are ready to enjoy greater achievement, fulfillment and success, get ready for major breakthroughs!"

Clearing Energy Engages The Law of Vibration

Using the **Quantum Energy Tools** (http://bit.ly/29WqnQk) on a daily basis is the basic foundation for clearing and resetting your energy for manifesting miracles. **Quantum Energy Tools #1, #2, #3 and #4 should be a minimum daily practice.**

Setting boundaries is a way of caring for myself. It doesn't make me mean, selfish, or uncaring (just) because I don't do things your way. I care about me, too."

Christine Morgan

Setting Healthy Boundaries Quantum Energy Tool #4
Guided Meditation
(http://bit.ly/22Ap2TW)

This **Quantum Energy Tool #4** works a boundary marker or a decoy. It serves by redirecting other people's energy into it rather than your energy field. Also, it helps you to stay inside your own energy field rather than jumping into other people's energy field. This helps to remind you to be present and mindful.

Bring your awareness to the edge of your aura. Visualize a rose on the edge of your aura. Ground it. Drop an essence of yourself, your picture and/or today's date and let it mark the edge of your space.

Clearing Mom's Energy:

Visualize two file folders symbols or icons out in front of you. Imagine one symbol represents you and the other symbol represents your mom (whether she is living or passed over). Begin to transfer any of your mom's energy that is stuck in your symbol back into her symbol. Just drag and drop or push the imaginary *'file transfer'* button. When you get the sense that all her files or energy is transferred, reclaim your energy from her symbol--either drag and drop, file transfer or whatever comes to your mind. When complete drag your icons into the trash.

Remember there's no right or wrong here...just use your imagination

Clearing Dad's Energy:

Visualize two file folders symbols or icons out in front of you. Imagine one symbol represents you and the other symbol represents your Dad (whether he is living or past over). Begin to transfer any of your dad's energy that is stuck in your symbol back into his symbol. Just drag and drop or push the imaginary *'file transfer'* button. When you get the sense that all his files or energy is transferred, reclaim your energy from his symbol--Either drag and drop, file transfer or whatever comes to your mind. When complete drag your icons into the trash.

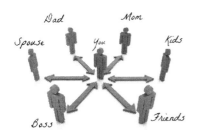

Clear Other Family Members Energy

Continue with any other immediate family members including children, pets and extended family members. Also, separate energies from wives, husbands (former and present ones), clients, colleagues, your boss, clients, etc.).

**This is a powerful exercise that you can complete after meetings with clients or at the end of every day, reclaiming your energy from other people where you left it and sending their energy back to them.

 Lack of boundaries invites lack of respect."

Anonymous

Healing Magic Wand Quantum Energy Tool #5
Guided Meditation
http://bit.ly/1Sg8ldA

Collect foreign energy stuck in your body that's creating dys-ease, dys-function or any undesirable situations and circumstances with Quantum Energy Tool #5. The Law of Attraction says, '**like attracts like**'. Whatever is stuck in your space is unconsciously creating for you on some level.

Wellness Color Quantum Energy Tool #6
Guided Meditation
http://bit.ly/1TWLQwT

Using the vibrational tone of color, you reset your overall energy frequency to attracting your desires. Resetting your body, mind and spirit with color changes your experiences. You can act or feel different day by day, by adjusting your color. Every moment you have a choice.

Like re-booting your computer, you reset your own frequency by using the tone or frequency of color. Consider:

> *What color resembles or is in affinity with you in this moment?*
> *What color brings your body to a state of wellness?*

Imagine that color dropping into your crown chakra at the top of your head as you set your body vibration to harmony. Notice what is different. Notice how that feels in your body.

Stress Buster Quantum Energy Tool #7
Guided Meditation
http://bit.ly/2a0DtAl

Stress Buster combines most of the tools and offers a well-rounded go-to practice tool if you are short on time. Running earth and cosmic energy is like having a '**energy shower**'—it's rejuvenating!

These tools are as powerful whether they are practiced individually or in sequence. One thing I can't emphasize enough is, '**the more you practice, the bigger the benefit'**.

With your awareness in the center of your head, imagine the energy centers at the bottom of your feet opening like a camera lens to about 20% open. Imagine bringing some neutral earth energy, from a place ½ way down from the center of the earth into your bottom of the feet, flowing into the ankles, up the legs, into the hips and the 1st chakra located at the base of your spine, and let the energy flow down your grounding cord.

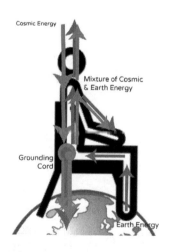

Let the earth energy flow up the legs and down the grounding cord. ***It might look like the golden arches***. The earth energy might have a color to it. It doesn't have to be brown...allow a color to appear. Allowing earth energy to flush out your leg energy channels. Notice how that feels in your body. Increase the flow of the earth energy and notice how it feels. Slow down the energy flow, and notice how that feels.

Imagine a ball of cosmic energy about 3 feet above your head and let it begin flowing down into the top of your head, down back of the neck, down the spine. Let about 20% of this energy flow down the grounding cord. Allow the remaining cosmic energy to mix with the earth energy in the 1st chakra at the base of the spine, and begin flowing up through each of the other 6 chakras in the front of the spine.

Let it flow up passing through the 2nd, 3rd, 4th and 5th chakras then split at the base of your neck, allowing approximately allowing 20% of the mixture to flow down each arm and out the palm of the hands.

Allow the mixture of cosmic and earth energy to flow up the neck into the head and the 6th chakra located behind the eyes in the center of the head. Notice the energy flowing out the top of the head like a fountain into your energy bubble.

Picture turning up or down the volume or flow of the earth and cosmic energy and notice how that feels to your body.

Commit to making this a daily practice and I PROMISE you will see profound changes in everything around you including how you perceive the world and how others perceive you. Also, people around you will be affected and healed through your practice.

> *Ask once, believe you have received, and all you have to do to receive is feel good."*
>
> Rhonda Byrns, <u>The Secret</u>

"Honestly, I've wasted so much time and money on useless programs that promise the moon; I was a little skeptical before buying another program that promises success. I've worked with many big name coaches and programs only to find they promise the moon and my results were less than sparkling. When I met Amirah, I thought I would give her training a try. I've seen a great improvement in how I feel everyday-- I feel like new person. I'm making more money than ever before, I'm soaring in my career and I know it's because of the effects of this program. ... Thanks for transforming my life."

Samer T, Abu Dhabi, UAE

Chapter 2 - Practice Guidelines

Practice the following tools this week:

1. Grounding – Quantum Energy Tool #1
2. Clear Your Mind – Quantum Energy Tool #2
3. Replenishing – Quantum Energy Tool #3
4. Setting Healthy Boundaries - Quantum Energy Tool #4
5. Healing Magic Wand - Quantum Energy Tool #5
6. Wellness Color – Quantum Energy Tool #6
7. Run Earth and Cosmic Energy – Quantum Energy Tool #7

GOALS AND HEALING WORKSHEET

WELLNESS COLOR _____

Physical Goal _____

Mental Goal _____

Emotional Goal _____

Spiritual Goal _____

MISSION STATEMENT

_____

WHAT ARE YOU NOTICING DIFFERENT?

_____

_____

WHAT ENERGIES **SUPPORT** YOU? (Colors, memories, beliefs, thoughts)

_____

_____

OTHER

_____

_____

Chapter

3

The Three Main Laws of Conscious Creation

Everything is about to brighten! Everything is about to clear! Sadness is about to become joy, sighs are about to become laughter, indecisiveness is about to become bold decisions, and your discouraged self is about to say goodbye to struggles."

Universal laws are funny things. We all have to learn them, whether we like it or not. Take for instance a baby just starting to sit-crawl-walk. We all went through this stage where we fell, hurt ourselves, watched how others did it, tried to copy them and eventually found out how to do it. Finally we got it right and started to walk. Whether we liked it or not, we had to learn to do it or we were stuck.

We then discovered a new freedom, but soon discovered there were certain responsibilities attached. You learned to watch where you are going, because if you fall down the stairs, or walk in front of the car, there would be no one to prevent you from hurting yourself. You have to take personal responsibility for managing how you walk about in the world.

If we do that, then what are the possibilities out there?

Taking Responsibility for Your Life

We can do whatever we want and go where ever we want on the condition that we take personal responsibility for our life every step of the way. Now, if we don't do that then we might get the feeling that someone is out to get us because every time you put a foot wrong, something happens. You then might think, "I best lock myself up in my room!" Does this kind of thinking ever come up in your life? Life is just too hard, it is unsafe, others have it better than me, I can't trust anyone, I just can't get it right, no matter how hard I work it just goes wrong, etc.

> *Have you ever wondered why some people are successful, while others spend their entire lives struggling?*

If you're like most people, these thoughts occur to you from time to time. What is the answer to these questions? Is it a question of luck, could it be fate or is there something else going on here of which most people are unaware?

It's All Around Us, Within Us

Just like there are Natural Laws that govern nature (such as gravity), there are other Laws which govern all that happens in the universe. From the spiritual to the physical to the mental to the emotional, everything that happens does so according to Universal Law.

It is our job to learn these **Universal Laws**. The quicker we learn them, the better it is for us! What is even more wonderful is that we can learn to use the Laws to our advantage. When we do that, we are able to achieve whatever it is that we want from life! On the flipside of that is that we struggle when we refuse to learn about them or when we think the only way forward is to manipulate, connive, steal, tell lies, and so on.

Nothing Happens By Chance

You see, the Universe is a very orderly place in which nothing occurs by chance. Even though one cannot see the Laws, or hear them, smell them or taste them, they are there. They apply to everything and everyone – nothing is exempt. Whether one is aware of these Laws or not, they still apply - just like the Law of Gravity. Even though one may not be aware of or understand Gravity, it always works. No matter who you are, if you decide to step off the top of a tall building, you will fall at an increasing rate of speed until you reach terminal velocity or until you impact the ground.

The Law of Divine Oneness

Within the Universe, everything is connected to everything else. What we think, say, do and believe will have a corresponding effect on others and the universe around us.

All of humanity and God are ONE. We are always connected to the force of God because the energy of God is everywhere at once, and permeates through all things living or material, just as the knowledge of God is infinite and always available to us. Each soul is part of God's energy.

Everything that exists, seen and unseen, is connected to each other, inseparable from each other in a field of divine oneness. Divine, all knowing, the matrix, pure consciousness or universal mind energy, sometimes also known as Life Force or God! **Everything is ONE.**

Increasing awareness of this Law will increase our awareness of God and awareness of being connected to everything. It is important for us as a human race to start realizing and understanding this Law. As we do, we will realize that what we think of each other should only for be good. As we think of the good in others, they will in turn think of the good in you. It is essential that the thoughts, feelings and actions be for good, as we *reap what we sow*.

Learning The Oneness

Before I was aware of this myself, years ago I can remember times when I caught myself thinking negatively about a co-worker. That co-worker continually behaved how I saw and thought of them: disruptive, arrogant and self-centered. Then I made the decision to experiment and pretended they were considerate, thoughtful and kind. To my ultimate surprise, the person began treating me exactly like I visualized. It was truly miraculous, and everyone in the office witnessed his surprising turn around. I will never forget that lesson. If you have someone in your life that challenges you, try this experiment. You just might be amazed.

As you gain a fuller understanding of the laws, you will see how they are all related, and how they overlap each other and govern the world we live in.

Everything is Energy

Everything consists of, and exists as, energy. Your subatomic particles aren't fixed. In fact, particles may be flowing into and out of you now from: this page, the sky, the floor, your best friend and your worst enemy. In other words, there is no separation. How would you behave if you really knew that you were not separate from life, your friends, colleagues and every being that has ever existed? The answer is this – probably differently.

> *We aren't solid beings living on this planet; instead this planet is a collection of energies which penetrate each other."*
>
> Hina Hashmi

Three Main Laws for Conscious Creation

They are the: Law of Attraction, Law of Detachment and Law of God Action.

When you know these three Laws, you'll be able to create your perfect reality like a master. This trinity of Laws forms the perfect creation of all reality. If you were to use these three Laws together, you would experience what you would call the perfect life. Perfection is the result of the perfect working of universal forces. Perfect understanding of universal forces enables perfect reality creation.

The Law of Attraction

The Law of Attraction states that '**energy attracts like energy**' and '**what you focus your mind on, is what you attract**'. Knowing the Law of Attraction is the first step that turns you into a conscious creator of your reality. Knowing that you create everything with the power of intention, you become conscious of how everything you experience is created by yourself. With the awareness of this universal law, you begin living life as if you were in a lucid dream. That is 'creating consciously, rather than unconsciously'.

> *You cannot solve a problem in the same frequency in which it was created."*
>
> Lynn Grabhorn

The Law of Detachment

The Law of Detachment states that creation is free to be worked on by the Universal Mind when you mentally and emotionally detach yourself from your intention. Knowing this law enables your creations to manifest without being sabotaged. Spirit is free and unbounded; therefore when you let go of your intention, you are expressing your true nature as a free spirit. In resonating as your true self, you allow Universal Mind/God to carry out the work of creation fully. Detaching from the how, when, where details allows your creative work to happen unhindered.

> *In detachment lies the wisdom of uncertainty . . . in the wisdom of uncertainty lies the freedom from our past, from the known, which is the prison of past conditioning. And in our willingness to step into the unknown, the field of all possibilities, we surrender ourselves to the creative mind that orchestrates the dance of the universe. "*
>
> Deepak Chopra

The Law of God Action

The Law of God Action states the Universe itself creates through you. Knowing this law enables you to allow all of your creation work to be guided by a Higher Power/God. Your existence in this dimension is simply a channel for the universal mind to express Itself as your personal creation is a portion of the universal creation that is in progress. When you create from this level, your intentions are in alignment with your Higher Self, therefore everything works out perfectly.

The Law of Action states that you must do the things and perform the actions necessary to achieve what you are setting out to do. Unless you take actions that are in harmony with your thoughts and dreams and proceed in an orderly fashion towards what you want to accomplish, there will be absolutely no foreseeable results. It is here that most people falter when pursuing success. Often times it happens that their fears or laziness get in the way and block success.

> *How it will happen, how the Universe will bring it to you, is not your concern or job. Allow the Universe to do it for you."*
>
> Abraham Hicks, The Secret

The Law of Cause and Effect

You can also relate this law to that of **the law of cause and effect.** The cause is your action, as you take the action there will be a corresponding effect. Only by taking actions corresponding with your free-will desires can the universe know what to bring into your life. For example, if you wish to learn something new and then take the action steps to learn - read, study or take a class--only then will the universe know what you are striving for.

When you take an action, even the smallest thing like writing a To-Do list in the morning, you set into motion corresponding effects that change your immediate future. If you follow up, day after day, it can become a habitual way of living and the results will be exponential. But if you fail to take that first action, then there won't be much in your future for results.

A mountain is composed of tiny grains of earth. The ocean is made up of tiny drops of water. Even so, life is but an endless series of little details, actions, speeches, and thoughts. And the consequences whether good or bad of even the least of them are far-reaching."

Sivananda

The Laws of Creation – Creating and Destroying

Most people lack the understanding of how the physical **Laws of Creation** work.

Consider for a moment...

> *Do you have fear, insecurity, anxiety, family programming or mental blocks that stop you from creating?*
> *Have you ever felt that you don't deserve to be loved?*
> *Are you putting off setting plans in motion because you might leave someone else behind?*
> *Do you think you are unworthy of having what you want?*

The reason so many of your thoughts fail to come into fruition in your life is that you judge them and discard them in your mind. Other thoughts that reached the emotional level were focused out, or you don't feel a strong desire to make them happen. Over time, your mind becomes **blocked or programmed** with negativity from your surroundings, and your ability to create is affected. Negativity is like a virus on your computer—it alters the natural flow of creation, creating more of what you don't want.

While growing up, parents, family, and friends bombard you with their thoughts, feelings, beliefs, habits and patterns. Most likely, you absorbed some of this unconscious programming. You stored it in your subconscious mind and body.

As time passes, storing this energy diminishes your own power to create. **Then we wonder: "why can't we attract what we want?"**

- Have you ever felt guilty when **releasing**, **destroying** or **ending** something, such as a relationship with a romantic partner, an agreement or commitment?

- Are you harboring old grudges, rejections or plans that never worked out? Is it difficult for you to let go of your old clothes or magazines?

- Maybe you feel guilty throwing out spoiled food or feel bad that you even let it spoil in the first place.

When you consciously or unconsciously are unable to release thoughts from former relationships or past situations, they create blocks to what you want to create in your life. Sometimes, you are so busy unconsciously creating blocks that you don't allow time or space for newer things to manifest what you want to create.

When you clear out the fridge of moldy, forgotten leftovers, you create room for fresh groceries to make delicious mouthwatering meals. The simplest way to put it is that the purpose of life is to learn to control energy. Learning to control your mental energy comes from using your thoughts and emotions to create the physical reality you desire. You then live successfully with the matter and events that are formed!

Visualizing is Creating Energetically

When you visualize an object or symbol, you are actually creating the object or symbol on an energetic level. This object or symbol has properties that can have an effect on the physical plane. When you imagine destroying the object or symbol, you are actually moving and changing the molecules that make up this energy form. When you create and destroy an object or symbol, an energy force is set in motion that affects all other energies surrounding it.

Therefore, you can use this process to move and release unwanted energies.

> **The Law of Detachment** *states that creation is free to be worked on by the universal mind when you mentally and emotionally detach from your intention.*

Knowing this Law enables you to allow your creation to happen unintentionally. Spirit is free and unbounded, therefore when you let go of your intention you are expressing your true nature as a free spirit. By resonating as your true and higher self, you allow it to carry out the work of creation FULLY. Detachment allows your creation work to happen unhindered.

> *Now the bigger question becomes, where are you resisting the natural rhythm of creating and destroying?*

Visualizations are Key

Your ability to create and destroy visualizations is directly related to the ability to create and destroy many other things in your life. When you create and destroy an object in your mind, you are moving energy and impacting everything around you.

There are all kinds of emotions and thoughts that affect a person's ability to **create or destroy. *Do you feel insecure about creating something different in your life? Do you feel blocked from starting something new? What perceptions are blocking your ability to create the love you want in your life? Are you ready to release their grip on a new perception of a present time reality?***

Think about what you are creating if you are walking wounded.

- *Is there something in your life you just can't seem to release? Anger, hate, shock, grief or apparent failures?*

- *How can you feel successful when you go through life dead on the inside?*

- *How can you create a loving relationship or business when you focus on resentments and past pain?*

Even if you think a former relationship is behind you, some of its effects might be hidden unconsciously.

All illness has its primary origin in the mind rather than in the body. Stress and pain result from an imbalance somewhere in your being. Mental pain expresses itself in scattered thinking, mental blocks, limiting beliefs, and misperceptions.

When you lock-in on your belief, feeling or thought at that moment it comes alive to you. This becomes part of what you are in the process of creating.

Clear Unconscious Blocks

Life is beautiful. Suffering is due to unconscious following."

Amit Ray

You don't have to be consciously aware of all your blocks to clear them and create room for what you do want. Clearing old thoughts and feelings from past experiences, disappointments, and resentments gives you a new sense of freedom and lightness. Discharging emotions, resentments or other stagnant energy restores your ability to manifest your dreams. Blocked energy that has unconsciously shaped your experiences can be released without effort.

The conscious alignment of your physical, mental and spiritual self, brings you into a state of being that is healthful and rejuvenating. Having good physical, emotional and mental health gives your spirit a more powerful and energetic place to dwell. You can be more focused on your life's dreams, vision, and goals. Recognizing your own worth and your true nature, without baggage, is self-loving and will change your life.

Releasing and Destroying Blocked Energy

Begin by creating a grounding cord. Visualize a rose and fill it with something (idea, feeling, situation) that you want to release from your life. Begin by reflecting on key external events that turned out to be the most toxic experiences of your life.

Imagine suspending another rose 6" in front of you and allow this symbol to absorbing this experience, releasing the blocked energy. Allow this symbol to draw out and absorb any foreign energy, stuck thoughts, emotions or pictures from your body and the space around you. Let the foreign energy appear as dark colors. Explode the rose.

Creating Mockups

Mockups are models or replicas used for instructional or experimental purposes. For example, architects create models of buildings to give a 3D conceptual view of them before they are built. Mockups for me are like energetic 3D printers. Imagine your thoughts are like an energetic blueprint that you send to a virtual 3D printer that creates an energetic form.

Creating energetic mockups can be helpful when we want to create something very specific. The mockup tool is used to clear energy blocks on any creation in order to guarantee its manifestation. The mockup tool allows you to set the energy levels of 'neutrality, enthusiasm, gratitude, clarity' in order to 'HAVE' the mock-up.

> *Answer the questions—who, what, where, when.*
> *If you don't care about some or the aspects of your mock-up—*
> *then choose!*

Mockups Quantum Energy Tool
Guided Meditation
http://bit.ly/1W4ZJJw

Think of something you want. Visualize dropping an image of that specific item into an imaginary rose 6" out in front of you. Ground the rose and begin draining everyone else's energy out of the symbol. Imagine your rose is a sponge or a French-press and squeeze out the energy. Drain any of your own energy as well as that of other's.

Havingness Gauge

Create a **Havingness Gauge** to the right of your rose. Visualize a simple gauge like a fuel gauge or your car odometer. Let there be a needle pointing to a number from 0-100%. This gauge is a ***present time indicator*** of your current ability to energetically 'have' something.

Check your Havingness Gauge—***Can you have this mock-up? Where is the needle pointing on the gauge?*** Visualize your gauge with a grounding cord and begin releasing any energy from the havingness gauge that is preventing you from having your mock-up, bringing your needle to 100%. This brings you to 100% energetically capable of ***having your mockup!***

Visualize a neutral Golden Sun filling in the Mock-up rose. Acknowledge that you have your mock-up and thank the Supreme Being. Step inside the mock-up symbol and feel yourself already having it. Release your symbol to the center of the Universe. Let it manifest!

> Note: *If your mock-up doesn't manifest in a reasonable time period—call it back and clear it off again, make any changes you desire and re-release it to manifest.*

Every great dream begins with a dreamer. Always remember, you have within you the strength, the patience, and the passion to reach for the stars to change the world."

Harriet Tubman

"Honestly speaking, I've wasted so much time and money on useless programs that promise the moon; I was a little skeptical before buying another program that promises success. I'm glad I gave this program a try. I've seen a great improvement in how I feel everyday-- I feel like new person... Thanks for transforming my life. I now know I'm well on the way to feeling stronger and more confident."

Roger, San Jose, CA

Chapter 3 - Practice Guidelines

Practice the following tools this week:

1. Grounding – Quantum Energy Tool #1
2. Clear Your Mind – Quantum Energy Tool #2
3. Replenishing – Quantum Energy Tool #3
4. Setting Healthy Boundaries - Quantum Energy Tool #4
5. Healing Magic Wand - Quantum Energy Tool #5
6. Wellness Color – Quantum Energy Tool #6
7. Run Earth and Cosmic Energy – Quantum Energy Tool #7
8. Release and Destroy Blocked Energy
9. Create Mockups

GOALS AND HEALING WORKSHEET

WELLNESS COLOR _____

Physical Goal _____

Mental Goal _____

Emotional Goal _____

Spiritual Goal _____

MISSION STATEMENT

_____

WHAT ARE YOU NOTICING DIFFERENT?

_____

_____

WHAT ENERGIES **SUPPORT** YOU? (Colors, memories, beliefs, thoughts)

_____

_____

OTHER

_____

_____

Chapter

4

The Law of Laws

> *Really think today about what you know, what you stand for...what you have learned and what you have taught... what you can share and what holds you together....the knowledge, wisdom and experiences that you have EARNED because you lived through them."*

The Law of Compensation guarantees that in the long run every '**integrity is rewarded**' and that each '**inconsistency is redressed**' - in silence, in certainty, and ultimately, in Divine Order. Ralph Waldo Emerson said The Law of Compensation or The Law of Cause and Effect is the **Law of Laws.** The most important lesson involving human conduct and interaction is seen in the Cosmic Law of Cause and Effect.

> *For what you give, you shall receive; and what you withhold will be withheld from you. You give love; you get love."*

For every action there is an equal and opposite reaction".

How?

Every Thought Creates Motion

With every thought of intention, action and emotion that is transmitted, a person sets into motion an unseen chain of effects which vibrate from the mental plane through the entire cellular structure of the body out into the environment and finally into the Cosmos. Eventually the vibratory energy returns to the original source upon the swing of the pendulum.

Every human thought, word and deed is a cause that sets off a wave of energy throughout the universe, which in turn creates the effect, be it desirable or undesirable. The law states that the effect must create a physical manifestation. This is why good thoughts, words, emotions, and deeds are essential for a better world for they all create good effects.

 When anger rises, think of the consequences."

Confucius

The law of cause and effect states that every cause has an effect and every effect becomes the cause of something else. This law suggests that the universe is always in motion and progresses from a chain of events. If you want to look at this law from a philosophical point of view, every cause and effect manifests into what we are experiencing in our physical world today. It's about creating a divine connection.

According to the nature of your actions, the Divine omniscient consciousness will assign corresponding effects. In order to benefit yourself and society as a whole, mankind should use their free choice and perform good deeds with the awareness that what they think, act and speak about will affect the entire universe.

Your prosperity of life is created by your own deeds in helping others through thoughts, feelings and actions. And so it is... you are here, refining your energy space to create more of what resonates in your heart.

> *Becoming aware of your own energetic space is a healthy first step in having healthy relationships. Setting and maintaining healthy boundaries with another person means that each of your energies remains distinct.*

Please don't make the mistake of thinking that something that you once deeply loved is beyond repair. If your heart tells you to stop and try to nurse a relationship, a job, your body, a skill, an old dream back to health, give it a shot and see what happens.

> *You might ask, 'How can I bring about that shift or change? Do I need a magical wand?"*

Shifts and Changes Are Occurring

You are shifting your energy, and you don't know how it's going to look until later on. That's what I call a *'**growth period**'* in which you might experience some growing pains.

One student of mine shared that she put both contact lenses in one eye and couldn't figure out why her vision was so weird one day. Another one was really confused as she got late and in a hurry, she put on one brown boot and one black boot and left for work. We laughed really hard because she traveled a long way that day and couldn't run home to change her boots. She just suffered the embarrassment and shifted to amusement as everyone commented about her new fashion statement.

Another client told me how she lost her cell phone and hunted all day long for it. Then went to get some ice for her drink and found her cell phone. I've told this story often in my classes and now all my students go to the freezer when they've misplaced their phones. The joke, however is that they have really left it somewhere else when they were NOT PRESENT and grounded.

Now, when we think about something not-so-good, our vibrations start changing. It's not that we shouldn't think about it; we are human beings and yes, we shift our mind in a jiffy. All we need to do is set a space!

Setting Communication Space in Relationships

Everybody seems to have an opinion about your relationships and your life, don't they?

Whose opinion counts?

It is so important to listen to the right voices. Many times, we must tune out almost every voice around us to be able to focus on what is true for our own lives.

You have within you the intuition to know which opinions can be gentle guides to you, and which are not helpful or are even self-serving or manipulative.

> *There are only two kinds of people who can drain your energy: those you love, and those you fear. In both instances it is you who let them in. They did not force their way into your aura, or pry their way into your reality experience."*
>
> Anthon St. Maarten

Act for yourself. Face your own truths and then act on your own truths. It's so important for you to set a communication space and to learn the best ways to tune out all of the voices not speaking your truth. Here are some ways to do this:

Re-setting Challenged Communication Technique

Identify a person with which you have challenged communication and imagine seeing you both inside a bubble with a grounding cord. When multiple persons are involved it is best to work with two at a time. (*i.e. You + other person.*)

Visualize yourself and the other person inside the bubble with a grounded rose between you both inside the bubble. This rose collects any charged energy between you and can hold a space for open and clear communication. Perhaps you will be able to express yourself easily or the challenge just melts away. This is a powerful technique to practice with anyone you have challenged communications with.

The bottom line is that there is an energetic reality to ALL our interchanges, interactions and attractions. If we understood and managed these energies consciously, we could significantly improve our communications at work and at home, as well as improve our health and well-being!

Setting Healthy Boundaries

People who don't have reasonable or healthy boundaries often experience life as a struggle and place excessive focus on exterior activities. Oftentimes people with unhealthy boundaries use body weight to create boundaries for themselves unconsciously.

Have you ever met someone who is constantly doing things for others and ignoring their own needs? That's a true sign of having unhealthy boundaries and they usually burn themselves out!

On the other hand, people with a strong sense of personal territory do not look outside themselves for self-worth, and their healing comes naturally. The idea of having and keeping healthy energetic boundaries enhances every aspect of communication and your overall ability to manifest miracles.

> *Energy work is priceless. It makes every day extraordinary and transforms the mundane to the holy.*"
>
> Silvia Hartmann

Defining Your Energy Space

Years ago open office space floor plans came into vogue. The cons are obvious: they're unhealthy, stress-inducing, and hostile to productivity, creativity and privacy. They create anxiety.

Much like an open-office space needs you to define your space; your energy body does as well. If you don't know where your energy space is then any old thing can creep in. This is why you might have days that leave you feeling like you were hit by a truck.

Healers, empaths and highly sensitive persons are particularly vulnerable to foreign energy. If you don't define your personal space you are going to soak up everyone else's problems, emotions, and pain like a sponge. Keeping out energy vampires who suck the life right out of you is much easier when you 'define and occupy' your space then this simply cannot happen.

It's not your job or responsibility to soak up or hold on to other peoples 'energy stuff'. I'm sure you have more than enough of your own to deal with. So how do you protect your space by defining it?

Protecting Your Space With Barriers

Walls are a way to define space; however, they can be closed in. We put a wall up here and a wall up there and pretty soon those walls actually point us in a different direction because we have to walk around them. Protecting your energetic space is very much the same thing. If you put up walls to protect yourself it doesn't just keep out the negative, it keeps out the positive too!

Putting up walls actually creates '*effort and resistance*'. It could be also that someone else created those walls for you. Are you walking around any walls that someone else built?

> *Considering you are like a home or office space, have you ever wanted to open up a wall that was already there so you could open up the space? Are there any pre-defined walls you must walk around that are possibly changing your direction? You don't have to put up walls to protect your space!*

Draw A Line In The Sand!

Protecting your space is much like drawing a line in the sand. You create a space (or boundary if you'd prefer to call it that) that defines where your energy space is. You allow others to come in by agreement. When you're in a relationship for instance you WANT to share intimate space with a special person but you can still own your space within the relationship.

Picture yourself in a gold bubble of energy that comes out about 3 feet all around you. Fully occupy the gold bubble and fill it with your happy thoughts. Consider it a safe, peaceful place. Fill yourself up with gold and allow everything else to fall away. Set a decoy rose on the edge of your aura also to define your space energetically. It tells YOU where your aura is and keeps foreign invaders outside of it. I can tell you from personal experience it is possible for personal energy to take up a whole room. I will also tell you that it doesn't feel good when you do that! When you clearly define your space not only will you feel more comfortable, you won't be affected by the energies of *everyone* in the room.

Practice Makes Perfect

> *Be the energy you want others to absorb."*
>
> A.D. Posey

Imagining yourself walking around in a bubble of energy takes a bit of practice, but don't just use it when you are with those who push your buttons and get to you. Practice when it doesn't count! Think of it as a fun game just to see what happens! There are many ways to define your space, and this is just one of them. No matter which method you decide to use, take time to practice until it becomes natural. Effort doesn't work, but your imagination and vision does. Define and create a beautiful space that you enjoy being in. Protect yourself by being in your own sweet, happy place.

How Is Your Growth Period? What Differences Do You Notice?

A good place to start is for you to tune into the shifts occurring around and within you. It's very helpful to make notes in your journal of what you are noticing and reflect on all the awesome work you are doing, because some of what is occurring may be subtle or hidden. As time passes, I guarantee you will have experienced such ongoing shifts and miracles that some of what's happening now might even appear as 'small potatoes'.

Alternative Ways to Protect Your Energy Space

In addition to these **Quantum Energy Tools** (http://bit.ly/29WqnQk) we discussed in the previous chapters including: Grounding, Clearing Center of Head, Replenishing with Golden Sun, Setting Your Crown Chakra to Wellness Color, Running Earth and Cosmic Energy, Separation Rose, Sending Other People Their Energy Back...

The following energy tools are especially helpful in setting healthy boundaries and separating from others energy.

Creating Neutrality

 A bridge has no allegiance to either side."

Les Coleman

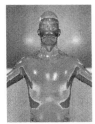 **Body of glass** is a quantum energy tool for creating neutrality in any situation. It allows energy to flow through you and doesn't get stuck within you. This is a fun tool to practice when you are around those people who know how to push your buttons.

Can you remember a time when you had a hard time standing your ground with a certain someone? Did you know you don't have to be a doormat and accept everything handed to you, or be apathetic or anything else?

Using the body of glass technique, allows foreign, controlling or dominant energy to flow through you. Rather than losing your space, you feel empowered and confident in who you are and what you want.

Many of my mentoring students have shared stories of feeling great and on top of their game and then went home to visit their family and **BAM** everything exploded. (Families can no doubt be challenging to holding our unique energy space.) It's as if they regressed and lost their balance. This tool, however, can be especially helpful in not taking on anyone's invalidation, their problems or decision and remain 'clear and calm'. That way you cannot get sucked down an emotional rabbit-hole and be compassionate for where they are coming from.

This quantum tool is as simple as *imagining you are a body of glass.* Give yourself a grounding cord and let any foreign energy flow right through your body of glass. Let other people's problems or decisions land elsewhere.

Separating and Clearing Foreign Energy

Before you can create something new or more in your life, you first must release previous energies and creations taking up space. It's like cleaning out your refrigerator before you can bring home new groceries to make a delicious dinner.

Creating and Destroying Roses

When you imagine you are destroying the object or symbol, you are actually moving and changing the molecules that created that energy form. Creating and destroying an object or symbol, sets energy in motion that affects all other energies surrounding it.

Simply imagining exploding or dissolving a rose or a symbol out in front of you is like throwing a pebble in a pond. It sends ripples out into the world around you.

Visualizing the same symbol consistently helps to identify changes as well as setting an unconscious pattern of release. I like to use a rose as my symbol; not only is the rose the highest frequency of any living thing on the earth plane, but it's a neutral symbol people around the world recognize. As you progress in the Manifesting Miracles 101, your rose/symbol gives you information on rogue energy. However, feel free to use what comes to you naturally.

Creating and destroying roses releases energy from thoughts in your space that have limited you. Such thoughts or pictures around not having enough time, not enough money, things I don't like, I'm not smart enough, etc. can be eroded by exploding or destroying roses. Simply imagine dropping the thought inside a rose and explode it.

You are in essence, clearing stuck pictures, beliefs or ideas that have been stuck or blocking the flow of your natural powerful you.

Collecting Your Energy Into Present Time

In collecting your vibes in a concentrated space, your aura, you magnify your energy. Not only do people notice you differently, but your energy is stronger and less receptive to 'energy invasions' or being influenced by outside sources.

Bringing your energy **'forward from the past'** and **'back from the future'**, brings you back into this moment. This helps anchor you in the present and releases energies that are taking valuable processing space in your energy field. To do that, just imagine looking at a time line from: birth to present time then into the future.

Birth ------------------------ **Present time**---------------------- **Future**

To bring your creative energy into present time, simply imagine a red dot lighting up on your time line for anywhere you left your creative energy … from the past all the way into the future.

Observing with neutral awareness, visualize a rose (or any symbol) starting at your birth, and begin sliding that symbol along your time line collecting all the red dots. Allow the rose to collect all your creative energy from anywhere you left it along your timeline. Then, simply dissolve your symbol.

Outlining Aura With Neon Color

Using color to outline your aura is helpful in *establishing* it for yourself and having a sense of where it is around your body. When using a bright color, it's easy to focus on it while you bring it around the body. Having an awareness of being present inside your aura helps set your boundaries and moves foreign energy out.

While you are grounded and centered inside the middle of your head, envision a large, oblong bubble completely surrounding you. Imagine lighting the edge of your aura with a very bright neon color. Then, gently begin bringing your aura in around your body and hold it there for a few seconds. Gently and slowly allow the aura to come back to approximately 3 feet around your body. Change the color of your grounding cord to match your aura bubble.

We all take different paths in life, but no matter where we go, we take a little of each other everywhere."

Tim McGraw

"I did a chakra energy program with Amirah Hall. She taught me to go deeper into myself, discovering and healing patterns and wounds that were stored in my chakras. I still use these techniques to this day and I have so much gratitude to Amirah for guiding and supporting me on my journey of self-healing, creating and manifesting goals that are truly in alignment with myself. This work has totally shifted my perception on living and where I am going in this life. I not only know myself better than ever before, I am much more at peace and love myself."

Monica Hill

Chapter 4 - Practice Guidelines

Practice the following tools this week:

1. Grounding – Quantum Energy Tool #1
2. Center of Head – Quantum Energy Tool #2
3. Replenishing – Quantum Energy Tool #3
4. Run Earth and Cosmic Energy – Quantum Energy Tool #7
5. Reset Challenged Communications
6. Setting Healthy Boundaries
7. Body of Glass
8. Collect Your Energy Into Present Time
9. Outline Aura With Neon Color

GOALS AND HEALING WORKSHEET

WELLNESS COLOR _____

Physical Goal _____

Mental Goal _____

Emotional Goal _____

Spiritual Goal _____

MISSION STATEMENT

_____

WHAT ARE YOU NOTICING DIFFERENT?

_____

_____

WHAT ENERGIES **SUPPORT** YOU? (Colors, memories, beliefs, thoughts)

_____

_____

OTHER

_____

_____

Chapter

5

The Universe Is In Constant Motion

> *You are precious, beautiful, and pure. Your life matters SO MUCH. YOU matter SO MUCH. Whatever has happened to you that tried to extinguish your light-- don't ever believe that there's not a flame. YOU are still in there. You are healing, overcoming and becoming everyday."*

The Power to Change is Within You

Give yourself some grace, and give all the grace you can to those around you. Receive this grace, too, and always seek out and go where there is peace. The energetic practices you are engaging in are shifting your energy. We all have the power within us to change as higher vibrations consume and transform lower ones.

In his book, The Science of Getting Rich, author Wallace D. Wattles talks about the Universal Law of Perpetual Transmutation of Energy.

Simply put, energy from the **formless realm** is constantly flowing into the material world and taking form. This energy is limitless and inexhaustible. As old forms are exhausted, they give way for new forms to emerge from the invisible hidden energy of the universe.

> *The energy of the Universe is always moving and transmuting in and out of form and is always in a state of motion.*

It will take one form and then move to another form, but it is always in motion and never stands still. This law relates to the universe and our consciousness through the realization that everything seen and unseen is constantly changing.

In <u>Manifesting Miracles 101</u>, you are harnessing this energy and transforming it into whatever form you desire.

By now I'm sure you are experiencing how your energy at the moment can be focused toward higher vibrations to cause the things around and within you to change for the better.

The energy is constantly flowing into our consciousness. You transform this energy into whatever you choose through your focus of attention at the moment. The formless energy is amenable to being shaped by your mind. All of the **Quantum Energy Tools** (http://bit.ly/29WqnQk) you have learned such as the ***Body of Glass, Golden Suns, Mockups, Exploding Roses, Running Earth and Cosmic Energy, Grounding*** – all assist you in transforming unconscious energy within and around you.

Change Is All There Is

Through learning **The Universal Law of Perpetual Transmutation of Energy** – you can understand that change is all there is. People often say, "***I like things just the way they are***", but they are just advertising their ignorance to this important law.

Everyone thinks of changing the world, but no one thinks of changing himself."

Leo Tolstoy

Everything is always changing. Resisting the change creates pain. Blocking the flow creates suffering and lack. But, being in the flow is where Universal Abundance and Power exists.

> **Where are you at in this moment?** *Growing and expanding? or Dying and shrinking?*
>
> **Visualize a Havingness Gauge for how much change and awareness shift you can HAVE today.**

How Much Can You 'Have'?

That is, ***how much growth can you 'HAVE' in this moment?***

Visualize a Havingness Gauge from 0-100%. **Where is your needle pointing in this moment?** Gently, move to 100% and allow yourself to HAVE what you desire right now.

By acknowledging that energy is in constant motion, you are aligning and engaging with the **Universal Law of Perpetual Transmutation of Energy.**

Sometimes good things fall apart so better things can fall together."

Marilyn Monroe

The Law of Polarity

Leading scientists have observed in the quantum world that light does not always behave in the same way. Wave Particle Duality is basically just a scientific name for the **Law of Polarity.**

Sometimes it displays particle-like behavior, and sometimes it acts like a wave. Interesting, huh?

So what is it? Is light a particle? Or is light a wave? Actually it's both!

Physicists refer to '**the wave nature of particles**' and '**the particle nature of waves**' when they attempt to describe the deep seeded duality of the nature of light.
The law of polarity states,

Everything can be separated into two wholly opposite parts, and that each of those still contains the potentiality of the other."

Hiram Pagen

In other words, particles have the potentiality of waves, waves have the potentiality of particles, white has black, low exists with high, slow is also fast. The same holds true for elation and depression, infatuation and resentment, kindness and cruelty, generosity and stinginess, and so on.

As the Late, Great Mythologist, Joseph Campbell once said,

No matter what good you do, it's evil for someone."

You see, no event is solely beautiful or solely tragic. It is impossible to have one without the other.

> *Is there bad in you? Yes. ...of course there is!*
> *There is both good and bad in all of us.*
> *No person is just good or just bad.*

The only thing labeling things good and bad does is help us talk about them, but it doesn't bring us to the source of love.

> *A beetle will chase after an opening of light, while a cockroach will scatter at a crack of it. How are we different from insects? Nobody is purely good or purely evil. Most of us are in-between. There are moths that explore the day and butterflies that play at night. Polarity is an integral part of nature — human or not human."*

Suzy Kassem

Going Back to Physics

It's been observed in laboratories that when you collide a Positron (e+) (a positively charged electron and also the electron's anti-particle) with an Electron (e-) (a negatively charged particle) there is an explosion. Both are annihilated and out of that annihilation, gamma-ray photons are created! LIGHT! ... and **LIGHT** at higher energies for that matter!

Positive + Negative = Light

When Positive and Negative come together, they birth light. Light is a metaphor for Love.

> *When you take a negative emotion in your life and see the equal and opposite, positive emotion that co-exists with it, the emotion you are experiencing is annihilated and out of that births love."*

Hiram Pagen

For example, when your girlfriend breaks up with you, a girl that you were deeply in love with, you may see the event as being tragic and then experience all the emotions of a tragic event such as sadness, anger, jealousy (i.e. if she's moved on with a new guy), depression, doubt, fear, etc.

But if you STOP and take note of your emotions, write them down and then ask yourself, "I'm feeling sad because I loved her and now she is gone, but what is it about this situation that I could be happy about?"

For instance …

Maybe she was a bit controlling and untrusting of you and always accused you of cheating on a daily basis. Now that she's gone, you can be happy about not having someone make false accusations against you all the time.

Maybe you like to save money and she liked to spend it, and as a result, every weekend she was draining your bank account. Now you can be happy that you can start saving money again and start accumulating wealth. Can you see how that works?

> *For every reason that you feel sad, there is going to be a reason to also be happy.*

By choosing to view life from this perspective, both life and your emotions become more balanced.

Realize that every time you allow yourself to feel an extreme emotion, you create the equal experience of the opposite. When you acknowledge that one-sidedness is merely an illusion and not actual truth, it opens the doorway to seeing the rest of world for what it truly is. A completely balanced system is fully equilibrated because of the divine order that exists in it.

As you allow yourself to perceive both sides simultaneously (the whole, positive and negative) you open yourself to the divine perfection of the universe.

> *Nothing is one-sided; everything contains its opposite. All is love.*

This is the essence of the **Law of Polarity.**

Sir Isaac Newton revealed that any action has an equal and opposite reaction; forces come in pairs. Why? It's because the purpose of the universe is '*equilibrium* and *synchronicity*'.

Energy cannot be created or destroyed, it can only be changed or transformed. You transform energy by applying its opposite pole."

Beverly Nadler

The Universe is Both a Creator and a Destroyer

If you were to look out into our universe with a huge telescope and see everything in real time, you would see stars exploding! Supernovae! But get this: the **death** of a star also means the **creation** of new planets, new solar systems, new life, etc.

Destruction Causes Creation -- Creation Ultimately Creates Destruction

When supernovae explode, they blast matter into space at some 9,000 to 25,000 miles (15,000 to 40,000 kilometers) per second. These blasts produce much of the material in the universe—including some elements, like iron, which make up our planet and even us. Heavy elements are only produced in supernovae, so all of us carry the remnants of these distant explosions within our own bodies.

The profane and ignorant masses looking from the outside might say, "*Oh, how sad...that star just exploded. It's gone.*" Their perception of the event is lop-sided.

> *...but the Adept, (the Master) sees both Destruction and Creation taking place simultaneously. He sees truth!*

As we progress in <u>Manifesting Miracles 101</u>, you will be taking a neutral look at energy that supports and doesn't support you in having your goals. What you observe one moment may not be the same the next time you observe it. Simply observing something, and realizing its opposite exists simultaneously, gives it permission to be different.

> *Tuning into yourself consider...*

Are you sick? Then focus on health. Talk about health and healing. Take actions that promote health. So many sick people enjoy talking about their illnesses. This is not an effective way to promote healing.

> *Life is whatever you make it, a heaven or hell on earth."*
> Steven Redhead

Are you having financial difficulties? Don't talk about (to others and/or yourself) how tough times are. That just puts you in vibrational harmony with more tough times. Focus on abundance, prosperity, beauty and luxury. Visualize yourself enjoying wealth, instead of focusing on lack. This doesn't mean you ignore your financial issues, it means you handle them as best you can, while you use your imagination to create wealth.

People who are sick, unhappy or struggling financially usually dwell on their undesired situations, and attract more of the same. It requires a conscious act of WILL to turn your attention to the polar opposite in the face of negative experiences.

Imagination is more important than knowledge!"

Einstein

Present Time Wellness Color

Resetting your vibration can be as easy and effortless as aligning with a color. Consider *what 'color frequency' will reset you into a feeling of 'harmony and wellness'*? In this moment, *what is the color as your 'present-time wellness color'*? Visualize a rose at that color. Drop it on the top of your head, into your crown chakra as you reset yourself to this wellness color. Allow yourself to *'vibrate at that color today'*. Quantum Energy Tool #6 - Wellness Meditation (http://bit.ly/2ait4Bh).

Creating Goals

 Setting goals is the first step in turning the invisible into the visible."

Tony Robbins

Reflecting on the concept of **creating goals, what does that look like to you?** Visualizing a rose, **what does it show you about the 'concept of creating goals'? What does it look like?** Observe it. Ask it to tell you about your understanding of creating goals.

You might have had exposure to what goals are, how to make them. Ground your rose and bring it into present time. Get a sense of what creating goals means to you and make notes in your journal.

As you progress in <u>Manifesting Miracles 101</u> and you proceed with the energy work, your body and spirit communication is enhanced. You begin to manifest into reality as you get aligned with your goals.

Owning Your Goals

Goals should be what are important to you as a spirit and the things you create on the path. Ask yourself: What's the **vibration of the concept of your ability to create goals**?

Is it creating and shining your light in the world? Or is it a **to-do list**?

Personal Mission Statement

Creating another rose next to your goal rose, allow it to represent your **personal mission statement** – or concept. **What feeling or sense do you get from the rose? What's your wellness statement for yourself**?

Some examples might be,

> *I am whole!*
> *I am aligned and radiant!*
> *I am balanced and a powerful creator!*

Goal for Manifesting Miracles 101

What is your goal for <u>Manifesting Miracles 101</u>**?** Visualize a rose for creating your own mission statement. Ground it. Observe it. **What is your havingness for this goal**? Bring it to 100%. Make note in your journal.

As you progress in <u>Manifesting Miracles 101</u>, you will add a new line of your mission statement regarding your ability to be in a state of wellness. (Chapter 24).

For example, since the 1st chakra relates to the body, family and survival, you might create a mission statement or a goal for this chakra such as one of the following:

> *"I am safe and secure."*
> *"I feel protected and self-confident in all I do."*
> *"My body is balanced, whole and well."*

By the end of <u>Manifesting Miracles 101</u>, you'll have eight statements for yourself, (for chakras 1-8) and a complete picture of where you are going. You will have a map per-se of your life mission as a guideline to steer the course.

The goals aren't just singular. They move you closer to the big picture while giving you more meaning for each step your take towards your goals and some value beyond the goals once achieved, they tie ones path to what is being created in the moment.

Using the Mockup Tools

Consider:

> **What do you need to do right now to achieve that goal?**

For example, let's say you want a new car. The steps to take to get that new car might include: 1) Organize your finances 2) deciding to sell the old car 3) decide what type of new car you want.

The mockup tool breaks down the smaller steps and the overall goal is the final accomplishment. (**Mockups Guided Meditation** - http://bit.ly/29Vd5FG)

Reset Energy of Creating Goals

Visualize a rose for your vision/mission statement. Visualize a rose for goals space. Set the relationship energy between them. Grounding them both, begin cleaning them off using a magic wand rose. Reset the roses with matching colors and connect the two roses together with a golden string.

> *One of the lessons that I grew up with was to always stay true to yourself and never let what somebody else says distract you from your goals."*
>
> Michelle Obama

Clearing Your Wellness Space

Visualize a rose with the color of your wellness. Ground and release foreign energy from your rose (i.e. if your rose is pink and it's got other colors flickering, using a sticky rose clean off the rose.) Bring the rose into your energy space. Set your crown chakra to vibrate your wellness color.

Re-Set Your Body Spirit Communication

Visualize a rose to represent body and spirit communication space. Clear all foreign energy with a magic wand rose. Ground it and reset it to your wellness color.

Consider: If you were to create a spiritual vision for your goals along your path...

What affect does that have on your body and spirit communication?

Visualize a rose that represents your spiritual path. ***Does the rose grow? Dance, expand or shrink? What does the rose do?*** Let it show you what happens. Set your crown chakra to match that vibration of the rose setting the body and spirit to communication with each other.

Manifesting Miracles 101 assists you with creating your own life picture. Having a mission (guiding value or picture of wellness) and integrating spirit and body to achieve your overall body, mind and spirit wellness.

Creating On Your Path In Harmony

When you are on your path, actualizing your vision – this is a ***BLAST***. You are manifesting and internalizing goals into alignment with your being. Manifesting Miracles 101 is all about releasing energy that takes YOU away from yourself and ***brings Heaven to Earth***.

To live in harmony requires that we be conscious of the hopes and needs that surround us and be flexible in our own course of action. We can be in harmony with others only when we are in harmony with ourselves--living true to our deepest sense of what is real and what matters.

ASK YOURSELF: *What ONE thing will help you take a step in wellness?*

If you are challenged comprehending some of these new concepts – don't worry because it's completely normal. That's because your left, logical brain is trying to understand it and there's so much unconsciousness energy clouding the subject that it can be challenging.

Have some amusement. Let go and try not to analyze. Trust that even if you don't know what you did, or should do, it's ALL working perfectly.

You can't start the next chapter of your life if you keep re-reading your last one."

Anonymus

"Working with Amirah's programs is like being on a magical journey. I'm feeling more joy and ease day by day, it's as if all my worries, doubts and fears are melting away in my sleep. I'm bubbling over with gratitude and feelings of abundance. Friends are telling me I'm 'glowing' but the best part is that I really feel 'beautiful'. There's no question that I want more of these high vibration feelings and continue feeling happy and light. These practices are truly a blessing to humanity".

Kara Upton

Chapter 5 - Practice Guidelines

Practice the following tools this week:

1. Grounding – Quantum Energy Tool #1
2. Replenishing – Quantum Energy Tool #3
3. Run Earth and Cosmic Energy – Quantum Energy Tool #7
4. Set Present Time Wellness Color
5. Set Goal for **Manifesting Miracles 101**
6. Reset Energy of Creating Goals
7. Clear Energy Your Wellness Space
8. Reset Your Body Spirit Communication

GOALS AND HEALING WORKSHEET

WELLNESS COLOR _____

Physical Goal _____

Mental Goal _____

Emotional Goal _____

Spiritual Goal _____

MISSION STATEMENT

_____

WHAT ARE YOU NOTICING DIFFERENT?

_____

_____

WHAT ENERGIES **SUPPORT** YOU? (Colors, memories, beliefs, thoughts)

_____

_____

OTHER

_____

_____

Chapter

6

The Laws of Rhythm and Relativity

> *Beautiful soul, it takes a lot of very important and contemplative listening to know for sure when it's time to hold on, when it's time to let go, and when it's time to just take a lot of extra care to get things back to healthy. Be brave and tune out all of the voices, except the voices that are speaking your truth."*

Everything in our life **just is** until we compare it to something. **Nothing in life has any meaning, except for the meaning that we give it.** It is all in how you look at your situation and what thoughts and perspective you choose to think about the situation with. When you focus on good thoughts and energies, more good things will come to you.

Likewise, if you focus on how bad your situation is, you will attract more bad.

The Law of Relativity

The Law of Relativity teaches us to compare our problems to other's problems in proper perspective. No matter how bad we perceive our situation to be, there is always someone who is in a worse position. It's all *relative*.

The spiritual and metaphysical aspects of the law of relativity tell us that everything in our physical world is only made real by its relationship or comparison to something else. Light only exists because we compare it to dark. Good can only exists because we compare it to bad. Hot can only exist because we compare it to cold!

You can always compare your life situation to someone else, and it will look better or worse depending on your viewpoint and how you look at it. If you compare your situation to someone's whose is worse, yours will look better. No matter the situation at hand, 'There is always someone worse off and there is always someone doing better'.

However, from a spiritual point of view, we can remove barriers of labeling and accept everything 'as is'. From A New Earth by: Eckhart Tolle: *"In form, you are and will always be inferior to some, superior to others. In essence, you are neither inferior nor superior to anyone. True self-esteem and true humility arise out of that realization. In the eyes of the ego, self-esteem and humility are contradictory. In truth, they are one and the same."*

Everything Has It's Own Vibration

Within the Law of Vibration every sound, thing or thought has its own vibrational frequency, unique unto itself.

Everything vibrates and moves to certain rhythms. These rhythms establish seasons, cycles, stages of development, and patterns. Each cycle reflects the regularity of God's Universe. Masters know how to rise above negative parts of a cycle by never getting too excited or allowing negative things to penetrate their consciousness.

Now, what you need to know is that the law works closely with the law of rhythm. What does it mean?

The Law of Rhythm

> *Everything flows, out and in; everything has its tides; all things rise and fall; the pendulum-swing manifests in everything; the measure of the swing to the right is the measure of the swing to the left; rhythm compensates."-*
>
> The Kybalion.

The Law of Rhythm states that the energy in the universe is like a pendulum. Whenever something swings to the right, it must then swing to the left. Everything in existence is involved in a dance--swaying, flowing, and swinging back and forth.

Everything is Either Growing or Dying

This law can even be seen in the cycles of economies; there's a high period and then a low period. Our seasons, you can see, are in a continuous flow of summer to winter. Everything goes through cycles, yet everything has a rhythm or a pattern. What seems to be random is actually very orderly.

The law of rhythm also governs our economy, health, relationships, and spirituality. Let's say that you're at peak potential with your health and fitness. If you realize you're at the peak, then you can foresee your health and fitness dropping some. However, instead of viewing this "drop in health" as something being wrong with you, you now view it as a sign to rest your body. Then, by law, you have to grow to a better and higher state of potential.

You have a *havingness* for everything. What's your ability to *have wellness?*

Havingness for Wellness

> *There is no one giant step that does it. It's a lot of little steps."*
>
> Unknown

How much wellness can you HAVE in this moment? Create a Havingness Gauge for how much wellness you can HAVE in this moment. Allow your gauge to show you how much of your energy supports your ability to '*have wellness*'? From 1-100 where is your needle pointing? Clean off your gauge and bring it up to 100% 'Havingness for Wellness'.

Havingness for Manifesting Miracles

> *Releasing resistance, you find that your miracles are waiting for you!"*
>
> Amirah Hall

Create a Havingness Gauge for how much '*manifesting miracles*' energy you HAVE in this moment. From 1-100 where is your needle pointing? Clean off your gauge and bring it up to 100% 'havingness for manifesting miracles'.

Physical Wellness

Visualize a gauge in front of you that represents your **Physical Wellness**

0_____Harmony _____0

Imbalance   **Imbalance**

Ask yourself what is it body desires for physical wellness?

Emotional Wellness

Imagine a gauge in front of you that represents your **Emotional Wellness**.

0_____Harmony _____ 0

Imbalance   **Imbalance**

Ask yourself what 'emotions' does it need? Make note.

Mental Wellness

Imagine a gauge in front of you that represents your **Mental Wellness**.

0_____Harmony _____ 0

Imbalance   **Imbalance**

Ask yourself what the 'mind' needs for wellness?

Spiritual Wellness

Imagine a gauge in front of you that represents your **Spiritual Wellness**.

0_____Harmony _____ 0

Imbalance   **Imbalance**

Ask yourself 'what does your spiritual wellness mean to you?'

Comparison and Competition

 Comparison is the death of joy."

Mark Twain

The thing about comparison is that there is never a win. How often do we compare ourselves with someone less fortunate than us and consider ourselves blessed? More often, we compare ourselves with someone who we perceive as being, having, or doing more.

Our minds **do** want to quantify. Our minds want to rank and file and organize information. Our minds want to know where we fit into the scheme of things. So we need to give our minds something to do.

Who you are today is a result of the decisions you made yesterday and you are in a state of constant creation. It's our human nature to continually expand. Ask yourself, **how have you continued to become a new and improved version of yourself?** Instead of submitting to the temptation to compare yourself to someone else, ask yourself a few questions instead.

Michelangelo said, "*Every block of stone has a statue inside it and it is the task of the sculptor to discover it.*" And, how well we do this is our measurement.

It doesn't matter what anyone else is doing with **their own** block of stone. The statue that they are liberating is one of their own intentions. **How well are you doing with your own block of stone?**

By tending to it with honor, care, compassion, and praise you allow for more self-expression and stand taller.

When someone tells you, "You've changed," it might simply be because you've stopped living your life their way."

Anonymus

Clearing Comparison

Create a timeline in your mind, from 'birth - present – future' and allow red lights to appear anywhere guilt is stuck anywhere **comparison energy** is stuck.

BIRTH_____PRESENT_____FUTURE

Allow any energy where you compared yourself to others, where you competed with someone else to be better than them or they competed with you. Using a magic wand or sticky rose, slide it along the timeline, collecting up all comparison energy from your timeline.

Why compare yourself with others? No one in the entire world can do a better job of being you than you."

Unknown

Feeling Guilty

I was always fraught with guilt, and it's such a waste of an emotion. It keeps you out of the moment of being where you are."

Kyra Sedgwick

Sometimes we can feel GUILTY that we are manifesting more than others around us.

As you begin noticing more effortless manifesting in your world, other people will start taking notice of you. Have you had anyone close ask you, "HOW DO YOU DO THAT?"

As others start noticing you are shifting, and something is seriously GOING YOUR WAY, they want your secret! My caution here is that you DO NOT teach them these **Quantum Energy Tools** (http://bit.ly/29WqnQk). Not because they are SECRET or anything like that, but what happens is that they jump into your energy field and start interfering with your own frequency.

It acts like static on the line. Or dropped calls! With a heavy load draining your connection, then things start getting messed up, stop flowing and you begin manifesting a slowdown in your manifesting momentum.

Maybe your desire is to truly HELP them. Yes, I understand. Better however, to send them to http://www.AmirahHall.com for the energy tools, or http://www.youtube.com/amirahhall1 they can begin practicing and you don't have a proverbial monkey on your back.

Guilty Emotions Block Your Flow

Guilt about money pushes money away."

Melody Fletcher

It may happen that as you manifest more and more, you begin feeling guilty. You may feel guilty for manifesting in the flow while you observe others struggle and suffer. Yes, I get it! Of course, you want to help them, but that can stop you manifesting. How? Well, there's an unconscious program not to move ahead or better yet, we don't want to leave our friends or loved ones behind.

Guilt is a two part belief – one part unworthiness (you're not as good as others and therefore don't deserve to have what you do), and one part thinking that there is a limited amount of resources and whenever you gain something, it means someone else had to lose.

Food, love, career, and mothers, the four major guilt groups."

Cathy Guisewite

Clearing Guilt Energy

Visualize a Havingness Gauge for how much of other peoples energy is in your space.

Visualize a timeline, from 'birth - present – future'.

BIRTH_____PRESENT_____FUTURE

Allow red lights to appear anywhere guilt is stuck anywhere guilt energy is stuck. Using a magic wand or sticky rose, slide it along the timeline, collecting up all guilt energy from your timeline.

Some of the guilt can include:

- Guilt for living if someone else died.
- Guilt for having a job. Or having something someone doesn't have.
- Guilt for not doing something you thought you should have done
- Guilt for not sharing something
- Guilt for not caring enough
- Guilt for not spending time with someone or guilt for spending too much
- Guilt for not spending enough
- Guilt for doing something wrong
- Guilt for not doing the right thing

You don't have to know specifically what you are collecting, or you may notice certain events coming to your mind.

Besides feeling guilty, we often compare ourselves with others. The point is however, that each person has a series of problems, life lessons and spiritual tests that ultimately strengthen the soul light within, challenging us to stay connected to our hearts as we resolve our problems.

Try not to get lost in comparing yourself to others. Discover your gifts and let them shine! Softball is amazing that way as a sport. Everyone on the field has a slightly different ability that makes them perfect for their position."

Jennie Finch

"I've struggled so much with manifesting the simplest things. What's easy for others was just plain 'not working' for me. My whole life felt filled with disappointment and the notion of having my goals felt impossible and exhausting. When I found this program, I felt I had nothing more to lose. Now I feel as if I'm walking on clouds and I'm more inspired about what the future will bring. I'm the first person who would have said 'it's impossible' but now I've gained an understanding of where my power has been blocked. Releasing the depression and sadness has been huge for me. I'm extremely grateful to this program and Amirah for her guidance and encouragement."

Dinesh Kumar

Chapter 6 - Practice Guidelines

Practice the following tools this week:

1. Grounding – Quantum Energy Tool #1
2. Center of Head – Quantum Energy Tool #2
3. Replenishing – Quantum Energy Tool #3
4. Run Earth and Cosmic Energy – Quantum Energy Tool #7
5. Reset Havingness for Manifesting Miracles
6. Clear Comparison Energy
7. Clear Guilt Energy

GOALS AND HEALING WORKSHEET

WELLNESS COLOR _____

Physical Goal _____

Mental Goal _____

Emotional Goal _____

Spiritual Goal _____

MISSION STATEMENT

_____

WHAT ARE YOU NOTICING DIFFERENT?

_____

_____

WHAT ENERGIES **SUPPORT** YOU? (Colors, memories, beliefs, thoughts)

_____

_____

OTHER

_____

_____

Chapter

7

1ˢᵗ Chakra Wellness Setting New Patterns

> When we wait for tomorrow to come before we enjoy all that life has to offer, we miss out on what life has to offer us right NOW. There is SO MUCH abundance in the world. There is enough for everyone, and you don't need to wait to enjoy what is in front of your face right now."

Did you know ...You are in the process of expanding, reconnecting, releasing, opening and grounding? It's through learning and implementing the **Quantum Energy Tools** (http://bit.ly/29WqnQk) and techniques, that you magnetize your goals effortlessly. Through these meditation practices, you will facilitate the connections of the spiritual and physical bodies and create balance within your chakra system.

Scientifically speaking, you are comprised of gazillions of atoms. You are energy. As such, you know what it's like to feel the intense energy in a room. Think of the chakra system as a reminder to pay more attention to the energy in your body, and a roadmap for self-care and personal growth in each facet of life.

In the last chapter, you looked at your 'Havingness for Wellness' within your whole being. That is − '**having**' an overriding sense of harmony for your entire system: physical, emotional, mental and spiritual. Being in a state of wellness is, in a sense, like a whole system reset.

> Without awareness of bodily feeling and attitude, a person becomes split into a disembodied spirit and a disenchanted body."
>
> *Alexander Lowen*

As you progress in <u>Manifesting Miracles 101</u>, we will continue to explore your personal energies and their roles in manifesting your experiences and desires.

We'll also continue to explore your Mind, Body, and Spirit.

This will include your physical survival needs, connection and belonging with place, family, and friends, sensuality and sexuality, sense of self and healthy ego strength, compassion, creativity and communication, intellect, and spirituality/intuition.

> *Manifesting ALL of your hearts desires is our goal.*

Setting New Patterns and Habits

Remember that good people have bad days sometimes. Smart people do dumb things sometimes. Bad things happen to good people sometimes. It's okay for you to have days like this. IT REALLY IS OKAY. YOU ARE OKAY. LIFE IS OKAY. And everything is going to turn out okay. You are going to make it.

Putting your wellness first takes some time and plenty of reminders, but it will become more pervasive throughout the day. Reminding yourself at the beginning of your day to reset your wellness color will eventually become a new normal. How are you reminding yourself to bring yourself to wellness? You might consider an alarm on your Smartphone or a red string on your wrist. Perhaps having a flower at your desk or wearing a piece of jewelry can be very helpful for recollection in the beginning. Setting new habits will soon become second nature, with practice.

Wait! There's one more important thing that needs to be considered... and it's the Universal Law of Resistance. Let's take a look at it:

Universal Law of Resistance

Every time we focus on something, we are 'calling' it towards us. Have you ever heard the expression, '**what you resist – persists**'? In his book, <u>SUPER BRAIN</u>, Deepak Chopra says,

> *Whatever you resist persists. There is the rub. As long as you engage in an inner war between what you crave and what you know is good for you, defeat is all but inevitable. In its natural state, will is the opposite of resistance."*

Amirah Hall

With our thoughts and beliefs we invite people, situations, experiences and material things into our life. When they arrive, if we do not really want them, we try to push them away.

Many people invoke the Law of Resistance without being consciously aware that they are doing it. Your subconscious mind and the Universal mind work similar to computers. You can't tell a computer 'not' to bring up a certain file if you have clicked on it, as it cannot accept negative instructions. It will assume you DO want that file and bring it up.

Your conscious mind CAN discriminate between a negative instruction and a positive one - but your subconscious mind is fully engaged and CANNOT tell the difference!

If you have a thought or make a statement often enough, it will access your subconscious mind. Some people have illness in their lives because they 'resist' illness. If you are continuously thinking, '*I don't want to be ill*' the word '*ill*' filters constantly into your subconscious mind. This, in turn, causes you to be ill.

'Don't', 'can't', 'won't' and 'not' are words that invoke the Law of Resistance.

For example, the thoughts:

> *'I won't ever find a perfect partner': resists the perfect partner.*
> *'I don't want to be poor': brings about poverty.*
> *'I can't live in that awful house': keeps you living in that awful house; and*
> *'I won't ever be like my mother': ensures that you will become just like her.*

On the positive side, statements such as '*I am healthy*'; '*I deserve a perfect partner*'; '*I welcome riches*'; '*I live in a beautiful home*', bring that energy towards you.

Never 'resist' failure or poverty. Instead attract success, wealth and abundance with positive thought instructions to your subconscious.

Always embrace the positive rather than the negative.

The Law of Resistance is triggered by *'victim'* consciousness. A victim is someone who blames others for their fate or believes that the world owes them, and they generally feel sorry for themselves. When someone is thinking **'Poor me'** or **'I am so unlucky'** they are being a *'victim'* who is resisting abundance and generosity. If someone blames another for what is happening in their own life, then they are a *'victim'* who is resisting taking personal responsibility for what they themselves have created. Clearing **'victim vibes'** from your aura allows the natural Laws of Attraction and Vibration to operate effectively.

Breathe in. Breathe out. Take a hot bath. Listen to your favorite music. And TRUST. And then keep trusting more.

When you hold resentment toward another, you are bound to that person or condition by an emotional link that is stronger than steel. Forgiveness is the only way to dissolve that link and get free."

Catherine Ponder

Clearing Victim Energy

Visualize a 'Havingness Gauge' out in front of you and allow it to show you how much victim energy is in your space in the present moment. Imagine a rose to represent victim energy in your space.

What does the rose look like? Is it small? Dark? Dehydrated? Sad? **Let it show you anything like, *'Poor me, unlucky me, failure, poverty, feeling sorry for myself'* inside of your space. Begin cleaning out the rose or symbol with an imaginary, sticky rose or sponge anywhere that you have not, or did not take responsibility for what you created.**

Collect up all the foreign energy that relates to this *'victim energy'* that creates resistance in your creations.

Fear Creates Resistance

When we feel fear, we resist the *'joy of life and the magnificence of 'Self''*.

Let's suppose you created an intention to manifest something, visualized in the proper way, opened your heart energy, and nothing happened. Your intention failed to manifest quickly because you had resistance.

Whenever your intention fails to manifest quickly, it's because you aren't a vibrational match to your intention. Instead, you're a vibrational match to things remaining the same...and you probably don't even realize it.

Resistance usually takes the form of subconscious fears and doubts. You don't even realize they're there. Yet, they sit in the background and prevent your desires from manifesting. They act as counter-intentions and the more attention and energy you give them, the harder it is to manifest what you want.

It isn't that the Law of Attraction isn't working. It is that you're giving it two different intentions to work on – what you want and what you're afraid of. Wherever you focus the most energy is what the Law of Attraction will create.

Remember,

- You probably don't give yourself enough credit for everything you already know.

- You are actually an expert about so many things. Just about every person you meet is an expert at something.

- Some are experts at making it through depression.

- Some are experts at living on a tight budget.

- Some are experts at making the most out of life when things don't go as planned.

- Everyone is an expert at something...and the best thing an expert can do is to share what he or she knows. That is how we help each other best. If you take some time to think about all of the things you have been through, it is really quite miraculous.

Clearing Fear Energy

Visualize a Havingness Gauge in your mind's eye and allow it to show you how much fear energy is in your space in the present moment. From 0-100%, *how much 'conscious and unconscious' fear is present in this moment?* Imagine, out in front of you is a rose or a symbol and allow it to represent the fear energy in your space. You might see or perceive black dots, rust or fog. Just know, that anything that makes that rose appear *'off'*, is fear energy. Imagine a sticky rose or sponge and start cleaning out the fear from the rose or symbol, collecting up all the fear energy that creates resistance when you're producing what you desire.

Becoming Happy

Have you ever walked into a room and felt negativity in the air? Feeling another person's energy is actually very common. If you give off positive energy, other people will feel better around you. In contrast, if you give off negative energy, others are likely to feel tense and maybe want to leave. Positive beliefs, thoughts and feelings turn into positive energy that you put into the universe. YOU control your energy. Whether it's positive or negative, your energy affects everyone you come in contact with.

Let's look at a Havingness Gauge for how much space you have for happiness. From 0-100%, how much room do you have for '**being happy**'? Using a sticky rose to clear off any energy taking space from your '**happiness**' area.

Without awareness of bodily feeling and attitude, a person becomes split into a disembodied spirit and a disenchanted body."

Alexander Lowen

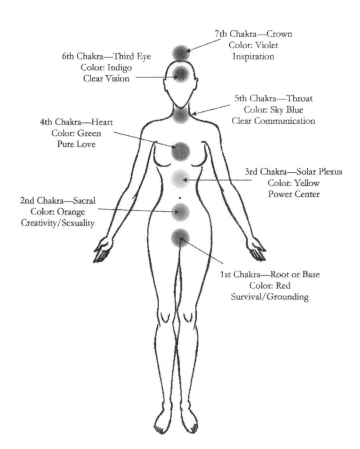

Chakra System

The concept of the chakras originated in the ancient Hindu spiritual text, the Vedas, and scientific research continues to support their validity of the mind-body connection. There is much written on this vast subject, but for the purpose of this book, I'm intentionally simplifying it and instead guiding you **'inside'** yourself to access your own information.

I'm not saying what's been written is incorrect or invalid; it simply keeps you in your head and out of where the magic happens -- the creative, intuitive side of yourself.

I firmly believe that to heal from any sort of trauma or to achieve meaningful personal growth, we have to approach the mind, body, and spirit in an integrated way. This is why pure **'talk therapy'** is not very effective, and why making changes to your physical lifestyle (like exercise and diet) is rarely sustainable without also addressing underlying psychological and emotional issues.

The chakras offer an ideal framework in which to map out and assess every facet of the human experience, both individually and as a whole, interdependent system.

Focusing on the characteristics of the 1st Chakra, and working to keep it balanced can help you actually follow through on your goals, rather than being all talk and no action.

> *To lose our connection with the body is to become spiritually homeless. Without an anchor we float aimlessly, battered by the winds and waves of life... is it any wonder that we equally ignore our physical surroundings, damaging the body of the Earth in order to perpetuate our dissociated survival? ... Only by recovering the body can we begin to heal the world itself, for as mind is to body, so culture is to planet."*
>
> Anodea Judith

Root Chakra Affirmations:
I am safe and secure.
I am grounded and stable.
I am connected to my body.
I am open to possibilities.
I trust myself.

1ˢᵗ or Root Chakra

What comes to mind when you see a chakra? Imagine a rose in your mind's eye and let it represent the '**concept of chakras**'. **What do you see? What does your intuitive self tell you about what chakras are, and how do they function**?

What is Your 1st Chakra?

Also called the **root chakra**, the 1ˢᵗ Chakra is a vibrating disc of energy that expresses itself near the base of your spine. It symbolizes your connection with the earth and with humanity. It affects your financial mindset and your sense of belonging.

When you strengthen and recharge your 1ˢᵗ Chakra, you affect these parts of your life. You feel supported by money and your community, as well as food, health and a general sense of wellbeing.

The **1st Chakra** influences our immune system, our energy, basic impulses, instincts, and endurance and fight or flight reactions. Grounding through the 1st Chakra makes the body feel safe and secure.

This chakra is the base of the six other major chakras and it deals with the body's survival including: food, shelter and protection. Relationships in our early life will influence the wellbeing of this chakra. It helps to activate our energy and stimulates activity, exercise, action and vitality.

If there was damage done to this chakra in early life and left untreated, then there will be problems encountered in the day-to-day life that prevents us from moving on though our development. The root chakra is relevant to achievements in the material world, money, permanence, character strength, patience, endurance and safety.

When this chakra is balanced we feel healthy, alive, free, optimistic, happy, steady and full of vitality. If the root chakra has too much energy flowing through it, this could cause selfishness, greed, an over-powering manner, irritation, aggression and sadism.

If there is too little energy flowing through it, this can cause anxiety, lack of confidence, and a lack of ability to complete things. There may also be an emphasis of feeling unloved and becoming masochistic. If this chakra is not working properly, it can negatively influence the legs, bones, adrenal glands, colon, kidneys and spinal column.

Unblocking and balancing aids to help realign the 1st or root chakra are physical activities such as cooking and cleaning in the home, sitting on the ground, being in nature, walking barefoot and, finally, dancing. All of these can help ground this chakra and help to make you feel safe. You're a human being.... so the truth is that you will continue to make mistakes throughout your life and you will have to re-calibrate and redirect. But each time this happens it will get easier and easier because you will have learned how to get yourself back on track. So even when you are redirecting your course, you can feel at peace!

The 1st Chakra is all about feeling safe as it stores all the spiritual information that you have gathered about survival.

Chakra Awareness

While tuning into your 1st Chakra, imagine a rose that represents your 1st Chakra. *What comes to mind when you say hello to your 1st Chakra? What does your 1st Chakra look like in the present moment?* Grasp a sense of what the rose is telling you about the chakra in the present moment -- *Is it open, closed – large, small – dark, light – depleted, fresh? Do you get a sense of a color, sensation, pictures or ideas?*

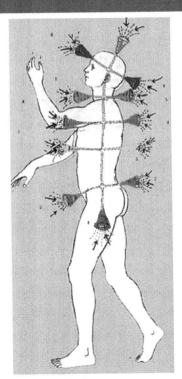

> *It is truly amazing how each brave new decision we make in our lives brings us to a more peaceful place on a soul deep level. As you grow and change and learn, you will become more peaceful inside. As you discover what is true and right for yourself, you align your life to live around that truth... and when what you believe aligns with what you do, you feel peaceful."*

As you progress through the chapters of Manifesting Miracles 101, you will look at your various chakras and connect with your own information by what you see. There's plenty written in books and on the Internet about what others believe chakras are, but it's empowering to receive your own intuitive insights on what they represent to you and the current state that your own chakras are in.

Personally, I see chakras as different colored, cone shapes with their widest part facing outward from the body and the points connecting at the spine.

Chakras are Energy Centers

There are seven major chakras that include the 1st Chakra from the base of spine to the top of the head, or 7th Chakra. The 8th Chakra is outside of the body approximately 6" above the 7th Chakra. There are hundreds of minor chakras in the body and they all relate to the energy meridians of the body. In this book, however, we will address the 7 major chakras plus the 8th chakra outside of the body where your higher self resides.

Just like our physical anatomy we have a spiritual anatomy and the major chakras are part of that. Each chakra has different energy levels and relates to a different part of you.

Chakras are connected to the glandular systems of the body and are where the spiritual being connects with the physical being. Bringing the chakra into wellbeing, in part, is bringing that communication of your spirit into balance and alignment. It also brings that chakra, or what that area represents, into balance for you.

The 1st Chakra, also known as the 'Root or Tribal' chakra is located at the base of spine.

You ground from the 1st Chakra and store information about your family connections and those connections that make you safe. This could be from when you are little and your survival depended on family (**tribes**). As you grow and develop, you still have those connections and what you learned from that tribe, but you may shift those connections and have a different tribe or different energy levels or rules.

It's all part of the survival idea and not just about surviving and making money. It's about feeling safe. ***How safe are you in your body? How connected do you feel to the earth? How grounded are you?***

This 1st Chakra has to be stable in order for you to develop higher spiritual consciousness because it always takes precedence.

Survival Overrides Everything Else

The main goal of the 1st Chakra is always to survive no matter what.

In terms of the physical body, the 1st Chakra is connected to ovaries and testes, which are the most basic level of survival for the body and species. Also, the adrenal gland (the fight or flight center) is affected. If there is a survival aspect in any chakra, there are a lot of different reactions that can happen, not just one.

Grounding and Feeling Safe

Visualize a rose out in front of you and allow it to represent your sense of grounding or being safe within yourself. Notice any colors associated with that. Let the first thing that pops up be that color.

Consider your family or tribal agreement. Make notes of what you saw. Some of the family agreements are in the past. Maybe there are limits. Look and see how some of these energies limit you in creating what you want, or limit you from having that chakra be comfortable.

Consider what you learned about being safe. *What is safety to you*?

What does being 'grounded' mean? What does it do for you in life?

What is survival? What is survival NOT?

Consider other ways you might ground yourself. This could be eating, exercising, nature, sex or through or being with other people.

With a magic wand, or sticky rose or symbol, begin collecting any past family agreements out of your 1st Chakra rose that are no longer supporting you. Set your wellness color into your 1st Chakra rose, bringing the 1st Chakra space into wellness.

In settling this space to wellness, you release those limits that prevent yourself from becoming grounded and safe.

Creating and Destroying Concepts

In Chapter 3, we discussed the **Universal Law of Creation and Destroying.** You have to release previous energies or creations in order to create space for new or different energies or creations. When you create and destroy an object or symbol, an energy force is set in motion that affects all other energies surrounding it. Even creating the rose is an aspect of '**creating a picture**'.

'**Mockups**' are the spiritual aspects of creating and putting out into the universe your visualizations of what you want to create.

> *Live by your own truth, sweet girl, and you will no longer worry about what others around you are thinking or doing. This is one way to freedom and peace, and you are getting closer every day."*

The Concept of 'Creating'

Visualize a rose and allow it to represent the energy space of '*creating*'. *What comes to your mind when you think of 'creating'? Does the rose change shape or give you an image or sense of what creating* means? Not only in terms of goals and things, it can also be about your feelings or what you want to do. *How much room do you have to create? Has someone put limits on your creation space?*

Visualize a rose for the concept of creating and let all things that would be limiting you to create go into the rose. (i.e. fears, concepts, other people's ideas about creating. When you sense it's full, explode the rose.)

Concept of 'Destroying'

In a spiritual sense, to destroy is a way of releasing. **Can you let go of things? Can you release?** In relation to the 1st Chakra, as its main function is survival and to make sure things '**persist**' or continue on, in many ways the wellness of this chakra would involve releasing, healing and letting go. Survival or energy on that level can stop us from changing and growing as a spirit. You stop growing when you can't let go of an old idea or concept. If there's anything there that says you can't let go because you don't know what's around the corner, then there's a survival consideration.

Ask yourself:

Is it safe for you to create and destroy? Explode roses around this concept; clearing any energy blocking you from creating or destroying.

Is there any 'fear of destroying'? Let go of any fear or anything that says you shouldn't be able to destroy. Let go of anything that limits you from clearing the clutter. Maybe you love roses and maybe when I suggest you explode a rose symbol, you might resist.

Consider that Universal Energy to create is unlimited and '**destroying**' is simply '**recycling**' stagnant energy to a new and useful form. Life is constant change and growth. Destroying is the natural and necessary partner with '**creating**' for all life to flow/grow.

> Visualize a rose that represents your '*ability to destroy*', fill it up with anything that stops you from destroying, or simply let it move through your body. Throughout your aura, collect any energy stopping you from destroying.

It can be as simple as someone taught you or said,

It's bad to destroy anything.

Save everything, you never know when you might need it.

Don't throw away any leftovers.

Don't buy flowers because they will die.

Ending a relationship means you are a failure.

I made an agreement that I can't cancel or change my mind.

Collect any and all the energy that stops you from '**destroying**' or '**releasing**' and explode the rose.

Finding Your 1st Chakra Wellness Color

> Visualize a rose that represents your 1st Chakra and bring your wellness color into the rose as you reset your wellness. Activating your grounding cord, get a sense of connecting to the planet and safe feelings and say '*hello*' to energy of wellness not just spiritually, but physically.
>
> Your 1st Chakra relates to the immune system. Get a sense of wellness within yourself and consider what supports that wellness for you. *What helps you bring your immune system into wellness? What can you do that helps set that energy of wellbeing for the 1st Chakra?*

> *What opposes that ability to feel safe or release negativity?* *(Colors, sensations, pictures or ideas)* **Set and vibrate your 1st Chakra to your wellness color, releasing any limits. Spin the chakra.**

Spinning your chakra at wellness helps it to harmonize with the body. You may notice that other chakras start adjusting towards wellness like an automatic reboot.

Sometimes we just need to '*put a hold on looking for what is wrong*' and do our very best to '*look for what is right*'. This is a wonderful break from the brain-bending burden of looking for what is wrong in situations, in people, in places and in us.

Setting Your Home and Workspace to Wellness

> **Visualize another rose and let it represent you at the present time.**
> **Send it into your home space. This will set your home to a present time wellness. Send another rose into your workspace as well.**
> *Congratulations on balancing your first chakra! Today... stop and remember just how brave, competent and strong you really are. You are watched out for, and blessed... and whatever happens... you will make it through.*

"I am very thankful to you for Manifesting Miracles 101! Having participated in many of Amirah's trainings, this is most helpful in having a deeper understanding to the foundation of the practices. At first I had no understanding of the effects of the Quantum Energy Tools, but have now gained a deeper respect and connection to them and also with myself. These practices get more profound in their effects the more I practice them. I can proudly say that now I feel more confident and magnetic than ever before. I feel my enthusiasm growing every day. Life is so much more beautiful being in the flow. Thank you so much!"

Carolyn Summit

Chapter 7 - Practice Guidelines

Practice the following tools this week:

1. Grounding – Quantum Energy Tool #1
2. Clearing Center of Head – Quantum Energy Tool #2
3. Replenishing – Quantum Energy Tool #3
4. Run Earth and Cosmic Energy – Quantum Energy Tool #7
5. Clear Victim Energy
6. Clear Fear Energy
7. Set Your 1st Chakra Wellness
8. Set Your Home and Workspace to Wellness

GOALS AND HEALING WORKSHEET

WELLNESS COLOR _____

Physical Goal _____

Mental Goal _____

Emotional Goal _____

Spiritual Goal _____

MISSION STATEMENT

_____

WHAT ARE YOU NOTICING DIFFERENT?

_____

_____

WHAT ENERGIES **SUPPORT** YOU? (Colors, memories, beliefs, thoughts)

_____

_____

OTHER

_____

_____

8

1ˢᵗ Chakra Wellness Activating 'The Secret'

> "No matter where you are, you can find something about that place that is beautiful, true or good, even if it is simply the lessons you are able to learn there. Look for what is RIGHT about where you are.
>
> No matter what situation you are in, there is something good to find inside of it. Look for what is RIGHT about a situation.
>
> No matter who it is you are with, you will be able to look in their eyes and see their value, finding something wonderful and good in that person. Look for what is RIGHT about others."

The Law of Action states that you must perform the things and actions necessary to achieve what you are setting out to do. In doing so, you employ the Spiritual Law of Action. Unless you take actions that are in harmony with your thoughts and dreams and proceed in an orderly fashion towards what you want to accomplish, there will be absolutely no foreseeable results.

It could be today, tomorrow or next week … but from this moment forward, you are creating space, taking spiritual action and bringing your desires closer.

Frustrated With 'The Secret'?

If you have seen the movie <u>The Secret</u> or read the book and tried to incorporate the concepts into your life, you may have had some frustrations along the way. It's okay! You're not alone.

That frustration stems from the fact that <u>The Secret</u> really only skims the surface of what you need to do in order to change your life. In previous chapters, we discussed the Law of Vibration, Law of Action, Law of Oneness, Law of Correspondence, Law of Cause and Effect and others. These are all active forces in creating your desires and being aware of how to consciously apply them, is the REAL SECRET!

To help you obtain the success that you're after, here are a few tips to help you achieve your deepest desires:

Applying 'The Secret' In Your Daily Life

The basic premise of <u>The Secret</u> is that you attract the things you constantly think about. To help make sure you stay on track with manifesting your desires, here are some helpful steps:

- **Make a list.** In your miracle journal, you might make a list of goals in the front of the book, and use the back for your list of miracles. That way you remind yourself of the coming and going of potential miracles and those already manifested.

- **Get crystal clear on what you want.** You may think you know what you want, but often these thoughts are vague or not put into the right perspective.

- **Get specific.** Instead of writing that you want to be out of debt, you need to visualize that you have all the money you could ever need and desire. Think of your credit card statements with a zero balance. Think about what you will do with the money. Have your list of wants become very precise, all the way down to the smallest detail.

- **Use visual reminders to help keep you focused.** If you want a new car, then find a picture of the exact car you want. You can even go to a dealership with a friend and take your dream car for a test drive and have your friend take your picture in the car. Print the picture out and post it where you'll see it each and every day. You can do this with anything you want. To attract more money, write yourself a check in the exact amount you want and post it everywhere you can see it. The mind works well with visual reminders and clues.

- **Create a personal mantra**. Create a screensaver or wallpaper on your computer. Post sticky notes on your bathroom mirror, leave yourself love notes under your pillow or set a daily alarm on your phone that will cement your personal motto in your mind.

1ˢᵗ Chakra Personal Mission Statement

As we progress we will make a <u>Mission Statement</u> or <u>Vision Statement</u> for each chakra.

> *What is your Mission Statement or Vision Statement for the 1st Chakra? For example, your overall MISSION statement could be:*
> *"I am safe and secure or I love and accept my body or my body is healthy and safe."*
> *I am present and feel secure on my path to creating what I desire.*
> *I am strong, healthy and whole. All my needs are met.*

Add this statement to your 1ˢᵗ Chakra Personal Mission Statement in Chapter 24.

Record this statement on your voicemail. SEND yourself an email reminder. Set an alarm with a message. Write it out on small slips of paper and post those papers everywhere so every time you start to slip into negative thinking, you have a positive reminder to help you re-focus. Be creative in how you remind yourself about re-setting your 1st Chakra with your Mission Statement.

Reprogram Your Mind

In <u>Manifesting Miracles 101</u>, you are re-programming your energy field and have an advantage over others who are simply thinking their **'conscious thoughts'** or creating mantras for what they want. Be patient, as this process does take some time, but you will be amazed by the many surprises coming your way and their far-reaching results.

I say this because, as you are aware by now, there's so much more to this work than what appears on the surface.

Always remember, worrying is a yucky habit that will suck the happiness right out of your life. Even when you have things that seem like legitimate worries, the fact is still true that worrying will not change anything for the better...not ever.

What helps when life is stressful and scary is to remember that every single day up until today, you have made it. You have gotten through all of those days. Today...you are wiser and more experienced than any day that you have ever lived.

So...the fact is...you made it through yesterday. You made it through every day before yesterday. You are making it through today...and without a doubt, you will make it through tomorrow.

Gentle Reminders

Making sure you have gentle reminders helps reprogram your mind and keeps you out of the habits of negative thinking or **'unconscious'** thought. It's easy to slip into the old way of thinking, worrying about money, or stressing over negative things. Disallowing your Self to get into that negative spiral by staying focused on **what's positive** is a big step in the right direction.

Being Grateful For the Abundance Already In Your Life

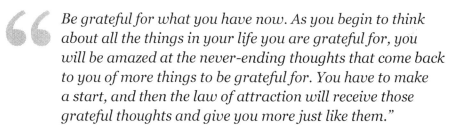

Be grateful for what you have now. As you begin to think about all the things in your life you are grateful for, you will be amazed at the never-ending thoughts that come back to you of more things to be grateful for. You have to make a start, and then the law of attraction will receive those grateful thoughts and give you more just like them."

Rhonda Byrne, <u>The Secret</u>

No, you may not have everything you want, but you have everything you need to succeed. Be thankful for each day that you wake up, for the fact that you're able to breathe and move on your own. Be thankful that you have a job, a roof over your head, and clothes on your back. Be gracious because you have someone who loves you. The only way to get more of good things, is to appreciate the good things you already have.

A lot of people feel like they're victims in life, and they'll often point to past events, perhaps growing up with an abusive parent or in a dysfunctional family. Most psychologists believe that about 85 percent of families are dysfunctional, so all of a sudden you're not so unique. My parents were alcoholics. My dad abused me. My mother divorced him when I was six...I mean, that's almost everybody's story in some form or another. The real question is, what are you going to do now? What do you choose now? Because you

can either keep focusing on that, or you can focus on what you want. And when people start focusing on what they want, what they don't want falls away, and what they want expands, and the other part disappears."

Jack Canfield

Attitude of Gratitude

We all have the ability and opportunity to cultivate gratitude. Simply take a few moments to focus on all that you have – rather than complain about not having all the things that you think you deserve. Developing an '**attitude of gratitude**' is one of the simplest ways to improve your satisfaction with life.

Gratitude may be one of the most overlooked tools that we all have access to every day. Cultivating gratitude doesn't cost any money and it certainly doesn't take much time, but the benefits are enormous. Research reveals that gratitude opens the door to healthier relationships, improves physical and psychological health, **enhances empathy and reduces aggression, improves self-esteem and your sleep patterns as well as improves mental strength.**

For just 5 minutes a day, write in a Gratitude Journal and begin noticing how your energy shifts, changing moods and emotions. Soon, you'll see the magic of The Secret at work in your life.

Setting Yourself to Wellness

Visualize, painting the middle of your head with a wellness color or anything that makes you feel safe and happy. Here you can find neutrality. Step back and reflect on this moment.

The 1st Chakra, a cone-shaped energy wheel located at the base of your spine, stores all the information about family, survival, group contracts and safety. This is the place where you set energy to feel safe and secure. Imagine putting your wellness color into your 1st Chakra. Simply visualize a rose at a wellness tone or color and drop it into your 1st Chakra.

Releasing What's Not in Alignment with Wellness

> **Imagine having an inner dialogue about letting go of anything that is not in alignment with your wellness. For example, *other people's problems, issues, trying to make them feel safe, fixing someone's job, etc.***

It's ok to let go of anywhere you tried to help anyone. Let go of any *'anti-wellness'*.

It might even be that you don't want a problem that you're invested in fixing for the family and any shift of energy at this level will affect everyone in this group. Sometimes you just have to find the space where *'it's ok to shift'* the energy of the 1st Chakra and then it can adjust.

Your own beauty shines brightest when you allow yourself to become exactly who you were meant to become...when you don't try to be something different from what you are. When you blossom into the exact person that your soul yearns to become, you are more beautiful than ever."

Releasing 1ˢᵗ Chakra Energy Blocks

Visualize a rose that represents your 1st Chakra. Ask the rose (or listen for what your inner voice says):

- **What is one thing in your family dynamics that keeps you out of wellness?**

  i.e., *co-dependency, alcoholism, poverty, resistance, competition, instability, not safe, dysfunction, judgment, disconnected.*

- **What keeps you in *'survival mode'*?**

  i.e., *fear, lack of trust, uncertainty, doubt, low self-esteem, loss, the unknown, never having enough.*

- **What keeps you from *'feeling safe'*?**

  i.e., *uncertainty, doubt, trust, shaky foundation, instability, criticism, not being good enough.*

Create and destroy these roses. There are no right or wrong answers here. You are just bringing your awareness into the situation and shedding light on where blocks might be.

Now, ask yourself or observe a rose:

- **What is one thing in your family dynamics that supports your wellness?**

  i.e., support, encouragement, love, education, kindness, compassion, connection, validation.

- **What supports you in 'survival'?**

  i.e., generosity, support, grounded, prosperous, loyalty.

- **What supports you in 'feeling safe'?**

  i.e., stable, secure, anchored, fully functioning, prosperous, grateful.

> *Is that really supporting wellness, or is it a detour toward wellness?*

What is the color of the 1st Chakra at the vibration of wellness?
Visualize a rose at your 1st Chakra wellness color and bring it into your 1st Chakra.

1st Chakra Goals

Professionalism: Stable, secure, anchored, earn more money, new business, write a book, and get promoted.

Spirituality: meditation, yoga, receptive to your body's needs, increased intuition.

Physicality: improved diet, exercise, activity, balance, sleep, being grounded, new hobbies, time for self, take action on projects.

Family: stable, loyal, supportive, engaging, validation, new home.

After working through the 8 chakras in Manifesting Miracles 101, you will have created your own personal prayer. We are spirits in bodies and when you practice the **Quantum Energy Tools** (http://bit.ly/29WqnQk), you are working on the spiritual level and it's important to make this effort valid on the body level. Then, as you clear your energy space, you get what you want.

1ˢᵗ Chakra Goals

Think of a goal that you want for your 1st Chakra. Visualize a rose for the wellness color of that goal. If you had that goal already, **what color would it be at wellness**? Set that goal to that color. **You can do that with any and all of your goals.**

For instance, maybe your goal is to write a book. Visualize a rose and ask what the wellness color is for that goal. Set that goal to a '**wellness vibration**', setting it in its best energy to manifest.

Take a look at the rose representing your goals for your 1st Chakra and what its focus includes: being grounded, the family, having a stable job, and being out of survival mode or feeling safe.

What are you working on? What would you like to have, experience or manifest considering: feeling safe, increasing your income, owning a home of our own, etc.? That can be included in your 1st Chakra goal. If you don't have words yet for your goals, imagine dropping a color into the rose.

Ground that rose and begin releasing any energy that prevents you from having that mockup. Notice what happens to your rose. How does it change? When you feel complete, release your rose.

Set Goals that Motivate You

When you set goals for yourself, it is important that they motivate you: this means making sure that they are important to you, and that there is value in achieving them. If you have little interest in the outcome, or they are irrelevant given the larger picture, then the chances of you putting in the work to make them happen are slim. Motivation is key to achieving goals."

MindTools.com

Staying Grounded and Balanced

Meditation facilitates the connecting of the spiritual and physical bodies for balance and harmony within the chakra systems. As you continue building your awareness of your 1st Chakra wellness, you create a sense of safety and become grounded in the body, mind, and spirit.

The 1st Chakra plays a very important role in supporting you and this cannot be emphasized enough.

Imbalance in your 1st Chakra can show up as '***less than***' feelings, such as insecurity, anxiety, nervousness, worry, suspicion, self-consciousness, isolation, and greed. In the process of trying to overcompensate for, or underplay, these feelings, a person may: overeat or under eat; be over stimulated or lack energy; be careless and sloppy or meticulously neat; be egotistical and domineering or weak in character and passive; or be extravagant and wasteful with money or a money miser.

A person with a balanced 1st Chakra feels safe and secure, protected and trusting. Self-worth, self-confidence, stability, and a quiet strength shine through in a calm, easy-going manner that affirms feelings of belonging in family, work, and community. With a balanced 1st Chakra, your physical needs are met with grace and ease. You will also have a sense of always having enough. This fosters a willingness to contribute and to share.

> *Well, there are two kinds of happiness, grounded and ungrounded. Ungrounded happiness is cheesy and not based on reality. Grounded happiness is informed happiness based on the knowledge that the world sometimes sucks, but even then you have to believe in yourself."*
>
> Andy Grammer

Most importantly, no matter what mistakes you have made, no matter how disappointed you are, no matter what has happened, you can ALWAYS find your own value, you can always look for what is RIGHT about yourself and take a break from looking for what is wrong. SEE what is right about you, beautiful amazing you.

> ***Consider a 'Wellness Statement for the 1st Chakra'. What color or phrase comes to mind? How do you want to feel in the 1st Chakra?***

What is your Mission Statement or Vision Statement for the 1st Chakra?

For example, your statement could be:

> *"I am anchored and grounded in present time."*
> *"I am safe and secure or I love and accept my body."*
> *"My body is healthy and safe."*

Add this 1ˢᵗ Chakra Mission Statement to Personal Mission Statements in Chapter 24.

When I met Amirah, I was in pain, broke and depressed. I was suffering with rheumatoid arthritis, had a very low paying unsatisfying job and had a restraining order on my ex-boyfriend. After working in the Miracle Mastery Mentoring Program and the practices in this book, I started a new successful business, bought my first home, got engaged and considerably reduced my medications. I began feeling better than I felt in years. Within a year, I moved cross-country and had a baby. My life looks completely different! And it's all because of what I learned in working with Amirah. She told me my life would change, and she was absolutely Right! It did and I love myself and my life more than I ever knew possible."

Jennie Wilson

Chapter 8 - Practice Guidelines

Practice the following tools this week:

1. Grounding – Quantum Energy Tool #1
2. Center of Head – Quantum Energy Tool #2
3. Replenishing – Quantum Energy Tool #3
4. Run Earth and Cosmic Energy – Quantum Energy Tool #7
5. Reset 1st Chakra to Wellness Vibration
6. Releasing What's Not in Alignment With Wellness
7. Releasing 1st Chakra Energy Blocks
8. Set 1st Chakra Goals
9. Create 1st Chakra Mission Statement

GOALS AND HEALING WORKSHEET

WELLNESS COLOR _____

Physical Goal _____

Mental Goal _____

Emotional Goal _____

Spiritual Goal _____

MISSION STATEMENT

_____

WHAT ARE YOU NOTICING DIFFERENT?

_____

_____

WHAT ENERGIES **SUPPORT** YOU? (Colors, memories, beliefs, thoughts)

_____

_____

OTHER

_____

_____

Chapter

9

2nd Chakra Wellness Feelings Set The Tone

*Make time by saying no, by prioritizing and reprioritizing.
You can make time by doing the things that matter first, and
by giving what you have left to the things that matter least.
You have time and it's yours to take care of.
You can do it...you've already begun."*

The mission of <u>Manifesting Miracles 101</u> is to support you creating goals in wellness as you grow and reconnect, release, open and ground through learning the techniques and practices of spiritual energy tools.

Move out of your survival mode from the 1st Chakra and start having fun. The 2nd Chakra is all about feeling sensual and sexy and engaging your creative self. This chakra attends to your desire for interpersonal relationships and invites others into your life to share your passions, sexuality, and creativity.

*No human relation gives one possession in another—every
two souls are absolutely different. In friendship or in love,
the two side by side raise hands together to find what one
cannot reach alone."*

Khalil Gibran

2nd Chakra - Emotional Center

Your present-time feelings dictate your vibrations and set the Law of Vibration into action. It's your feelings in the moment that become your vibrations.

> **Positive Feelings = Positive Circumstances**
> **Negative Feelings = Negative Circumstances**

The 2ⁿᵈ Chakra level primarily focuses on emotional and sexual energies. Balanced emotions promote a sense of self-worth that allows oneself to accept all the good, including abundance and prosperity, into his or her life. Balanced sexual energy generates romance and healthy sexual relationships. The craving to create something physical, outside of oneself, develops at this level, and drawing, painting, writing, and music are excellent outlets for this desire.

Balanced 2ⁿᵈ Chakra

A balanced 2ⁿᵈ Chakra leads to feelings of wellness, plenty, pleasure, and joy. You can see this exemplified by those who are fully connected and attuned to their physical and emotional centers. They are comfortable with their bodies and their emotions. Sexual and non-sexual relationships are healthy, and they are based on trust and mutual respect. There is a passion for life that is expressed in everything they do.

I don't want to be at the mercy of my emotions. I want to use them, to enjoy them."

Oscar Wilde

Imbalanced 2ⁿᵈ Chakra

Imbalances in the 2ⁿᵈ Chakra are characterized by '**living too much inside your head**,' and being out of touch with what your body is telling you will deny yourself pleasure. Anorexia, bulimia, drug and alcohol abuse, and other addictions are attempts to nurture oneself in this kind of emotionally disconnected or detached state. Sexual dysfunctions are also directly related to imbalances in the 2ⁿᵈ Chakra.

An overactive 2ⁿᵈ Chakra can result in lustful, arrogant, or conceited behavior, and an aggressive desire to control others; whereas an underdeveloped 2nd Chakra can manifest as distrust, resentment, fear, apathy, pessimism, and anti-social conduct. It can also show up as continually worrying about what others think and always following the crowd.

The 2ⁿᵈ Chakra is a very important building block in your spiritual anatomy. It's perfectly positioned and proportioned right above the 1ˢᵗ Chakra, which is the foundation or base of the chakra system. Emotional awareness and connectedness will become more and more important as you ascend up the chakras, because emotions are the magnifying glass through which you will examine, study, evaluate (and ultimately communicate with) all of your chakras.

The only currency in this bankrupt world is what you share with someone else when you're uncool."

Philip Seymour Hoffman

Passion and Pleasure Center

The 2nd Chakra is your passion and pleasure center and it is located in the pelvic area. While the 1st Chakra is satisfied with survival, the 2nd Chakra seeks pleasure and enjoyment.

> *The gift of this chakra is experiencing our lives through feelings and sensations.*

The 2nd Chakra is the center of feeling, emotion, pleasure, sensuality, intimacy, and connection. The energy of this chakra allows you to let go, to move, and to feel change and transformations occur within your body. It allows you to experience present moments as they are, in their own fullness.

Main Challenge is Society Conditioning

The main challenge for the second chakra is the conditioning of our society. We live in a society where feelings are not valued; where passion, and emotional reactions are frowned upon. We are taught not to '**lose control**'. In doing that, we turn down our true feelings, getting disconnected from our bodies and our feelings.

As if this were not enough, we also experience the wounds of our collective cultural struggles over many sexual issues of our society. On the one hand, sexuality is magnified and glorified, and on the other hand it is rejected. This results in either blocked or excessive 2nd Chakra issues.

Let's not forget that the little emotions are the great captains of our lives and we obey them without realizing it."

Vincent Van Gogh

No wonder we have so many issues with our passion center; the wellspring of feelings, enjoyment, and sensuality.

Sexuality has become burdened with many judgments, fears and emotions. Hardly any aspect of it is spontaneous or self-evident anymore. The aspect of freely exploring it in a childlike manner has been lost. Most people are full of fear and tension when it comes to sexually expressing themselves.

> *Do you love your body?*
> *Do you enjoy feeling your body?*
> *When was the last time you walked barefoot on the grass and felt the sensation of ground underneath your feet?*

Center of Creativity

Passion is the fuel of creative energy. Everything you create, a poem, a drawing, or a website, originates from the energy of 2nd Chakra. It is also where your fertility originates. After all, conceiving a child is a creative process.

A person with a healthy 2nd Chakra, is passionate, present in their body, sensual, creative and connected to their feelings.

 Never apologize for showing feeling. When you do so, you apologize for the truth".

Benjamin Disraeli

Growth Periods Can Be Tricky

At this point, you might be working on a growth period of the 1st or 2nd Chakra. A growth period is the lag time between the change in your energy and the realization of that change in your body. As your energy begins to change and you create a new space, things begin feeling different. It's like changing your furniture in your living room but when you turn off the light you might run into the furniture. Everything is in a new place. That's what's happening with your energy field.

Your growth period is the outward expression that you are taking a '**big energetic step**' and trying to catch up to yourself while adjustments are being made.

> *Don't get too serious as you stir your energetic pot.*

Most people avoid growth periods, but you have chosen to shift your energy and your experiences. It's very important to have and to keep some amusement in this process. If other people are criticizing you for *'having the dropsies' or 'running into walls' or 'suddenly forgetting things'*, try and ignore them.

It's important though NOT to criticize yourself! Instead, ask yourself, "**What can I give myself to feel better?**"

Step outside of yourself and observe these changes without judgment or attachment. Notice what's different with you, as you most definitely reflect how you are growing.

Notice what is shifting. Notice also what you are shifting away from. **New habits, behaviors, feelings...?**

Emotional Center – Radar Central

Ask yourself questions. Dig into your heart and your stories and your past to find the parts of you that were lost along the way. Claim your own story and honor it.

People change over time. We forget what we knew once. We take roads that others are taking and try to be like they are...we forget who we are.

Take the time it takes to get to know your beautiful self...look for the truth in your story and experiences. Honor each part of your story...the good, bad, beautiful and hard. Have some space!

If you don't have a good sense of your own space, you will take on the energy of other people around you. If you are unaware of taking on other's energy and being in the effect of others, you can really get knocked around. Remember the primary instruction of almost all ancient teachers and temples; "**KNOW THYSELF!**"

> *How do you 'feel' others out?*
> *How do you interact with others?*
> *Do you read or sense others through your feelings with the 2nd Chakra?*

That's all part of the 2nd Chakra -- The outside world coming into you and from the inside going out, expressing yourself. Other people around you also might be doing the same thing--connecting with you. Energetic exchanges go both ways. It's not really a problem, rather its part of recognizing how we connect with others.

Emotion always has its roots in the unconscious and manifests itself in the body."

Irene Claremont de Castillejo

Separating From Other's Energy

Some of the tools we use are roses by using them to separate from matching with other people's energy. We do connect and match, but when we are complete, we need to separate and step back from that energetic space.

You are unique. How you express yourself in the world is unique. You have unconsciously collected other people's energies that control and limit how you express yourself.

In general, if a couple cannot expand their original rules and boundaries to accommodate personal growth, the relationship disintegrates."

Caroline Myss

Releasing 2nd Chakra Energetic Limits on Self-Expression

Ask yourself:

> *How much can you move or shift your own energy from the inside to the outside?*
> *What energetic limits are put on your emotional expression?*

Looking at that energy of your self-expression from the 2nd Chakra, in terms of colors, visualize a rose or consider a color that represents your emotions.

Visualize a rose 12" in front of you that represents the energy of your body.

> *Is it open or closed? What color is it?*
> *Let it represent your body's ability to reflect energy.*
> *What color is unique from the others?*

Release any energy that is not yours. Let that foreign energy go so your energy becomes even more visible. Observe what happens to your rose.

> **Did the rose open? Or close?**

Ground and release other people's energy and any energy that's stopping you from being in your own vibration. Let your body be set at its own energy.

> **Release anything that limits your freedom or ability to express things freely. i.e.: that it's not ok to express yourself, tension, restrictions, and limits.**

Allow your wellness color to completely fill up the rose as you bring your wellness vibration into the space of feeling and expressing yourself.

> **Now, how much room do you have to express yourself?**

If you don't have enough room, simply allow the rose to expand and give yourself room to express yourself. When you get the sense that you've reached your full capacity to express yourself, allow your rose to dissolve. Allow all your **'own energy'** to be in your 2nd Chakra. Notice how your body feels.

We are challenged every day to say yes to the movements of life, to see it all through, without pause, staying in relationship to the music of life and each other, adjusting as we go, not knowing what will happen next."

Mark Nepo

> Visualize a rose that represents your 2nd Chakra. Ask the rose (or listen for what your inner voice says):
> - What are one or more levels of expression where you've had limits?
> - *i.e., joy as a child was limited to how much fun you could have.*
> - *What energies give you joy or freedom?*
> - *What color allows you to be joyful or amused?*
> - Notice if you have any energy of judgment against it.

Accepting means you allow yourself to feel whatever it is you are feeling at that moment. It is part of the isness of the Now. You can't argue with what is. Well, you can, but if you do, you suffer."

Eckhart Tolle

Sexual Wellness

Sex appeal is a wonderful, warm, womanly healthy feeling . . . it comes only from inside, it's from nothing that's manufactured. It has nothing to do with measurements or lipstick color. To me, it's cleanliness, and youth, an effervescent desire to enjoy life."-

Jayne Mansfield

Sexuality is the dancing together of male and female energies. Sexual union is a deeply emotional act and if you ignore this aspect, you are not fully present in the act and you cut yourself off from the real meaning of sexuality.

> *Is sex an uplifting, rejuvenating, life-affirming, deeply pleasurable and transformative experience for you?*

If it isn't, you're 2nd Chakra is not in a state of wellness.

We live in a culture with a wildly bipolar relationship to sex. Sex is everywhere: in movies, pop songs, advertising. Yet, we're also told that we're not allowed to have it and enjoy it.

It is understandable that most people have conflicting beliefs about sex.

Unless you take the time to examine what stands in the way of you and the ideal I described above, you won't get there.

Everyone can have an intimate relationship with themselves and their partner that is soul-nourishing and infuses every part of their lives with powerful and revitalizing energy.

This is natural.

Avoiding sex, feeling like it's a minor or inconsequential part of an intimate relationship, experiencing guilt and anxiety:

Not natural.

Sex is the glue in your relationship. Sex is your vital, life force energy. If it isn't being channeled and enjoyed, chances are that you are living a lackluster life. I guarantee that you'll have a lackluster marriage or relationship.

Clearing your sexual blocks will open you to your true, radiant and sensual nature.

Releasing Past Emotional or Sexual Energy

Clearing stuck emotional or sexual energy through time brings this chakra into wellness.

As you release energy from past where you had **limits on your expression, judgments, criticism, fear, shame, guilt, lust, doubt, rejection, etc.** you create space for a fuller expression of yourself.

Visualize a timeline in front of you that represents where you had **high emotional or sexual energy turned on.**

Birth_____**Present Time**

Allow bright lights to ignite anywhere you had high emotional or sexual energy turn on.

Visualize a wellness rose for your emotional self in the 2nd Chakra and slide the rose from birth to present time collecting all the spots on your timeline, releasing anyone else's energy that was stuck on your time line. Roll up your timeline and drop it inside a rose and explode rose.

Maybe some people just aren't meant to be in our lives forever. Maybe some people are just passing through. It's like some people just come through our lives to bring us something: a gift, a blessing, a lesson we need to learn. And that's why they're here. You'll have that gift forever."

Danielle Steel

Physical Side of 2nd Chakra

Sex isn't just physical; it is every bit spiritual. Energy flows through everything around us. It is the life bearing force that makes living possible for every living thing imaginable. Although energy is limitless and formless, its vibration can be experienced consciously and unconsciously.

For many, sex is seen simply as a physical act, but it's more than that. Every time sex is occurring there is also an energy exchange. Each person deposits energy into the other during the experience. Through the connection of the genitals, the spirit also connects with that of another.

When two people decide to sleep together they are making the decision to share not just body parts but also everything else that is contained within that body. Sickness and disease can be passed off to the next person during sexual contact, and the same applies to attitudes as well. Anger, joy, sadness, irritation, excitement and the like are vibrational energies that can pass onto the next person.

When having sex with a partner it is healthy and helpful to be aware of the energy you're exchanging. Lower vibrational energy (anger, sadness, fear) manifests themselves as headaches, body aches, cloudy thoughts, irritation and poor attitude after having sex. The next day you may wake up feeling any of these conditions and not know where they came from. Believe it or not, your body is telling you that you've picked up bad energy and need to get rid of it.

High vibrational energy can be exchanged and experienced during sex as well, but it is the lower vibrational energy that, if not cleared, can become trapped in areas of the body and cause imbalance and disease. This is called '**energetic debris'** or simply speaking, '**foreign energy'** that can and should be cleared.

The corresponding organs to the 2nd Chakra are the reproductive organs (ovaries in women and prostate in men) and the bladder.

 Emotional vampires suck the energy right out of you. I want you to think about the vampires in your life, people who make you feel depleted, insecure, or just plain angry. You don't need to hang onto these people. You can wean them from your life, just as you do with sugar."

Sara Gottfried

Resetting Hormone Levels and Clearing Glands

You might not be able to see your hormones but they play a constant role in how your body's function. Your hormones are chemical messengers that travel, via our bloodstream, to every organ and tissue in the body. They influence fat storage, sex drive, energy levels, brain health and a host of other vital functions.

Clearing and resetting the hormones and glands associated with your sexual center brings your the energy level of your emotions, creativity, relationships and sexuality into balance.

Progesterone:

Visualize a rose that represents progesterone and its effect on your body. Ask yourself: *Is it open or closed? Is it shut down by your energy or someone else's? Are there any limits that freeze the rose?* Consider the wellness level for that hormone. Notice if this hormonal level fluctuates.

Grounding the rose, begin releasing anyone else's energy from your space. Allow the rose to come to your wellness color. Release any limits or blocks. Explode the rose into a million pieces.

Estrogen:

Visualize a rose that represents estrogen and its effect on your body. Ask yourself: *Is it open or closed? Is it shut down by your energy or someone else's? Are there any limits that freeze the rose?* Consider the wellness level for that hormone. Notice if this hormonal level fluctuates.

Grounding the rose, begin releasing anyone else's energy from your space. Allow the rose to come to your wellness color. Release any limits or blocks. Explode the rose into a million pieces.

Testosterone:

Visualize a rose that represents testosterone and its effect on your body. Ask yourself: *Is it open or closed? Is it shut down by your energy or someone else's? Are there any limits that freeze the rose?* Consider the wellness level for that hormone. Notice if this hormonal level fluctuates.

Grounding the rose, begin releasing anyone else's energy from your space. Allow the rose to come to your wellness color. Release any limits or blocks. Explode the rose into a million pieces.

Re-setting Female and Male Energy

Visualize two gauges in front of you – One that represents female energy in your body and one that represents male energy in your body. Without judgment,

- Allow the **Female Energy Gauge** to show you how much female energy you run in your body.

- Allow the **Male Energy Gauge** to show you how much male energy you run in your body.

Play with the gauges by adjusting this energy and notice it's affect on you and others.

If you are a female, try turning up your female energy and notice how that feels. If you are a male, try turning up your male energy. And, then reverse it.

Sleep has been provided by nature to do the body's healing work, and it takes seven or eight hours for this process to happen. Commit to getting at least seven to eight hours of good quality sleep every night to keep your body and hormones in balance."

Suzanne Somers

I know some of this might seem a little foreign and maybe even difficult, but it's important that you have fun! Play as a little boy or girl. Get out your toys and pretend for a little while. Who cares what anyone thinks! It's YOUR 2nd Chakra! Give yourself permission to play and keep playing. Continue creating what you want in life.

Words of Wisdom!

Many times, however, the problems we have in life contain deep and powerful lessons to help us grow and heal and gain valuable wisdom. We will not gain all of the wisdom that is available if we do not own our part in our problems. We do not get to a place of freedom until we admit that there were things that we could have done differently.

- So today, forgive yourself and forgive others.

- Own your part even when others do not own theirs.

- Do better today than you did yesterday and use what you have learned to make everything around you better.

- You can mend what is broken, even the things that are unfair and unjust, and you can start by owning your part fully.

If you're happy, if you're feeling good, then nothing else matters."

Robin Wright

"Meeting Amirah in Dubai has been an amazing experience for me. I met her for a private session and was impressed with what she told me about my life situation and circumstances. My work and business is highly stressful and I began practicing the Quantum Energy Tools and Stress Buster Guided Meditation, and them the Miracle Mastery Mentoring Program. It has been a most enlightening journey that has given me an anchor during death of my father and relationship challenges. I highly recommend Amirah's practices to anyone who struggles with stress, focus and needing clarity. There isn't one part of my life that has not been positively affected by using the program and after using it a few short months, my business doubled and we opened a children's dentistry center. With a very busy practice and business, I cannot go a day without using the Quantum Energy Tools. My family, staff and business depends on me being centered, focused and grounded."

Dr. Michael, Dubai, UAE

Chapter 9 - Practice Guidelines

Practice the following tools this week:

1. Grounding – Quantum Energy Tool #1
2. Center of Head – Quantum Energy Tool #2
3. Replenishing – Quantum Energy Tool #3
4. Run Earth and Cosmic Energy – Quantum Energy Tool #7
5. Release 2nd Chakra Energetic Limits on Self-Expression
6. Release Past Emotional or Sexual Energy
7. Reset Hormone Levels and Clearing Glands
8. Re-set Female and Male Energy

GOALS AND HEALING WORKSHEET

WELLNESS COLOR _____

Physical Goal _____

Mental Goal _____

Emotional Goal _____

Spiritual Goal _____

MISSION STATEMENT

_____

WHAT ARE YOU NOTICING DIFFERENT?

_____

_____

WHAT ENERGIES **SUPPORT** YOU? (Colors, memories, beliefs, thoughts)

_____

_____

OTHER

_____

_____

Chapter

10

2ⁿᵈ Chakra
Range of Emotions

> *Your heart and your gut know exactly what you need to let go of, even if your brain is giving you all sorts of reasons to clamp your fingers around it. There are seasons and times to have different things, relationships and situations in your life...and then the seasons change and it's time to let go of many of those things.*
> *Change is hard ... but change is absolutely necessary."*

Each person has a chronic or habitual emotional level that determines the overall, and more or less constant, behavior in life. As we experience success or failure in our activities of life, the emotional level moves up or down accordingly. It tends to rebalance, going back to our habitual emotional level. In this chapter, we clear your 'range of emotions' increasing your energetic frequency and activating the laws of attraction and vibration.

It's the chronic or habitual '*mood*' or emotional level we have to raise by increasing our own energy frequency. The more we do that, the higher and higher our habitual emotional level becomes and our sensation of happiness boosts and stabilizes into higher levels.

Your emotional level or '*frequency tone*' is the manifested frequency level of everything and anything that is '*real*' (perceivable) to you in your world and life's experiences. "*We reap what we sow*".

The Law of Attraction has become very popular lately, as The Secret points out very clearly how '*attraction*' draws events and circumstances toward us that match the essence of our '***feelings***' or emotion level. This is another way of saying our '***emotional frequency***' or vibrational level.

Our emotions are our life's power and vitality; the '***carrier wave***' upon which our projected thoughts are sent to create or modify our reality. As the Law of Vibration is activated, and the more potent our '***carrier or emotional wave***' is, the more quickly and effectively it will affect and transform our reality.

The happier we are, the more 'attractive' power we have.

Remember, however, that your lower frequencies will also attract to you the things you probably least desire. So my bet is that most of us desire feeling happy and being 'attractive' to our heart's desires, and not the latter.

Your happiness level is a direct measurement of your creative and attractive power.

All you need to live in **Authentic Happiness** is to learn how to increase the vibrational frequency of your energy and your emotions at any '***now***' moment in time.

You don't have to wait until tomorrow to be happy. You can be happy right now by self-generating the right emotions and feelings.

The formula for constant authentic happiness consists of just ONE STEP:

INCREASE YOUR FREQUENCY!

Increasing your frequency will change your behavior,
Increase your creative power, and you'll live an exceptional life.
This sounds so amazingly simple. It is! Yet so devastatingly effective and do-able!

You are NOT at the mercy of your emotions where it feels and appears like you have no control.
Yes, emotion control is in your hands.
Yes, You can set your emotions in motion.
Yes, emotion regulation is one of your natural abilities.
Yes, you can handle your own energy.
Yes, you can feel happiness NOW!

Range of Emotions

There are only two basic emotions that we all experience: love and fear. All other emotions are variations of these two emotions. Thoughts and behavior come from either a place of love, or a place of fear. Anxiety, anger, control, sadness, depression, inadequacy, confusion, hurt, lonely, guilt, shame; these are all fear-based emotions. Emotions such as joy, happiness, caring, trust, compassion, truth, contentment and satisfaction are love-based emotions.

There are varying degrees of intensity of both types of emotions. Some are mild, others moderate and others strong in intensity. For example, anger in a mild form can be felt as disgust or dismay, at a moderate level can be felt as offended or exasperated, and at an intense level can be felt as rage or hate. The emotion that always underpins anger is fear.

What are you willing to let go of today? Life is so much about knowing what to hold on to, and what to let go of...and having faith that it will all work out in the end.

If we just get quiet, get brave, and listen very closely.... our hearts will tell us what to let go of. This doesn't mean it will be easy...it just means that it is what is meant for now.

You can do this. Listen to your heart. Be brave."

Physical Effects of Emotions

Emotions have a direct effect on how our bodies work. Fear-based emotions stimulate the release of one set of chemicals, while love-based emotions release a different set of chemicals. If the fear-based emotions are long-term or chronic, they can damage the chemical systems, the immune system, the endocrine system and every other system in your body. If this happens, our immune systems can weaken and many serious illnesses set in. This relationship between emotions, thinking, and the body is called Mind/Body Medicine today.

Your intellect may be confused, but your emotions will never lie to you."

Roger Ebert

Controlling Your Emotions

You cannot change or control your emotions. You can learn how to be with them, live peacefully with them, transmute (release) them and manage them, but you cannot control them.

Think of the people who go along day after day seeming to function normally, but then all of a sudden they explode in anger at something that seems relatively trivial and harmless. That's a sign of someone who's trying to control or repress their emotions, but their repressed emotions are leaking out.

The more anyone tries to control their emotions, the more they resist control and the more frightened people eventually become at what is seen to be a *'loss of emotional control'*. It's a vicious circle.

 If you don't think your anxiety, depression, sadness and stress impact your physical health, think again. All of these emotions trigger chemical reactions in your body, which can lead to inflammation and a weakened immune system. Learn how to cope, sweet friend. There will always be dark days."

Kris Carr

Your 2nd Chakra is the place from where you express your emotions. As a spiritual being within your body, it also expresses itself through emotions.

Energetically speaking, **how much permission do you** 'have to **express yourself'?**

Rules Restrict Your Access

When a person has a *'narrow range of emotions'* there tends to be lots of rules around the right or wrong ways to express themselves.

Imagine a piano keyboard for example. The piano is versatile and has a wide range and ability to play chords, along with the ability to play louder or softer. It has a row of 88 black and white keys.

In any musical composition, there are high notes and low; loud and soft. People might put judgments on lighter sounds or the black, deeper sounds, but in music they all work together to make a beautiful composition.

In terms of your own emotional range of expression, as judgments are placed on certain sounds and how people feel around you, you end up responding to that. The consequences then, are that maybe you start to decrease the range of what you allow yourself to receive. Or maybe you have 60 or 40 keys in your range of expression rather than access to the full 88 keys.

There is no 'wrong' way to express yourself. Don't limit your emotional range based on the rules and judgments of others. You need only express yourself fully, honestly and clearly for your personal growth (without intent to cause others harm).

Colors, like features, follow the changes of the emotions."

Pablo Picasso

Balance is Everything

As with most health-related barometers, balance is everything. The pH scale is another example that measures how acidic or alkaline a substance is. This scale ranges from 0 to 14. Seven is neutral. Below 7 becomes increasingly acidic, above 7 becomes increasingly alkaline.

Proper pH varies throughout your body for many reasons. For example, your bowels, skin and genitals should be slightly acidic – as this helps keep unfriendly bacteria away. Saliva is more alkaline, while your urine is normally more acidic, especially in the morning. In addition, your body regularly deals with naturally occurring acids that are the by-products of respiration, metabolism, cellular breakdown and exercise. So clearly, the goal is not to think of acid as '***bad***' and alkaline as '***good***'. Rather, they are a delicate balance.

In terms of your emotions, you must be able to function both on a negative and a positive range of emotions. Some people judge the negative side of things, avoiding '***anger***' at all costs. Some people will even be upset when others get really '***excited***'.

To have extremes, you have to have both. Not to say that you '***have to have***' anything.

You may have a wide range while others do not.

> **What's your natural range of emotions?**
> **Do you have permission to explore them?**
> **Where are your blocks?**

If you resist negative range, you may resist certain feelings. For example if you become joyful, get all excited and then feel guilty for having joy. Maybe sometimes you feel angry and shame, but then feel happy for feeling that way.

That's your body's way of telling you what energy level you are at, in relationship to your world. Confused and conflicted.

> *How do you feel about those things?*

There are a lot of reasons, because everyone is different. When you create a sense of emotional wellness, it is giving yourself permission to have a full range of expression. If you can't open the door to explore, then what's happening for you?

> *Can you get your answers, open this space and go there to solve it?*

Becoming neutral to your own feelings means not judging yourself if you feel joy and then guilt. The energies do not match, but clearing off the confusion will create the space for wellness.

Working with the **Quantum Energy Tools** (http://bit.ly/29WqnQk) is especially important while working through the exercises in this book. Allow neutral energies to stabilize your body, releasing what you are ready to. The practices outlined in this book also assist you in observing energies without getting lost inside them, by keeping your unconscious to them. Give yourself permission to observe "you" and your own vital energy-creating solutions for '*manifesting miracles*'.

 Shallow men believe in luck. Strong men believe in cause and effect.'

Ralph Waldo Emerson

Clearing Range of Emotions Gauge

Visualize a scale or gauge (range for you) maybe like a piano, with the center-point being 0 or neutral and extending to 100 on either side of 0.

100 _____ **0** _____ **100**

Ask yourself:

> *How wide is your range when you express yourself?*
> *If you were totally free as a new spirit, with NO limits, what would be your range?*
> *What is the range where it's acceptable for you?*

> *Where is there energy of 'non permission' stuck?*
> *Where is energy stuck that says, "it's not ok to be happy, don't be*
> *sad, don't be too happy" or anything that says you can't feel what you*
> *want to feel."*

Give your body permission to release '***sadness, loss or incompleteness***' when you can't have your range of emotion. Notice any body pain or stress and release it. Visualize a magic wand or sticky rose and begin clearing any energy that is not yours. If you have freedom to experience emotions freely and move them out, that's excellent! Create and destroy roses, clearing your space of foreign energies, blocking the freedom to express a full range of emotion.

The ultimate goal is for you to have a full range of freedom without judgment. ***What would your goal be for full, emotional self-expression?***

> *The beautiful truth about YOU is that you are infinitely valuable, wonderful, and one-of-a-kind...there is a plan for you...and you are so very beloved. You don't have to do anything to earn this love...it just is. It is.*
>
> *Truth comes quietly.... take some time to turn off the distractions and really listen. It's trying to tell you something."*

Re-setting Wellness throughout Your Body

Tell the body it's ok to release fears, resistance or whatever else. Simply allow your wellness color to run through your body channels. Use **Stress Buster** (Quantum Energy Tool #7 - http://bit.ly/2a0DtAl) as your guide and reset your wellness using color.

Consider:

- *What are the two or three things that could support you in taking the step of being emotional wellness– i.e. being w/friends, dancing, spending quiet time alone, watching a funny movie, etc.*

- *What makes it ok for you to expand this part of yourself?*

- *What energy resists you from being in wellness? i.e. colors, feelings, thoughts, etc.*

Being neutral is not about being judgmental. It's OK to just have a feeling with no reason. Getting neutral with yourself allows you to have your feelings and let them have you. Moving out any energy that stops you from having your emotions is the goal in achieving freedom of emotional expression.

Releasing Resistance

> *What you resist you become.*

An emotion needs a cycle to be complete. It can stick to you, and when it sticks it can't move until you solve it to finish the cycle.

For example, when anyone gets stuck on some form of anger that is not expressed, it creates a deep seat of resentment. Then, when other situations arise, there's a build-up and it becomes about something different than the immediate reason for their anger. The body is communicating to you about what's going on *right now*.

2nd Chakra Goals Can Include:

Professional: increased integrity, increased confidence, morally aligned, networking

Spiritual: art class, writing, poetry, journaling, increased excitement, being more flexible

Physical: improve diet, healthy sexual activity, balance, more sleep, starting new hobbies, taking a class.

Family: supportive, engaging, passion, validation, setting healthy boundaries, making new friends.

2nd Chakra Goals

Think of a goal you want for your 2nd Chakra. Visualize a rose for the wellness color of that goal. If you had that goal already, *what color would it be at wellness?* Set that goal to that color. **You can do that with any and all of your goals.**

For instance, maybe your goal is to *'feel passionate about living'* or *'developing new social skills'* or *'being more flexible'*. Visualize a rose and ask what the wellness color is for that goal. Set that goal to a *'wellness vibration'*, keeping it in the best energy for manifesting.

Take a look your 2nd Chakra goals and what their focuses are. This includes: emotional freedom, creativity, sexuality and relationships. Visualize a rose and drop your 2nd Chakra goals into that rose.

What are you working on? (ie. *Feeling happier and more confident? Improving your relationships with healthy boundaries? Increasing your creativity or enhancing your passion*?) All these and more can be included into your 2nd Chakra goal rose. If you don't have words yet for your goals, imagine dropping a color into that rose.

Ground that rose and begin releasing any energy that prevents you from having that mockup. Notice what happens to your rose. How does it change? When you feel complete, release your rose.

Spiritual Mission Statement
2nd Chakra Personal Mission Statement

What is your Mission Statement or Vision Statement for the 2nd Chakra? For example, your overall MISSION statement could be:
"I am balanced and have healthy boundaries"
"I fully, openly and easily express myself"
"I am confident, happy and creative."

Add this statement to your 1st Chakra Personal Mission Statement in Chapter 24.

On a regular basis, remind yourself of your 1st and 2nd Chakra statements and use them to help you re-focus in a positive way. Be creative in how you remind yourself about re-setting your 2nd Chakra with your Mission Statement, such as sending yourself a voice message or leaving post-it notes on your fridge.

Visualize dropping your 2nd Chakra Personal Mission Statement into a rose, and begin releasing any stuck energy from it. Imagine dropping your wellness color into that rose.

Visualize a goal you would like to create in a second rose and, using a grounding cord, begin releasing any foreign energy from the goal.

Please note: goals don't have to be 'grandiose'; they can be as simple as going for a walk.

Continue creating and destroying roses and keep dropping your 2nd Chakra goals into the wellness rose while still clearing off any stuck energy. Be amused as energy flows out of rose, creating space for your goal to manifest.

What's Different?

Visualize a rose that represents your energy at the beginning of this chapter. Beside it, visualize a second rose that represents your energy now. Notice the differences and the energetic steps that you took. You can't go backwards; you are not the older version of yourself. You can have this new energetic space.

Congratulations on taking this giant step!
EVERYONE has wonderful things about them that we can focus on. If nothing else, focus on the fact that they are a fellow human being. That should be enough to compel all of us to speak with only kindness. Spreading gossip never feels peaceful. Stopping it by refusing to spread it will truly make a difference, far and wide and deep. Let it stop in a peaceful place.

"What Amirah Hall brings to the table is pretty much 'everything'. Amirah utilizes core knowledge from many spiritual traditions – from the very oldest Upashadic revelations of the forest dwelling yogis 5,000 years ago in India through the ecstatic practices of many traditions such as Sufism, Christianity, Cabalism, Yoga, and wide esoteric knowledge - to the deeply shared Love and Oneness of all people of this current age as taught by my guru, Maharajji Neem Karoli Baba, and of course Jesus Christ. Through the five years that I have worked with Amirah, I have come to realize that she possesses many divine attributes that she well uses to heal, attune, clear and indeed free her clients ... and I'm pretty sure she knows the way to lead you to the Real You that dwells joyfully within.

Jai Ram Ransom, Author 'It All Abides in Love.'

Chapter 10 - Practice Guidelines

Practice the following tools this week:

1. Grounding – Quantum Energy Tool #1
2. Center of Head – Quantum Energy Tool #2
3. Replenishing – Quantum Energy Tool #3
4. Run Earth and Cosmic Energy – Quantum Energy Tool #7
5. Clear Your Range of Emotions
6. Re-set Wellness Throughout Your Body
7. Create 2rd Chakra Goals
8. Create 2rd Chakra Personal Mission Statement

GOALS AND HEALING WORKSHEET

WELLNESS COLOR _____

Physical Goal _____

Mental Goal _____

Emotional Goal _____

Spiritual Goal _____

MISSION STATEMENT

_____

WHAT ARE YOU NOTICING DIFFERENT?

_____

_____

WHAT ENERGIES **SUPPORT** YOU? (Colors, memories, beliefs, thoughts)

_____

_____

OTHER

_____

_____

11

3rd Chakra
Power To Choose

> *Your mind is like a fertile garden and it will grow and grow and grow and grow whatever is allowed to be planted there. So plant seeds of beautiful truth, endless potential, optimism, beauty and gratitude. If you plant those things thickly enough, they will choke out all of the weeds. Pull out the yucky stories when they try to invade, ok?*
> *You are important. You are enough. You are amazing. Your life matters."*

The overall theme of the 3rd Chakra is, '**You have the power to choose.**' We've each been provided with a number of incredible and irrevocable gifts that are oftentimes overlooked and/or taken for granted. One of the most incredible gifts provided to everyone on this planet is our '**power to choose'**. What we choose, we receive -- unconditionally.

What's most common, however, is that many people '**unknowingly and unintentionally'** choose to apply this power '**unconsciously'**. At best, most people use this power on a very shallow and superficial understanding of this treasure that we each have. Remaining '**unaware'** of how and why our every thought molds, shapes and impacts, at varying degrees, every event, every condition and every circumstance, limits your freedom to choose.

> *Every decision you make--makes you! Never let other people choose who you're going to be."*

Cassandra Clare

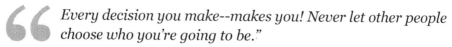

This is why so many '*perceive*' themselves as '*powerless*', to create desirable change. This is why they view themselves and others as victims or creatures of circumstance, rather than what we ALL truly are: '*creators of circumstance*.'

You can choose to achieve your life purpose or you can live out your karma or past experiences.

What Do You Choose?

* *Do you choose love, light and healing?*
* *Do you accept that you have the power to choose?*
* *Do you feel a sense of freedom when you make a choice?*

Regardless of how you answered these questions, and whether you currently '*believe it*' or not, it's far more than possible, *it's your birthright*! We can '*consciously*' want something and yet be '*unconsciously sabotaging*' it.

The choices that you are currently and consistently making everyday are the result of your previous programming and conditioning. Since **you have the power to change**, whenever you choose to do so, you can create an entirely new life for yourself!

When we clench old things in our hands, we prevent new things from being able to hold hands with us. New experiences, new things to learn, new relationships, new things that we don't even know exist yet.

Today is a great day to finally let go. It will be okay. In fact, it will be incredible. Feel the unlimited Abundance and Happiness.

Unlimited Abundance and Happiness

You have the power to choose, to create and live any kind of lifestyle that you would like. You have the ability to be as happy or unhappy as you choose to be. You have the power to choose to live a life that most people only dream about, as well as the ability to experience struggle, disharmony and discord from day to day.

The **only difference** between someone who is experiencing '*abundance and happiness*' in every area of their life, and someone who is not, has nothing to do with what's going on outside of you, but rather with what's going on within you.

> *Yet, it's outside where so many people look for the changes they seek.*

Unconsciously, they use their power to choose to engage in the physical activity of **'doing...doing...doing'** themselves into living in abundance. Utilizing your power to choose **'consciously and intentionally'** begins by deciding to take an inside-out approach using principles in <u>Manifesting Miracles 101</u> on the short path to harmony.

The beliefs you've acquired come through a number of channels. Your parents, who simply taught you in the best way they knew how, were taught to be logical, practical, realistic, right and true.

Loving, caring and well-intentioned parents only want what's best for their children, but they are innocently and unknowingly passing on and teaching their children the same self-sabotaging, self-limiting beliefs that they have been previously taught. These things they believe to be true without ever realizing that there is a Higher Truth!

Whether you explore the latest in scientific discoveries of quantum physics or enlightened wisdom of the ages, a common theme holds true.

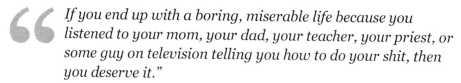

> *If you end up with a boring, miserable life because you listened to your mom, your dad, your teacher, your priest, or some guy on television telling you how to do your shit, then you deserve it."*

Frank Zappa

Perceptions Determine Reality

> *What is done is done. What is over is over. We are meant to move forward; we are meant to progress. Everything natural and beautiful and true and living was designed to constantly be renewing itself, progressing, living, living, living and then dying -- going on to the next step of its life cycle. When we clench old things in our hands, we prevent new things from being able to hold hands with us."*

We exist in a belief-driven universe. The conscious and unconscious beliefs that you have determine how you **'feel'** about any given circumstance and mirror a reflection of choice(s) in the various aspects of your life.

Depending on the quality of beliefs acquired and held, you interpret everything around you through the lens of your own individually acquired belief filters which determine your perceptions regarding life, yourself and what's available or not available to you individually.

This is where your power to choose '**c*onsciously***' becomes so crucial. Choosing to become '***conscious of***' the beliefs that are creating how you '***feel***', determines the quality of what you think, say and do. This can collectively determine the quality of your tangible and measurable results.

Once we choose to become keenly aware of our unique filters (beliefs) and make a choice to discern which are moving us forward and which are holding us back, we can make a conscious choice to enhance and elevate those that previously held us back and create the desired forms of change.

In essence, we can utilize our power to choose consciously, which in turn elevates our quality of consciousness (our beliefs). Our beliefs change how we '***feel***' and enables us to think, speak and act in such a way that aligns and harmonizes with what we desire to see and experience. This enhances the quality of results that we experience.

It's not a requirement of life, yet it is a choice we all have the ability to make.

Always continue the climb. It is possible for you to do whatever you choose, if you first get to know who you are and are willing to work with a power that is greater than ourselves to do it."

Ella Wheeler Wilcox

Anything and Everything You Want Is Available

It's not until you shift the perception and eliminate the belief-filters, that you will be able to access what you want.

This overall lack of understanding keeps people around the world stuck spending countless hours in unfulfilling jobs they despise. They're stressed out, investing in and using billions of dollars worth of '***over-the-counter quick fix medications***', '***perceiving***' themselves as victims of circumstance, unable to achieve any sort of harmony in life while constantly struggling to put food on the table and pay the bills.

If you consistently find yourself experiencing '***lack luster***' results, ***Take Heart.***

Overwriting and Eliminating False Beliefs

The first step here is: becoming aware of, overwriting and eliminating whatever false and self-limiting beliefs that you've been programmed to believe. You need to reprogram yourself with a **'Higher Truth'** regarding **who and what you truly are**, the gifts provided to you and **what you are 'truly' capable of achieving and becoming.**

You have the Power to Choose. You will explore, learn and discover the immutable and unwavering governing power that depicts our entire universe, but you still have the authority to choose to ignore and remain oblivious to that power. Exploring the Law of Vibration and Law of Attraction, you discovered your true ability to create your life by design and consciously utilize their incredible power to attract the life you desire.

 We are stardust . . . we are golden"

Joni Mitchell

3rd Chakra – Power of Transformation

The Solar Plexus, or the 3rd Chakra, located between the navel and solar plexus is the core of your personality, your identity and ego. It's a source of personal power and governs self-esteem, warrior energy and the power of transformation.

While the 2nd Chakra seeks pleasure and enjoyment, the 3rd Chakra is all about the perception of who you are. It's the center of willpower. The gift of this chakra is sensing your personal power and being confident, responsible and reliable.

It's the center of your self-esteem and self-discipline as well as warmth in your personality. The energy of this chakra allows you to transform inertia into action and movement and allows you to meet challenges and move forward in your life.

If we listened to our intellect, we'd never have a love affair... or go into business. You've got to jump off cliffs and build your wings on the way down."

Annie Dillard

Balanced Personal Power

The main challenge for the third chakra is to use your personal power in a balanced manner.

What does that mean?

It means '**consciously**' harnessing the energy of the solar plexus chakra. Rather than being **reactive** or **inactive**, you are proactive.

Every child is an artist. The problem is how to remain an artist once we grow up."

Pablo Picasso

Out-of-Balance 3rd Chakra

Persons with excessive third chakra energy react to life circumstances with emotional outbursts and are often stressed out. If a person's 3rd Chakra is blocked or deficient they typically allow life to just pass them by while they do nothing. Every time you judge or criticize yourself, you deplete this chakra and weaken your willpower.

Over-Active 3rd Chakra

If a 3rd Chakra is over-active, a person may be '**judgmental and critical**', easily finding fault in others. They are demanding, have extreme emotional problems and are rigid or stubborn (either my way or no way). Often anger or aggressiveness results from an over-active chakra. This person may always be planning to do things, but never do them. Their job or interests become a priority over other things – basically a workaholic. Often, they are also perfectionists and things are '**never good enough**'.

Under-Active 3ʳᵈ Chakra

If this chakra is under-active it can cause severe emotional problems. This can generate a lot of doubt and mistrust towards other people and excessive worry about what other people might think. It's typical that a person with an under-active 3rd Chakra runs on '**auto pilot**' to avoid feelings of depression or anxiety and the fear of being alone. This person may also feel that they are not good enough and constantly seek approval from others, leading to a life of '**dependency**'.

Balanced 3ʳᵈ Chakra

Having a strong and healthy 3rd Chakra reflects the ability to move forward in life with confidence and power. It reflects the ability to make conscious abilities to choose and to act. Having self-love, self-acceptance, and acknowledgement of your own worth are the building blocks of the third chakra.

A person with an open and balanced 3rd Chakra values themselves, their work and is confident in their ability to do something well. These individuals love and accept themselves, are willing to express themselves in a powerful way and know they have the freedom to choose to be themselves and direct their own life.

The only way to deal with an un-free world is to become so absolutely free that your very existence is an act of rebellion."

Albert Camus

Releasing Control

Considering the 3rd Chakra is your power center, a lot of competition or control energy (control of others, control of energy) can be stuck here.

If you are not comfortable or do not feel welcome, it's very easy to fight for your energy space to exist and rev up your 3rd Chakra. What's really happening is you go into '**competition**' with the foreign energy in your space.

From the spiritual side of things, the 3rd Chakra is where your spirit connects to your physical body. It's the main contact point and where your astral body (spirit) leaves when you dream. The physical body always wants to know if you are coming back or '**how committed are you to being with your body?**'

Great changes may not happen right away, but with effort even the difficult may become easy."

Bill Blackman

Commitment to Yourself

Our commitment to ourselves begins from the inside of the body and everything flows out from there. The competition and fight for control that the body generates happens when it's challenged or threatened by some foreign energy. When your body is invaded by foreign energy, it fights to have **'control of its own space'**.

When the 3rd Chakra is wide open, you are very energetic. When you quiet yourself in meditation, it usually closes down somewhat. However, there is a point where it can be closed down too low and you don't have enough energy. On the other hand, someone else's energy might be blocking you from having the chakra open enough to get what you want done.

Have you ever nodded off during a meditation? You might have closed it down too much and fallen asleep. You have to keep enough energy in your 3rd Chakra to keep from sleeping.

Your Commitment to Your Body

To determine how much foreign energy is controlling your commitment to your body, visualize a rose or a gauge. **What percentage of you is committed to your body?**

If your 3rd Chakra is closed down, there is foreign energy controlling your space. You don't have to change it. You may only need to create a little awareness or benchmark where you're at today.

 One, remember to look up at the stars and not down at your feet. Two, never give up work. Work gives you meaning and purpose and life is empty without it. Three, if you are lucky enough to find love, remember it is there and don't throw it away."

Stephen Hawking

Releasing Judgment Energy

> *Are there any judgments on how you energetically occupy your body or run your energy?*

Judgments on having too high or low energy, out of control energy, bouncing off the walls or being told you're dull? Simply **let go of any judgments of how you use your body**. Some of those judgments might be self-judgments: not positive or not even yours. Judgments, control and invalidation can cause you to withhold some of your spiritual energy from the chakra. This can be demonstrated through your **need to control situations** or **your behavior.**

Can you remember being in kindergarten? It was a safe environment where anything could happen. Having the freedom to express and explore your energy is true power. Not letting people have their energy and run it how they want in your space gives you the freedom to choose.

Let yourself release that energy out of your body and down your grounding cord. Using a sticky rose, begin collecting up all the foreign energy that is controlling your commitment to your body. Explode the rose or gauge.

 Get up, stand up. Stand up for your rights."

Bob Marley

Clearing Invalidation Energy

Over time, we all have situations or experiences where we withdrew from our body and relinquished our commitment to it. Oftentimes, very serious events caused us to give up our personal power or right to control our energy space. Maybe where you put a lot of energy into something, but it didn't happen? Feeling let down, disappointed or failure are examples of a time when we give up our own energy commitment.

> Imagine a timeline from birth to the present time and allow a light to appear anywhere along the timeline where competition energy came in, controlled or invalidated your 3rd Chakra.
>
> **Birth _____Present Time**
>
> If you start to get a million lights, just let the places start to light up where that shift started to occur. You may recognize or recall some situations, but it's not necessary to be effective.

Create a rose at birth and slide it along the timeline collecting up all lights. Create a wellness rose in present time and slide it along your timeline, back to birth, filling all the spaces where you released energy and reset it to your own wellness.

Visualize a rose for your original commitment to the body. Start to bring that rose toward the 'Present' – bringing your commitment forward to present time. Admire that rose – as you bring it into the present time, re-own your spiritual commitment to your body. RE-OWN it for yourself. Consciously own that commitment and vibrate at your wellness in the present.

Bring that rose inside your space and let it go wherever it wants to go (i.e. 3rd or 4th Chakras) Take a deep breath and allow your time line to dissolve.

When we least expect it, life sets us a challenge to test our courage and willingness to change; at such a moment, there is no point in pretending that nothing has happened or in saying that we are not yet ready. The challenge will not wait. Life does not look back. A week is more than enough time for us to decide whether or not to accept our destiny."

Paulo Coelho

The Physical Side of the 3rd Chakra

The sun shines not on us, but in us."

John Muir

Having explored the spiritual side to the 3rd Chakra, the other part of the equation is the physical body. There's a relationship with each chakra, organs and endocrine glands. The 3rd Chakra affects the adrenals, pancreas, liver and kidneys.

The spiritual energy of the 3rd Chakra comes into the chakra and communicates to the body through the glands. As long as the communication is clear, then the right energy will get to the body. The body knows what to do and the energy is translated perfectly.

Consider the relationship between the energy level of the 3rd Chakra and the energy level of the hormones (chemicals) released from the adrenals (adrenalin/aldosterone).

- Visualize a rose for the energy level of the hormones of the adrenal glands.

- Visualize a rose for your physical body.

- Visualize a rose for the energy level or chemicals emanating from your adrenal glands.

You may notice a vibration around that part of your body and the adrenals.

Alongside of the roses, visualize a rose for your wellness vibration and start to bring the rose for your adrenals in sync with the wellness vibration. Notice what happens in your body (changes, sensations) as you bring that space to wellness. Ground the rose for the adrenals, allowing any foreign energy to release out of that rose. Dissolve the wellness rose.

Visualize a rose representing your 3rd Chakra. Set that alongside of the rose for the physical body and your adrenal glands. Observe and allow your wellness to flow between the two roses. Once that space is cleared, allow the adrenal rose to dissolve keeping the rose for the 3rd Chakra.

Begin bringing your wellness color into the 3rd Chakra space. Visualize it at your wellness for this chakra. Visualize it coming out of the chakra through a silver line of energy, the silver cord, and connect it to your body.

What does it look like to you – what comes to mind?

Spirit Resides on Astral Plane

Let your awareness go to your astral body, the non-physical part of you that leaves the physical body and the third dimension that goes to a different dimension.

This also happens in dreams, astral projection, near-death experiences and death. A lot of the work we do in Manifesting Miracles 101 is done on the astral plane.

After getting a sense of your astral body, start allowing your wellness energy to flow through the silver cord and clear off any communication between the spiritual body and the physical body. When they are at wellness vibration, dissolve the images in your mind.

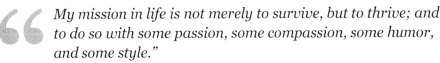

My mission in life is not merely to survive, but to thrive; and to do so with some passion, some compassion, some humor, and some style."

Maya Angelou

Thanks for continuing to believe in a better way...for working towards big things while enjoying the little things along the way....for continuing to seek for sweet fabulousness, and when you can't find it...for creating it."

"What I can most definitely say I feel the most out of everything is more centered and peaceful at the root of myself. Before our sessions together and working with the Quantum Energy Tools, I felt as if I was masking too much on top of my true aura that I couldn't really feel myself anymore. I'm feeling more sensitive and vulnerable possibly because I had been without my period for over 63 days. It came a couple days after our last session. That was totally powerful and such a relief.
My feelings for my boyfriend have intensified and although I feel as though I have been protecting my heart for so long, I'm starting to see the man I fell in love with again. I can tell I truly want to move forward with him and make things work. Besides all of that, I feel I'm healing my relationship with my mother and gives me peace knowing her cancer is advancing. I know divinely working with you was meant to overlap with this to help me through the process. I'm truly grateful for that."

Linda Martin

Chapter 11 - Practice Guidelines

Practice the following tools this week:

1. Grounding – Quantum Energy Tool #1
2. Center of Head – Quantum Energy Tool #2
3. Replenishing – Quantum Energy Tool #3
4. Run Earth and Cosmic Energy – Quantum Energy Tool #7
5. Reset Your Body Commitment
6. Release Judgment Energy
7. Clear Invalidation Energy
8. Reset Adrenal Glands

GOALS AND HEALING WORKSHEET

WELLNESS COLOR _____

Physical Goal _____

Mental Goal _____

Emotional Goal _____

Spiritual Goal _____

MISSION STATEMENT

_____

WHAT ARE YOU NOTICING DIFFERENT?

_____

_____

WHAT ENERGIES **SUPPORT** YOU? (Colors, memories, beliefs, thoughts)

_____

_____

OTHER

_____

_____

12

3rd Chakra Competition Destroys Creations

Not only are there others who have been through the same kinds of experiences you are going through, and felt the same kinds of pain you have felt, or worked towards the same kinds of goals you have worked for, or who want the same things out of life that you do...you also have unseen angels around you and the same hands that created you are watching over you, protecting you, and keeping you company every minute of every day.

You are cherished, loved, and watched over. You are never alone."

You are a bright shining star. Live colorfully...

Clearing, balancing, and opening your third chakra can help you develop a healthy sense of self-worth, to stand up for yourself, grow as a leader, become more effective, successfully set and reach goals and create the life that your soul longs for.

When energy is flowing freely through your 3rd Chakra, you are more able to pursue your destiny with a sense of personal power and are more able to be spontaneous and enjoy your journey with ease and laughter.

When foreign energies invade or get stuck in the 3rd Chakra, you go into '**competition**' with something or someone. You set up a '**win-lose situation**', and that changes how you express personal energetic power. Competition energy destroys your own spiritual validation and affects how you use your personal power, sending it away where it is not supportive to you.

I'm in competition with myself and I'm losing."

Roger Waters

Sky-High Expectations

In addition to competition, having '**expectations**', '**needing to be right**' and '**fighting for control**', '**the blame game**' energetically destroys your creations and self-growth.

Having sky-high expectations of yourself and / or others can devastate what you create for yourself.

Expectations are a good thing when they drive productive, incremental change, positively guided by grace and acceptance. However, unreasonable expectations begin to undermine, or sabotage, relationships and your own growth once they become immovable standards that must be met. Trying to chisel out of stone the ideal perception of yourself, but in reality it blocks your real beauty and natural abilities.

Do you struggle in life? Many of us are masters of our own sabotage and wonder why. We ironically destroy the vital pieces of our own lives -- our careers, friendships, integrity and even trust.

 Nature is based on harmony. So it says if we want to survive and become more like nature, then we actually have to understand that it's cooperation versus competition."

Bruce Lipton

Early Childhood Influences

Early childhood plays a heavy role here. We are passive recipients of what happened to us as children. All of us, to some degree, have experienced damage and learned behaviors that result in brokenness and mistrust for others. It has made us skeptical, weary, critical, fearful, and worried. These energies affect what we expect and ultimately attract into our lives. We developed distorted impressions and deductions from what is happening inside ourselves toward what's happening around us.

We interact and create our own personal reactions to the stimuli we see, forming conclusions that may diverge greatly from the reality of what is happening. These conclusions grow into fixed negative messages and expectations about oneself and others.

Here's an example of how competition and resistance can destroy your creations:

> **Bob and Karen are attempting to help their daughter, Sarah, with her homework. Sarah interprets the intervention as, *'I'm not smart enough to figure it out on my own'*. She feels bad and resists co-operating with her parents. Bob genuinely has Sarah's best interest at heart and hopes she will benefit from their help. Sarah however perceives *'their help'* as *'she's incapable and inadequate'* not aware of her hidden willingness to be judged negatively, she unconsciously accepts that she's *'defective and unworthy.'*
>
> **Sarah may feel that something is happening that is unpleasant with her family and begins to passively act out. Then, as she reaches adulthood she most likely *'resists support and love from others'*.**
>
> **Can you relate to how you may have formed conclusions that created different results from what you really wanted?**

In the above example, Sarah goes into **'competition'** with herself. Her perceived reality conflicts with her soul's truth. Resisting her parents support also creates competition between them for control over her space and the information and them needing to be right. If Sarah had been aware of what was happening, she might have chosen the option to come into harmony with the experience of being helped and make it work toward her benefit.

> *Do your work with your whole heart, and you will succeed - there's so little competition."*
>
> Elbert Hubbard

> **Sometimes we just have to keep sacred things to ourselves until our resolve, decision or goal is not feeling so wobbly and timid and fragile. Sometimes we have to give it time to grow and to become strong and solid and clear before it is safe enough to share it.**
>
> **Remember the peace you felt when the decision was finally made. Remember the clarity you felt when you knew the answer for sure. Remember that you knew it was right.**
>
> **What made it muddy was the outside opinions, preferences and judgments that really have no business making these kinds of decisions for your one beautiful, precious life.**
>
> **Stay strong, dear one. You know the way to go. You know what to do. It won't be easy, but it will be worth it.**

External Factors Influence Your Energy

The body's external energy field, known as the aura, is an outward manifestation of a dynamic internal energy system. The human energy system is a highly sensitive, complex phenomenon that is affected by the mental and physical state of the individual. It's also a host of external factors including social influences and our interactions with others and their energy system.

Your energy system is flawlessly and exquisitely engineered and flexible in its development. Our greatest challenge is to figure out ways to promote its evolvement, enrich overall growth, inner balance and sense of wellness.

Similarly, the conditions that impair your total growth likewise impair the energy system and its functions. If someone or something affects you, you are allowing them to affect you. If you feel **controlled, criticized, rejected** or **deprived**, it's because you consciously or mostly '**unconsciously**' allow it.

Rather than being passive receivers of what life or other people dish out, you are a co-creator by virtue of your energetic makeup.

Energy Vampires, Spoil Creations

Psychic or energy vampires are emotionally immature individuals who drain the time and energy from those around them. It's most likely too that you've experienced one or two in your own life. They are usually highly self-interested and lack empathy and are largely self-serving. The best way to deal with energy vampires is by identifying them in your life, setting firm boundaries (using Quantum Energy Tool #4) and working on your own sense of self-esteem and self-worth.

Energy vampires impair your aura's function and seriously damage its capacity to energize growth.

I recently worked with a client whose energy was completely immobilized by foreign energies and his own resistance. It was as if his spirit wanted something yet his body said: '**you want what?**' The other thing that can happen is thoughts like '**that will never happen**', '**you can't do that**', '**you can't have that**' or self-imposed or subconscious limits to how much you can have or what you can do, squashing your best intentions and efforts.

That's how those very thoughts get in the way and keep you from manifesting your desires.

You wanna know what scares people? Success. When you don't make moves and when you don't climb up the ladder, everybody loves you because you're not competition."

Nicki Minaj

Creating Chakra Balance

As collecting pools of subtle energy, chakras are very sensitive to mental, emotional, physical and spiritual inputs. Our chakra system is the energetic component of being human and unites us by the fact that we all have them and they behave the same way for everyone. The better you understand your chakras, the better you will be able to notice when things are out of balance and do something to bring them back into alignment.

It's easy for chakras to get out of balance just in the course of daily activities. The good news is that it is also very easy to do simple things each day to bring them back into balance, if you know what to do. Simple energy practices restore your chakras to their proper balance and are the basis for what **Quantum Energy Tools** (http://bit.ly/29WqnQk) and Manifesting Miracles 101 were designed to help you do. Miracle Mastery Mentoring takes these practices and tools and turns up the dial for producing miracles on steroids.

I'm not in this world to live up to your expectations and you're not in this world to live up to mine."

Bruce Lee

Having a balanced 3rd Chakra allows you to be in complete control over your emotions and thoughts. Your ego and mind are not influenced by foreign energies and you know without a doubt your place in the Universe. When in-tune and balanced, your 3rd Chakra center radiates warmth, joy and self-confidence to all you come into contact with.

3rd Chakra – Energy Distribution Center

It could be that in order to create something in the world, you are using someone else's energy to support you. Since your 3rd Chakra is your energy distribution center it may be set with foreign energy that is dictating the output of your goals.

The sun's energy warms the world. But when you focus it through a magnifying glass it can start a fire. Focus is so powerful!"

Alan Pariser

How It Is - Not How It Will Be

It's helpful to remember one of the tenets of kindergarten – having no expectations! Have no expectations about '**how you are supposed to be or feel**', '**what's going to happen**', '**where you are supposed to be**' – because all of those things will become self-fulfilling prophesies, or a series of limits on how things will be.

When you explore a new arena with expectations, you set limits about what can happen or how it can shift and change. When you have an expectation of where you should be for example, you '**invalidate**' where you are.

Considering '**everything is perfect**' in this moment—how can it be wrong? Releasing expectations out of your energy field liberates your energy to exploring possibilities that you have not yet discovered.

The problem with competition is that it takes away the requirement to set your own path, to invent your own method, to find a new way."

Seth Godin

Know Thyself

Constant invalidation may be one of the most significant reasons a person suffers from emotional blocks. Can you remember a time in your life where you were **invalidated, rejected, criticized, mocked, teased or judged?**

There is an interesting dynamic between healing and clearing, growth and improvement.

Referring to it as '**self-improvement**' implies '**you are broken and need fixing**.' Expecting that there is something wrong with you invalidates you as a spirit, and then you view yourself through that defective lens.

Instead you should be viewing yourself, '**for who you are**' – Know thyself! Yes, there is improvement in self-growth, but from this perspective you don't have the expectation of not being good enough. Rather than being from a place of '**problem solving**' you are in a place of '**acceptance** and **expanded awareness of who you really are**'.

Having Growth without Rules

What are your REAL goals as a spirit? What can you 'have' or 'allow' yourself to experience?

Take five minutes to center yourself in the morning - set your intention every day."

Oprah Winfrey

The 3rd Chakra can be set at a lot of different energies. For example, **win or lose, control or expectations, support, control or competition.**

Returning to your 3rd Chakra and its wellness vibration, have in your mind the idea that as you release energy, you are letting yourself move to an energy space of wellness in the 3rd Chakra and your whole self.

The big secret in life is that there is no big secret. Whatever your goal, you can get there if you're willing to work."

Oprah Winfrey

Consider what type of expectations you have for the 3rd Chakra:

Work/Career? *I'm not smart enough, I can't achieve that, I'm not educated, I don't deserve it, I'm not capable, I don't have enough money*

Family? *I'm alone, I have no freedom, I don't fit in, I'm not included, I'm not worthy, I don't deserve to be happy, He's/she's out of my league, I will always struggle*

Health? *I'm afraid that, it's hereditary, I'm worried*

Relationships? *He's/she's out of my league, I don't deserve love or support, I'm not worthy, I'm not enough, I always struggle with love*

On finances? *I always struggle, I don't deserve money, I can't handle $$$, I don't know how, my wallet is always empty*

... like most guys, you carry around this girl in your head, who is exactly who you want her to be. The person you think you will love the most. And every girl you are with gets measured against this girl in your head."

Rachel Cohn

What sense do you get on that 3rd Chakra? Visualizing a rose, begin releasing any of these or other thoughts, feelings or beliefs that come into your mind into that rose then dissolve the rose.

Releasing 'Have To Be'

Visualize another rose in front of you and imagine releasing any expectations into the rose. Let go of any considerations in the 3rd Chakra or in your space that put an expectation on your energy.

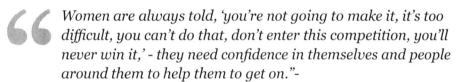

i.e. I have to: be perfect, on time, have a partner, be a lawyer, be smart, be thin, achieve, control, be free, analyze everything, know, be in charge, have what I have to have...or any 'have to be's',

Notice or think about what kind of message those expectations say to you and consider letting go of those expectations. Using a magic wand rose, imagine collecting all the **'have-to-be's'** inside your rose and explode it.

> *Women are always told, 'you're not going to make it, it's too difficult, you can't do that, don't enter this competition, you'll never win it,' - they need confidence in themselves and people around them to help them to get on."-*

> Zaha Hadid

Releasing 'Shoulds'

Imagine another rose in front of you and imagine releasing any **'shoulds'** from the rose. Notice what happens to that rose. ***Does it change or get bigger?***

> *We have this chance to make the most of where we are now. We have this chance to be the best we can be right now. We have this chance to put on a smile, to see the good, to spread joy, to give ourselves a break, to give everyone else a break....to tell others that it's ok if they didn't get everything done that they were wanting to get done."*

You are OK

Visualize the idea or picture that you are "OK" right where you are. Consider that idea and create that for yourself. You are right where you are supposed to be. Bring that consideration or message into the rose and put it into your body and 3rd Chakra in your solar plexus.

Creating the energy that lets you step out of any pressure and expectations, let the 3rd Chakra relax into your body and enjoy being right here in this moment.

Visualize your wellness color coming into your 3rd Chakra and let it match the idea that *'you are ok right where you are at'*. Replenish your energy and let go of whatever you are ready to release.

You have competition every day because you set such high standards for yourself that you have to go out every day and live up to that."

Michael Jordan

Creating 3rd Chakra Goals

This energy center fuels leadership. When energy is flowing freely through your Solar Plexus chakra, you are more able to pursue your destiny with a sense of personal power and self-worth. With a healthy sense of your self-identity, you will be more able to act spontaneously and enjoy your journey with ease and laughter. These are fabulous benefits of a strong 3rd Chakra.

Visualize a rose out in front of yourself and allow it be for a 3rd Chakra goal for yourself.

Think of a specific goal such as, *increasing self-esteem, standing up for yourself, being confident, being assertive or for a new job.*

Consider creating one goal for your healing in the 3rd Chakra and one for your space of creating things in your future.

3rd Chakra Mock-up

Visualize another rose for something you can do for yourself that will support you setting this 3rd Chakra at wellness for yourself, being at a vibration for having your growth and letting that 3rd Chakra be just for you (not set by any of your expectations).

What would be something you can create for yourself over the next week or two?

Visualize that goal inside a rose and ground it. If it's just a color that's ok, you might get a clear idea about something you want to do. Own that. You can have that. Imagine bringing it inside your aura, inside your body. Allow your body and energy field to adjust to the idea of 'having' that mock-up.

Let that mock-up go outside of your aura and allow the universe to manifest it into physical form.

Spiritual Mission Statement

3rd Chakra Personal Mission Statement

What is your Mission Statement or Vision Statement for the 3rd Chakra? For example, your overall MISSION statement could be:

"I am worthy of living my hearts desires."
"I am open to receiving all the good that is coming my way!"
"I am balanced and joyful and have all that I desire."

Add this 3rd Chakra Mission Statement to the previous 2 Chakras Personal Mission Statements Chapter 24.

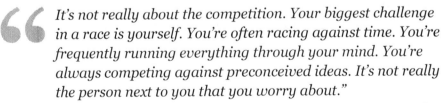

It's not really about the competition. Your biggest challenge in a race is yourself. You're often racing against time. You're frequently running everything through your mind. You're always competing against preconceived ideas. It's not really the person next to you that you worry about."

Summer Sanders

What is beautiful is that when we finally start to see ourselves in the light of the truth....we begin to seek out and attract people and situations and the beautiful life that is meant for us, and life proves itself right.
What a wonderful thing. But it's all in what we believe. Please believe in the truth."

"Working with Amirah, I'm feeling the resurgence of my passion for my career as the calling that has always been present has resurfaced. I have always been so scared to follow my heart and tried really hard to mask it and pretend I didn't want it. This TRULY feels like just the beginning and I am so excited to move into hyper-drive and begin what really feels like my true life."

Michelle Clemons

Chapter 12 - Practice Guidelines

Practice the following tools this week:

1. Grounding – Quantum Energy Tool #1
2. Center of Head – Quantum Energy Tool #2
3. Replenishing – Quantum Energy Tool #3
4. Run Earth and Cosmic Energy – Quantum Energy Tool #7
5. Release Expectations
6. Release Shoulds
7. Create 3rd Chakra Goals
8. Create 3rd Chakra Personal Mission Statement

GOALS AND HEALING WORKSHEET

WELLNESS COLOR _____

Physical Goal _____

Mental Goal _____

Emotional Goal _____

Spiritual Goal _____

MISSION STATEMENT

_____

WHAT ARE YOU NOTICING DIFFERENT?

_____

_____

WHAT ENERGIES **SUPPORT** YOU? (Colors, memories, beliefs, thoughts)

_____

_____

OTHER

_____

_____

Chapter

13

4ᵗʰ Chakra
It's All About You!

> *It's brave to keep dreaming big dreams, to keep posing big questions, to decide not to settle for the status quo. It's brave to seek for more beauty, goodness, joy and light in a world when it's often so hard to find. It's so courageous to keep your heart and mind on the good stuff and to ignore the fears that try so hard to keep us from all that our hearts are begging to have and experience."*

Let me ask you something…

Is there a relationship in your life that you're having trouble with? Are you lonely or do you have a hard time connecting to others in a meaningful way? Do you have a broken heart or emotional wound that won't heal? Is there someone (including yourself) you'd like to forgive? Are you on a path of spiritual growth? Would you like to rise to a higher level of compassion and non-judgment for others?

If any of this resonates with you, it might be helpful to learn some ways to clear and balance your heart chakra, the 4ᵗʰ Chakra.

Having moved past the physical needs of your first three chakras, raising yourself to the 4th level is a breeze. The 4ᵗʰ Chakra or the Heart Chakra is all about you. It's about writing your future your way and creating your life with your heart as the driver.

Having heart is about stepping outside what feels stifling or constraining to your nature. The 4ᵗʰ chakra is all about "***doing aliveness***."

> *When we develop the heart chakra, we begin to influence the surroundings with our spiritual presence. When we develop the communication chakra, we begin to influence the country with our spiritual presence. When we develop the seventh chakra, we begin to influence the world with our spiritual presence without doing anything."*
>
> Swami Dhyan Giten

In this chapter, you will discover and clear the energetic blocks around '**giving and receiving**' and discover the aspects or **'rules'** about receiving. If there is resistance in the 4th Chakra between giving and receiving for instance, '**I can't give out or receive from wellness**', you will clear the blocked energy. Also, you will look at your '**affinity**'. In other words, being able to connect/link with a deeper part of yourself within the 4th Chakra and clear it.

When you have '**your own affinity'** with yourself, it's like a sensor that tells you what you are in affinity with inside yourself, and what's in affinity with you outside of yourself. The problem is we don't follow what our heart tells us and the rules intercept us and intervene.

Clearing this chakra space allows you to listen to your OWN voice. That is, finding your wellness and affinity so that you listen to your heart, the louder voice.

> *We suffer when we give others the ultimate responsibility of making sure that we are happy and comfortable and that we have everything we need. Not only do we suffer, we cause others to suffer, too... because no matter how much others want us to be happy no one can make us happy and content. No one can make us feel fulfilled. This is a job that is ours and ours alone."*

4th Chakra – Affinity with Self

The 4th Chakra is located at the center of the chest and includes the heart, cardiac plexus, thymus gland, lungs, and breasts. It also rules the lymphatic system. The Sanskrit word for the fourth chakra is **Anahata,** which means: **"unhurt."** The name implies that beneath the pain and grievances of past experiences lies a pure and spiritual place where no hurt exists.

When your heart chakra is open, you are flowing with love and compassion, you are quick to forgive, and you accept others and yourself.

 Our hearts resonate at the same frequency as the earth and the universe. Therefore, we are all valuable instruments in the orchestration of the world and its harmony."

Suzy Kassem

A Closed 4ᵗʰ Chakra

A closed heart chakra can give way to grief, anger, jealousy, fear of betrayal, and hatred toward yourself and others.

Some people choose to live in the place of grievances. Perhaps they've been hurt in the past by parents, siblings, classmates, or loves. Maybe you've been there too. It's impossible to avoid situations where someone may try to hurt you, but you get to choose what to do with that hurt. Some people might try to hurt the other person in return. Yet, that is not living from a place of *an open 4ᵗʰ Chakra*. The person who inflicts pain on others is coming from a place of fear, ignorance or hatred, all of which represent a closed 4ᵗʰ Chakra.

I remember a situation that happened to me. A longtime friend, who didn't understand my work and considered it the work of the devil, informed me that she could no longer be my friend. Although I was sad to lose what I thought was a deep friendship, I surrendered to her decision.

It was when I was working with my own 4ᵗʰ Chakra energy that she contacted me again and shared that she started to understand where I was coming from and that she had some similar life experiences that she wanted to share. She said she didn't have anyone in her circle of friends that could understand like I would. That was a wonderful surprise of how powerful the 4th Chakra healing can be.

To hand others the keys to your life fulfillment -- is to give away your power. To take responsibility is the very best kind of freedom. It is worth it."

Now you might be thinking ... **how do I create openness**? It's easy, right!?

Empathy and Compassion Create Openness

Walking in another person's shoes is not easy to do, but it can be helpful in fostering a sense of empathy. To help create empathy and compassion, I like to play a game called '**the what-if scenarios**'.

When encountering a person who is being unpleasant or who has treated me poorly in the past, I quickly take my mind through a host of '**what ifs**'. For example, ask yourself,

- *"What if that person is just having a bad day?"*
- *"What if that person just lost his job?"*
- *"What if she just learned her husband was having an affai*r?"
- *"What if he was just diagnosed with an illness?"*

As you create these stories, of which the possibilities are endless, you begin to empathize with the other person and his or her situation. This method takes you away from yourself and self-pity and instead, places compassion onto the other person.

Now, let's suppose that there's a family member or a close friend who just repeats a pattern of inflicting hurt on a constant basis. As you release your previous 4th Chakra programming, pain and stuck energy, you can still offer love and compassion, either from a distance or by setting boundaries. In any case, know that when someone chooses to hurt you, it's almost never about you. It's about them.

When you begin to touch your heart or let your heart be touched, you begin to discover that it's bottomless."

Pema Chodron

Give Love to Receive Love

The best way to receive love is to give it. Author and motivational speaker, Leo Buscaglia, used to teach that we should give and receive 12 hugs a day for optimal health. So give hugs and kisses. Other ways that you can give love include:

- Smile at everyone you see daily, even if you don't feel like smiling. It's contagious.
- Forgive and move on. Life is too short to hold grudges.
- Give friends, family and co-workers positive affirmations and feedback.
- Try to go one day a week without criticizing anyone or anything, including yourself.

Take any opportunity you can to foster love and loving feelings. Love is a currency, and whatever you give, will come back to you.

This chakra's main issues are about relationships and love. That is, loving yourself or having affinity with self. Most important, it is the bridge from the physical part of you, to your mental and spiritual dimensions. Love and its many expressions (passion, caring, rapport, unity, understanding, and forgiveness) are the means to and the rewards of a clear 4th Chakra.

Ultimately, the objective of an open 4th Chakra is unconditional love—starting with self. This is a love so pure, that it is not quantified by any restrictions imposed on it, such as your ideals or the way you think others should act or respond to you. So, in addition to your family and friends, the 4th Chakra also makes it possible for you to 'love your neighbor (or fellow man) as yourself.'

Life is like riding a bicycle. To keep your balance, you must keep moving."

Albert Einstein

Now before showing the ways to balance this chakra, it is very important to know the two aspects of the 4th Chakra.

Two Aspects of the 4th Chakra

There are two sides to the 4th Chakra. 1) Affinity with yourself and the *'harmony or conflict'* with the spirit and the body. 2) Affinity with yourself and the outside world in terms of *'what you can attract to yourself'*.

If there's any resistance in the 4th Chakra between giving and receiving **for instance, "I can't give out or receive from the vibration of wellness"**, then it is BLOCKED. You can say what you want, but there's a rule or tone that sets the vibration, and to whatever degree you can '**give and receive**', will determine how you attract what you desire.

> *Some people are just givers and won't let themselves receive.*

Healers are most often like this and it's always an issue because they burnout '**giving, giving, giving**'! If you find yourself **giving** to '**fix or solve a problem**' then you can't receive until it's done. **AND … It's never done!** You put all of your energy into an issue and get nothing back.

The **giving and receiving** I'm looking at is not that part of you giving of yourself. It's the energy you are giving out to the world, the energy you put out from the 4th Chakra. When you give from a place of '**wellbeing**', you are not giving your own energy. When you're healing the issue, situation or person, you often give away your energy.

When you give from a place of recognizing the other's 'soul presence' in the world, you give freely without diminishing your energy. Being able to be in your own affinity is what **giving and receiving** or getting back is all about.

Most people think about love with the 4th Chakra: **open hearted, love the world, all is love**. Really it's about your attraction, affinity for yourself or your attraction ability. Love is really **affinity, communication and reality** all together.

It's more than just attraction in the 4th Chakra -- it's a much bigger idea! It's a better picture of love and strong attraction. If you are missing all the other stuff, you really don't have love. To receive love and compassion, it is very important to listen to your heart.

Listening to Your Heart

> *What if? WHAT IF today was the day that you chose to stop blaming yourself for choices you have made, (choices that you would make differently today, knowing what you know now, and being who you are now) and instead put your arm around yourself, kissed yourself smack on the cheek and said...*

We know better now, so we can do better now!"

I want to take the *'love picture'* out of the 4th Chakra so that you can have your own affinity with yourself--wanting to be nice, be liked etc. but ultimately we don't follow our heart. Rather, it's about listening to our own voice.

When finding our 4th Chakra wellbeing and affinity, **we listen to our heart – the louder voice**.

So when we talk about *'listening to our heart,'* it means being mindful of our soul's perspective, our inner knowing, our intuitive feeling and our essential loving core.

Balanced 4th Chakra

A person with a balanced 4th Chakra has a loving presence and is accepting, warm, friendly, gracious, compassionate, and charismatic with the ability to LOVE SELF. Healthy, loving relationships based on a balanced give-and-take dynamic are the benchmark of this chakra. Being able to gracefully 'receive' as well as to give is incredibly important.

> *In a maize field choose to be a flower. In a garden of daisies choose to be a rose."*
>
> Matshona Dhlio

Deficiencies in this area surface as feelings of isolation, withdrawal, paranoia, fear of commitment, lack of self-esteem, and/or depression. Heart defenses may manifest as a tendency to 'give everything away,' or to be totally focused on others while depriving oneself, or as addictions (such as drugs or alcohol), which are used to suppress or deaden feelings from the heart.

A closed or shielded 4th Chakra can stop your ascension from getting to the higher-level chakras immediately, so it is easy to see how important it is to open your heart. Unconditional love is the reward, while forgiveness is the key.

> *Your heart is the source of all of your dreams of all that can make you happy. Your heart draws and connects you to whatever is divine, in yourself, in your life, in the world."*
>
> Elana Peled

Communication Bridge

The 4th Chakra is the communication bridge between the upper chakras (5th, 6th, 7th and 8th chakras) that are the spiritual centers, and the lower chakras (1st, 2nd and 3rd chakras) which are the physical body centers. The 4th Chakra is a pivotal point of where the other chakras come together to communicate with each other and trigger a state of '***being in the flow***'.

> *Pay attention to whatever inspires you, for it is 'spirit' trying to communicate with you, that's why it's called 'inspiration' as 'in-spirit'. Listen to it, believe it, and act on it.*

The biggest thing about the 4th Chakra energy space is your AFFINITY! That is, your attraction to things. Often, what we tend to do is give and receive to/from the world based on what you are feeling. This all happens in the 4th Chakra.

What you get from the outside <u>WORLD</u> is based on what you feel within your 4th Chakra.

Holding Back

As humans, we tend to hold back when we perceive that we are running low on something. We believe thoughts like '***I don't have enough time to volunteer***' or '***that person doesn't show me love***, so I'll withhold my love too.' Maybe you can relate to keeping clothes you haven't worn in years or hiding the last piece of cake. Although you might think you are being safe or frugal, there is '***unconscious fear***' hidden within these actions—You fear that you won't have enough for yourself.

When you truly understand the principle of ***giving and receiving***, you will give more with an open and joyful heart (without fear), and actually receive more as it truly is one constant flow of energy.

As you go about your day, try your best to '***give something to everyone you meet***'. It might be a smile, a compliment, money for a snack, or some other simple gesture of kindness. Remember to receive with a happy heart as well.

As you continue to give without a fear of losing your resources—and simply enjoy the knowledge that what you give will come flowing right back to you— you will open up the door to a new and joyful way of living that you'll never want to close.

Giving From the 4ᵗʰ Chakra

To truly hear your heart, you must quiet your mind. When your mind is quiet, the whispering voice of your heart can be heard."

Elana Peled

Consider the concept of *'giving from the 4ᵗʰ Chakra'*. Reflect on what that is for you. What does *'giving'* mean to you?

Visualize a rose for this concept and observe:

How open is it? What color is it? Are you feeling comfortable giving?

Do you resist the idea? Do you trust it? Let the rose show you how you feel about giving.

Rules about Giving

Are there any rules around giving? Do you always have to give? Does giving mean love and care to you? I must give? It's better to give than receive?

Visualize a rose that represents *giving.* Begin releasing any rules that aren't yours. (i.e. mom's, dad's, society's, a former teacher's, etc.).

Release any resistance such as: *I have to do this or I must give in a certain way.*

As you release any resistance from the rose and your body, allow your wellness color to pour into the top of the rose. Allow this energy space for giving to shift into wellness by setting your *Havingness Gauge to 100%.*

When you *give* from this wellness vibration, you aren't giving a part of you away when you do. Notice how it feels to give in a place of wellness and how releasing any resistance changes the space. Bring the *giving* rose (set at your wellness color) into your 4ᵗʰ Chakra.

Every Giver Needs a Receiver!

So, why does receiving make most of us feel uncomfortable?

Have you ever been offered a compliment only to find ways to brush it off and NOT ACCEPT it? Maybe you've experienced someone offering to help and you quickly jump into the "**No thanks, I'm fine ... I'll manage it...**" mode.

Most people associate '**receiving**' with shame and weakness.

Receiving requires you to open up and become **a vessel** for letting go of your control, by letting the Universal Principles operate. Practicing the **Quantum Energy Tools** (http://bit.ly/29WqnQk) and the exercises within Manifesting Miracles 101 is guaranteed to be an effective way to erode whatever blocks that are keeping you from receiving.

> *In terms of RECEIVING, what frequency are you set at? What rules are influencing your energy space of receiving? Imagine that there's an energetic space that you can give and receive from a vibration of wellness.*

Can you recall a time when you felt obliged to give because it was the nice thing to do? Maybe you received something and it felt proper to give something in return. Those unspoken rules dictate how you give and how you allow yourself to receive. Whatever the rules, maybe you gave something to get something back.

Now it's important to learn how to receive from the 4th Chakra...

Receiving From the 4th Chakra

> Consider the concept of '**receiving** from the 4th Chakra'. Reflect on what that is for you.
>
> Visualize a rose for this concept and observe:
>
> *How open is it? What color is it? Are you feeling comfortable giving? Do you resist the idea? Do you trust it?*
>
> Let the rose show you how you feel about *receiving.*
>
> Having And Receiving Gauge

Rules About Receiving

> *What unconscious rules do you have around receiving? Does 'receiving' mean that you are weak and not capable?*

Who taught you how to *receive?* Visualize a rose that represents *receiving.* Begin releasing any rules that aren't yours? (i.e. *mom's, dad's, society's, a former teacher's, etc.).*

Release any resistance or foreign energy about *receiving* from the rose. Allow your wellness color to pour into the top of the rose. Allow this energy space for *receiving* to shift into wellness. Allow your *Receivingness Gauge to be set at 100%.*

When you *receive* from this wellness vibration, you aren't giving a part of yourself away. Notice how it feels to give in a place of wellness and how releasing any resistance changes the space.

Bring your *receiving* rose (set at wellness) into your 4th Chakra.

"WHAT IF????
Wouldn't that be so much easier, so much more peaceful, so much more loving and merciful, and SO MUCH MORE PRODUCTIVE and RIGHT? Yes, it would. But YOU are the one who has to do it."

Physical Aspects of the 4th Chakra

Location of the Thymus

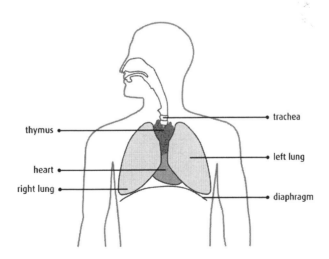

The gland associated with the 4th Chakra is the thymus, located just below the collarbone, on either side of chest. Bending your arms and pounding your chest is about where it's located. Thumping your thymus works to boost your immune system and release t-cells for a healthier you.

Visualize a rose for your thymus. *What is your wellness color for your thymus? Has anything changed?*

Consider: *How does the vibe of T-cells and thymus affect the wellness of your body?* Begin releasing any energy of your thymus by grounding your rose and reset the thymus to the energy of wellness.

Receiving Goals in Affinity

Visualize a rose for '*something*' you don't have yet (a dream or goal) and notice its vibration. Sometimes things we are working on have someone else's energy on them. Bring that rose closer to your body. Notice what it feels like. Notice your reactions. *Do you resist it?* Move it outside your aura again.

Bring that goal into affinity with your 4th Chakra wellness. Let everything else fall away from it. When it comes into affinity with you, bring it into your aura. Notice how that feels to your body.

Is it easier to have? Do you like it? Do you own it as if you already have it?

Imagine the energy that you need to reach that goal. Visualize dropping it in your crown chakra. Explode the rose outside of your aura.

Sometimes goals don't come because we're not in affinity with ourselfves.
Dreamers are not always treated with kindness and understanding. Visionaries are rarely taken seriously. People who seek for what is good and true are often scoffed, laughed at or shut down.
Are you willing to dream big dreams anyway? Are you willing to believe in the vision you have of what you want the world to be, or what you want your life to be? Are you willing to keep seeking the kind of life that others might say is unrealistic?

Give Yourself This Healing Affirmation:

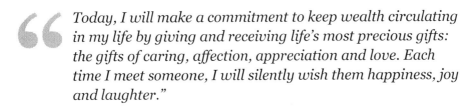

Today, I will make a commitment to keep wealth circulating in my life by giving and receiving life's most precious gifts: the gifts of caring, affection, appreciation and love. Each time I meet someone, I will silently wish them happiness, joy and laughter."

Amirah taught me useful meditation techniques. Her insights helped me to heal and to better understand myself in relation to my family. I strongly recommend her to anybody. She is an excellent clairvoyant and healer and her energy healing skills are powerful. Her insights were always very accurate."

Elijah Toumi

Chapter 13 - Practice Guidelines

Practice the following tools this week:

1. Grounding – Quantum Energy Tool #1
2. Center of Head – Quantum Energy Tool #2
3. Replenishing – Quantum Energy Tool #3
4. Run Earth and Cosmic Energy – Quantum Energy Tool #7
5. Review Concept of Giving for Yourself
6. Clear Rules About Giving
7. Reset Having/Receiving Gauge
8. Reset Receiving to Wellness Vibration
9. Reset Goals to Affinity

GOALS AND HEALING WORKSHEET

WELLNESS COLOR _____

Physical Goal _____

Mental Goal _____

Emotional Goal _____

Spiritual Goal _____

MISSION STATEMENT

_____

WHAT ARE YOU NOTICING DIFFERENT?

_____

_____

WHAT ENERGIES **SUPPORT** YOU? (Colors, memories, beliefs, thoughts)

_____

_____

OTHER

_____

_____

Chapter

(14)

4ᵗʰ Chakra
Learning Self Love

> "Sometimes we forget that there are people around us that we might not even know who wish us the best just because we are alive. Sometimes we forget that there is air to breathe, and plenty of it, and that we get to breathe in as much of it as we want, whenever we want to. Sometimes we forget to watch how the trees sway back and forth in the breeze as if they are saying hello every time we walk by. Sometimes we forget all of the incredible color that is all around us, in every form imaginable. Sometimes we forget that ALL of the beauty, truth and light is there for us...every single day...just for us."

Let's start with a very basic yet important question: **What's the most important relationship in your life?**

Well, it is your relationship with yourself. **Do you take yourself for granted? Or do you function on autopilot at the whims and desires of others, without knowing exactly what you want until something happens that you definitely don't want?** Then you wonder, "**What's going on? How did I get into this mess?**"

When we don't pay attention, the Universe has its way of waking us up. The good news is that these challenges can push you in a new direction. When you get so sick and tired of being sick and tired, you change! You WAKE UP!

In this chapter, you will discover a deeper affinity with yourself and clear energy to be able to validate yourself from the inside out. As you continue exploring and releasing any 4th Chakra energy or pictures that other people have about you '*not fitting in*,' you gain greater self-love and learn more about your place in the world.

We Create Everything in Our Lives

> *What have you been creating? What are you allowing in?*
> *What are you letting happen? "Because that's the way it's always been," or "I can't change them" or any number of excuses?*
> *Are you doing what you do because of conditioning; because of 'shoulds' 'ought to haves'?*
> *Do you disregard yourself? Do you give others the power to hurt you?*

Accepting and allowing yourself to be where you are without judgment is key. Consider this as '*just information*'. You have to know where you are to move in a different direction. You are the main hero in your life. You are THE STAR!

Star in Your Own Movie

Are you a player in someone else's movie or the STAR in your own? This is your life, and the most important role you have, is taking care of yourself. *How are you doing at it? How about getting in touch with you? Do you know who you are?*

A good way to begin getting to know yourself is to ask yourself these questions about **everything** you contemplate doing:

> *Does this increase my joy, loving and abundance?*
> *Is this something that will fulfill me?*

If the answer is no, ***STOP!***

That is, STOP AND MAKE A CHANGE!

Change Starts With You

> *The old world is constantly trying to make us forget that everything we need to be happy is almost always right in front of our face. Please, be one of the brave ones who notices the love that has gone into every creation around us."*

I'm not saying that you should abandon your current responsibilities, but instead take a fine-tooth comb and consider your actions. Change starts with you. If you're not centered and balanced, how can you assist others? When you function with strength, grace and peace, people respond positively and that makes you the '**actor**' rather than the '**reactor**'.

Before you start your day, take some quiet time for yourself and bring yourself to wellness. Consider what you want to create? Complete? Or, participate in? Setting your intentions to wellness sets them in motion. Practice reminding yourself throughout the day to '**come to your wellness color**' and reset the energy for affinity with yourself.

> *And if you forget, laugh. Be amused with yourself.*

At the end of your day, ground and release the activities of the day including your '**mistakes, shouldas, couldas and wouldas**'!

Get plenty of rest, exercise and eat healthy foods. Associating with people who are positive and supportive, friends and family is nurturing. Practice staying centered and focused and don't give others power over you. Practice awareness and patience, especially with yourself. If you usually go outside of yourself to find worth and validation, go inside instead. Validate yourself. Live through your own opinion.

We are all conditioned in certain ways. Ask where your usual thoughts and emotions are coming from. Are you allowing something that happened years ago to dictate your actions today?

When you are allowing the changes… the first change should be the LOVE for yourself.

Loving Yourself First

Everyone's heard this self-help platitude: **We need to love ourselves before we can love anyone else.** Learning to love yourself is a very powerful 1st step! The wounded child resides in the 4th Chakra and if it's closed down, your core essence suffers. Your breathing becomes shallow and your metabolism slows down. All in all, it lowers your physical energy.

The heart of life is a sphere quiet and serene, and the star that shines therein is fixed for evermore."

Khalil Gibran

When blocked at your 4th Chakra center, you are divided between mind and body; you withdraw into a closed system. On the other hand, when your 4th Chakra is too open you have the tendency to give all your time and energy away, focusing on others instead and losing your centeredness.

People with an over-active heart chakra give away all their resources without reason. They withdraw from their own emotional bank account until nothing is left and they find themselves unable to relate to others and risk losing friendships.

When the 4th Chakra is blocked, it's hard to stay balanced and have the energy to flow freely between the physical and non-physical bodies. As the heart is healed, you can give and receive better. Love is felt automatically. It's from this place of being that we reach out to each other with compassion and healing.

As your 4th Chakra begins changing using the exercises and **Quantum Energy Tools** (http://bit.ly/29WqnQk) congratulate yourself for allowing this BIG STEP to occur. Continue to release any 4th Chakra energy or ideas that other people think you don't fit in. Consider that whatever happens you will continue to let go of any beliefs, notions or pictures of what others have of you.

> *What are you calling or drawing to you? Is it in affinity with you? What might affect it from being in affinity with you? Sometimes you might want something, but the energy isn't right and it won't manifest. Maybe you can remember a time when you had a dilemma of wanting it and at the same time resisting it.*

Meditation is to become aware about this internal life energy. Meditation is the procedure to rearrange, harmonize, activate, and integrate the individual life energy with the cosmic life energy."

Amit Ray

You also risk your heart energy when you cling to old wounds without working through them. You lose out when you stay jealous or cling to relationships. All the while, you're forgetting to take care of yourself and maintain a healthy balance so that you have enough to give to others.

The heart is not only the location of the 4th Chakra, located at the center of your chakra system, but also the center of your conscious universe and is able to create and define life in its true essence."

Steven Redhead

And believe me, it's not just about loving ourselves, it's also about the magical power of forgiving!

Forgiveness Is a Must

Every good story has opposition...tragedy...and the overcoming of it all. YOUR STORY is a beautiful big rich story. You are the brave hero. You are the main character. You have such a beautiful, beautiful story and there are so many incredible chapters still to come."

Relationships can be difficult with someone who has closed their heart to the world.

Forgiveness is a must. When this chakra is in a negative state, physical illness is brought about with heartbreak and requires an emotional healing to occur alongside the physical.

Ideally, the 4th Chakra should radiate love with a strong solid center of self-acceptance. It should reach out in support for others with care and compassion to others. The central message of the 4th Chakra is: balance, self-love and love for others with these being equal or interconnected with others.

With a balanced and healed 4th Chakra you are united by the beautiful gifts of grace and peace. Love teaches you to let go and trust in the world. Having a healthy 4th Chakra is a devotional journey that paves the way for healing on a global scale.

From The Outside In

What are you calling or drawing to you? Is it in affinity? What might be keeping it from being in affinity with you? Sometimes it might be something you want, but the energy isn't right. Or it might be the dilemma of wanting it and having the goal while still resisting the energy of it.

Reclaim Your Validation

What the superior man seeks is in himself; what the small man seeks is in others."

Confucius

We all want validation. We all need healthy validation from others, because it's one of the ways that we communicate acceptance of our Self and others. However, there is a point to where we *'give up our personal power'* in exchange for approval. Seeking validation outside your Self is the ultimate way of giving away your POWER.

On a spiritual level, you can reclaim your ability to validate yourself. In many ways, we learned to put validation outside ourselves and seen it from sources such as: teachers, doctors, schools, institutions, etc. Really it's always been there, we just aren't looking for it in the right place. Once you can reclaim that inner space, you can let go of where you look outside of yourself for validation. Release those old places into the Universe.

Ask yourself:

- *How often do you seek someone else's approval on how you look?*
- *How often do you seek someone's help in making a minor decision?*
- *Do you jump through hoops to please others?*
- *Do you change your appearance based on the approval of others?*
- *Do you become depressed if no one gives you accolades, approval or compliments?*

Visualize a rose out in front of you for the first person you were attracted to from a 4th Chakra basis. Not attraction in terms of as in *'chemistry'*, but whey they acknowledged or approved of you. Considering this person, were they the first person where you created self-approval or validation from/with? Maybe there are several people. Consider:

What did they have that you admired?
Was it a teacher?
What were the qualities that you admired?

Consider, as we look at this person or the composite of many persons, and begin calling your validation back from where they became your source of validation for you.

Visualize two roses. One that represents yourself and one that represents anyone you gave your validation to. Imagine reclaiming all your validation from their rose into your rose. Begin calling back your validation and return it to your body or chakras.

Bring all of your validation inside of you so that it's not outside of you.

When you begin to relinquish your ego, you will no longer feel compelled to prove to people how busy you are in an attempt to validate your sense of worth."

Miya Yamanouchi

Now here, I am about to discuss a great concept about energy space that will give your life a required boost. Yes, I'm talking about the MOCKUP space.

Validation in Mockups

Your MOCKUP space is the energy space where you energetically create. The reason we are looking at this is because whatever energy goes out on your mockup, the same comes back to you. So if the energy says, 'it's **hard work'** even if it's something you really want and it doesn't require a lot of work... well, that's an experience!

When you have validation from within, you won't create validation to chase your validation. **Have you created a mockup that is never enough?** With that, there's always an energetic void that means it can never fill you up.

I have a friend who always wanted a Mercedes and thought that once she received it, she'd be forever happy. However, within just thirty days of finally having her prize, she felt unsettled and unfulfilled because she was not in affinity within herself, or with the mockup.

There are no voids in the spiritual universe. When you gave away your validation, something else filled up your body. When you called back your validation, you needed to release something first. That is what grounding is used for.

Releasing Foreign Energy from Mockups

Visualize a rose for where you energetically create things – your mockup space. Let it represent your overall creative space and get a sense of it (thoughts, colors, senses, etc.). This is a space where you go to for goals.

Notice: *Is it hard work, fun, enthusiastic...yeah let's do it? What sense do you notice?*

Is it comfortable, disappointing or is it blank?

Begin releasing other people's energy, for instance: *'creating is hard, need effort, not enough, etc.'*

Sometimes you might create something and afterwards look back at it and say: *"why was that so hard? "Why was there so much energy set there?"*

Consider your wellness color for your own vibration or affinity. Set the mockup energy space to that color: your own vibration or affinity. Then, as you work on your goals, all that's left is your energy instead of programming such as: *It's hard, this is boring, can't do it, it's a struggle, etc.*

Visualize another magnetic rose out in front of you. Allow it to move through your body and collect energy that *'won't let you change'*. Send the magnetic rose through your aura, collecting up any energy that says, *'it's not real, this is weird, etc.'* Explode the rose.

Consider replacing all the negative space and replenish yourself with a Golden Sun filled with self-validation, *'it's easy, I have support, I'm validated, I have what I want / know what to do, everything flows, and I trust the universe.'*

Forgiveness

 Forgiveness is a gift you give yourself."

Suzanne Somers

Begin a new day today with letting go of the past, forgiving it and yourself. Forgive those who have hurt you, and forgive yourself for allowing it. Then move on and truly forget it. **Let it go**. Don't let the past dictate your present or your future or analyze it to death. Who did what, why they did it and why you did something IS OVER! It's DONE. Move past it. Release it. Love yourself – then it's easy to love others.

Forgiving others often starts as a decision of surrender-an act of your will. This surrender invites deeper levels of healing and opening yourself to **'be in the flow'**. Negative emotions disrupt the flow of your 4th Chakra just as easily as boulders in a stream. How many boulders have piled up in your heart over time? Each boulder represents a major hurt, a major resentment, a major betrayal or disappointment, a deep wounding, shame or grief.

When the flow is disturbed or slowed, stagnation happens. Stagnant heart flow breeds anger and resentment, depression and self-loathing. It muddies the clear waters of the heart, and dirty water spills over into everything you do.

 Forgive or be unhappy. Which do you prefer?"
William Fergus Martin.

> **Visualize a rose for your goals, cut it in half lengthwise, from top to bottom. Consider that one side represents your affinity and the other side represents what resists you from being in affinity with yourself.** *What colors do you see and which one is the most dominant color?* **Set your goal rose to your wellness vibration.**

 When you do not forgive you are blaming someone else for the pain you are actively maintaining in yourself."
William Fergus Martin.

Wellness for the 4th Chakra

> **Create an image of yourself. Visualize a picture of yourself with a grounding cord. Imagine a rose in your wellness color and bring it into the 4th Chakra, re-setting it to wellness. Consider dropping the idea into it: that you are going to connect with your wellness color each day.**

Personal Spiritual Mission Statement

> **What is your Mission Statement or Vision Statement for the 4th Chakra?** *What color or phrase comes to mind? How do you want to feel in your 4th Chakra?*

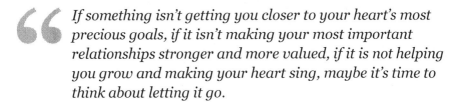

For example, your statement could be:

"I embrace all that I am!"
"I love and forgive myself!"
"I love me. I have all that I need."

Add this 4ᵗʰ Chakra Mission Statement to the previous 3 Chakra's Personal Mission Statements in Chapter 24.

> *If something isn't getting you closer to your heart's most precious goals, if it isn't making your most important relationships stronger and more valued, if it is not helping you grow and making your heart sing, maybe it's time to think about letting it go.*
>
> *If you will listen very, very, very closely, you will know for sure what to hold on to...and what to let go of...and where to spend your precious minutes and energies."*

"I grew up in a communist regime where freedom of speech was repressed and anything away from materialism was roughly judged. Through working with Amirah, came the confirmation of the challenges I have to face and master, the beliefs I have to work on to overcome the blockages that keep me stuck and it confirmed some spiritual gifts I thought I had but was not sure if it was just in my imagination."

Ramona Kuzinsky

Chapter 14 - Practice Guidelines

Practice the following tools this week:

1. Grounding – Quantum Energy Tool #1
2. Center of Head – Quantum Energy Tool #2
3. Replenishing – Quantum Energy Tool #3
4. Run Earth and Cosmic Energy – Quantum Energy Tool #7
5. Reclaim Your Validation
6. Releasing Foreign Energy from Mockups
7. Reset 4th Chakra to Wellness
8. Create 4th Chakra Personal Spiritual Mission Statement

GOALS AND HEALING WORKSHEET

WELLNESS COLOR _____

Physical Goal _____

Mental Goal _____

Emotional Goal _____

Spiritual Goal _____

MISSION STATEMENT

_____

WHAT ARE YOU NOTICING DIFFERENT?

_____

_____

WHAT ENERGIES **SUPPORT** YOU? (Colors, memories, beliefs, thoughts)

_____

_____

OTHER

_____

_____

Chapter

15

5th Chakra
Seat of Self-Expression

> *Each of us was born with a lovely inner compass ... it's there to guide us. We must tune out almost every voice around us to be able to focus on what this inner voice tells us is true for our own lives."*

I f you're searching for answers in life (and really, who isn't?), you might not have to look any further than yourself. Learning how to tap into your inner voice for guidance is key with the 5th Chakra.

Do you struggle with listening to your inner voice? Do you doubt yourself and every inner signal you get? You're not alone.

Over a decade ago, I didn't know that I could follow my heart. I'd never heard of the concept of inner wisdom, or inner voice. Then, I started following my interests and doing what made me feel good. This is the essence of doing what you love and listening to that subtle voice inside of you.

The problems start when we listen too much to outside sources.

We start to think that we're doing it wrong. I went through one of these periods myself. Looking back, I see that while it was a period of struggle, it also helped me go deeper into what worked for me.

Prescription for Fitting In

We were taught, when we were young, "*If you haven't something good to say (read, what the person wants to hear), don't say anything*", "*Children should be seen and not heard*", *etc*. While such expressions have within them kernels of truth, their intent was to get us to learn to speak and

Amirah Hall

act in socially acceptable ways. A person with a fully functioning 5th Chakra speaks their mind without forgetting their heart.

It's a lot to swallow...

We were given, over the first 16 or so years of our lives, a prescription for fitting in and not rocking the boat. We were taught to look outside of ourselves for both the source of our problems and their solutions.

Communication Conditioning

 Act for yourself. Face your own truths ... then act on your own truths. Plug your ears when there are annoying, loud, negative voices that have no business giving you opinions about your own life. Turn off the confusing lies, and be brave enough to tune in to that inner voice that speaks your truth. Those feelings in your gut are your deepest wisdom, and you will recognize the voice of truth by the warm and peaceful feelings it brings."

We were conditioned to bite off our words, lest the big people offend themselves. We were programmed to see life as a '***burden to be shouldered***', which is mainly '***a pain in the neck***'.

Along the way, we lost our spontaneity, our zest for life and our voice. The Bible describes '***stiff-necked people***' as people who lived by rules and regulations, looking down their noses at others.

The tension in the 5th Chakra space is almost always the result of unspoken or un-enacted expression.

Most men have been conditioned to be authoritative and angry in their words and actions when confronting a blockage. Women have been trained to shove things down for the good of those around them, and to always try to make things better for others. One of the curses of the sexual revolution is that you now have '***ball-breaking***' women using a male approach, and '***sissified***' men in whose mouths butter wouldn't melt. We now have masses of both sexes doing what doesn't work for either.

And, of course, repeating what doesn't work, over and over. God forbid we try something new.

Because of the great intuitive nature of the human body, the energy of wholeness continues to flow (either as a trickle or a torrent) for as long as we are breathing air. In the depths of us, we know that there is another path, another way.

Choosing from fear transgresses our trust in Divine guidance."

Caroline Myss

Now, as we progress, it's very important to tap into the power of detachment.

Learning Detachment

One of the qualities that we need to develop for our spiritual growth is that of staying detached from the problems that we face every day, whilst trying to survive in the modern world. The flowering of the 5th Chakra provides us with a sense of detachment that lets us witness the 'Play of Life'. As a result we avoid being brought down by things which seem traumatic, but are in fact simple '**events**' or '**coincidences**' which we must pass through to reach the Other Shore.

This does not mean that we stop accepting responsibility for our actions, or that we '**give up**' on life. It simply gives us a means to maintain a sense of perspective when we are faced with overwhelming emotional situations. We become a witness of the game, and can keep a distance from our involvement and thoughts, from our planning and conditionings, from our emotions.

- Does your life reflect the fullness of who you are?
- Are you speaking your truth and saying the things that really need to be said?
- Are you hearing others' truths-- Are they hearing yours?

The 5th Chakra is located at the base of your neck and governs self-expression, both verbally and in all of the ways we interact with the world. It includes: **creativity, communication and truth.**

You are song, a wished-for song."

Rumi

The 5th Chakra is the seat of self-expression, and similar to the 4th Chakra being a bridge, it can be viewed as the mediator between thought and emotion.

The 5th Chakra is one of the most interesting chakras and **also the one most likely to be blocked.** This is the throat chakra, and relates to the neck, upper shoulders, the mouth and the jaw. This chakra is the source of expression and manifestation. What is expressed or made to manifest (made real) is *me*.

The wellness of this area directly reflects **how true I am to *who* I am**. It also directly reflects your willingness to be true to yourself without losing sight of the thoughts, understandings and concerns of those around you.

And, it's rare for anyone to not carry some tension in the neck, shoulders or jaw.

We are driven to seek wholeness, then we block ourselves when that path leads (*as it always will*) to letting go of everything, and grasping on to something new.

Affirmations Alone Are Not Effective

I don't believe that mumbling any affirmation will change anything. On the other hand, if I say to myself, "*I am ready to meet the person that I described in my list of qualities, characteristics AND I haul my butt out of my house and head to a 'logical place,'* (i.e. not a bar) -- then what I'll likely notice is that, '*magically...*' I start to meet people who match what I have said I am looking for. The clarity of my thought and my willingness to '*go and do what is necessary'* allows what is new to come into being.

I was just talking with a client about this very subject of finding herself and dropping her perceived roles. She said, "*I just want to find someone I can be a good wife with.*" I replied that it might be more interesting and truthful to say,

> *I want to be me, as I understand myself, and I want to share me with others who will appreciate me and share themselves with me to be appreciated.*"

I suggested she drop her **acting *role*** and begin to engage her 5th Chakra. In other words: **begin to be real.** That is, without the need to manipulate others, of course.

I treat others with dignity and respect, not because I think they'll then be **'*forced'*** to treat me that way. **I treat others with dignity and respect because that's the way I treat myself**. I can say things cruelly, or clearly. I can blame or I can take responsibility for myself. I can be centered and grounded, or head over heels.

If you notice tension in your neck (the 5th Chakra region) consider:

- *What you are doing that you don't want to do?*
- *About what you are not saying that needs to be said?*
- *Seek the compassionate action and word, with clarity.*

Within the 5th Chakra, there are 4 different parts of your Self:

1. **Inner Voice** - When you find that voice that you might NOT ever listen to, you'll know when you start arguing with it.

2. **Clairaudience** - Clear hearing, hearing your spirit guides or higher self.

3. **Telepathy** - Narrow band telepathy is connecting with one person. Wide band telepathy is communicating with a large group of people.

4. **Verbal Communication** - As you communicate, the tone of the words you use, express feelings and the energetic/emotional vibration. It's not necessarily the content.

As part of those things I mentioned, there's that part of you that communicates to your Self – your inner voice and the part you share with the world, your verbal communication. It's your **hello** out to the world, your telepathy.

It's funny to be around someone who communicates telepathically-- you don't know who communicated WHAT.

Saying One Thing – Something Different Comes Out

Sometimes I might say something and my intent is different than what comes out. When I was young, I often recall my mother telling me that '*it was the tone in which I was speaking*' that bothered her. I guess you could say, '*it was my 'tude.*' There's a tone behind our communication and it's not uncommon to hear students tell me that they are commonly '*mis-understood*'. Usually that's where different or foreign energy is stuck. As you make that connection, notice how sensitive you are and be aware of what communication comes out.

Acknowledging Yourself

> **Visualize a rose out in front of you and let it represent your own spiritual essence.** *What color is it? What vibration is it? What does it look like?*

Consider: *When do you use it? Do you say 'hello' or acknowledge self often? Do you go through the day without acknowledging yourself mentally, spiritually and physically?* Just consider that by bringing awareness to it.

Notice if there's anyone else's energy inside it. Release any foreign energy using a grounding cord. Ask yourself: *Whose energy might be there? Is there a certain way you learned to acknowledge yourself?* Reset the rose to its wellness color.

To learn who rules over you, simply find out who you are not allowed to criticize."

Voltaire

Communication to Others

There's a lot of energy on '**communicating**' to someone else and not having a clear direct flow of communication. Sometimes this communication can be uncomfortable, awkward and sometimes it can be regarded as if you **had been trampled on**.

One of my clients recently expressed that most of the time when she composed any email she had difficulty forming the right sentences to express. She also noticed that others had difficulty understanding what she was saying. Having a clear communication space can change everything.

Visualize another rose out in front of you and let it represent your communication to others. *What does it look like? Is it opened or closed? What color(s) do you see? Is it resistant? Is it free flowing?*

Ask yourself: *when and how do you use this rose or communicate to others?*

- *Do you withhold?*
- *Only give it to certain people?*
- *Can you speak to people without acknowledging their spirit*?

Consider a wellbeing color and set your '**communication rose to others**' to a wellness vibration. Visualize a magnet rose and imagine it collecting whatever energy lights-up when someone says '**hello' to you**. Let it collect up any and all of the energy in your space from other people. Explode the rose.

Visualize another rose out in front of you and consider:

- ***What would be different in your communication with others if your space was set to wellbeing?***
- ***Would you be more patient or open?***
- ***Would you talk nicer?***
- ***What would be different for you?***

After setting your communication to wellness, notice what comes of it as you set forth on your path.

> *You can talk with someone for years, every day, and still, it won't mean as much as what you can have when you sit in front of someone, not saying a word, yet you feel that person with your heart, you feel like you have known the person for forever.... connections are made with the heart, not the tongue."*

C. Joy Bell C.

Challenging Communications

I'm sure you've experienced communication challenges that block you from being heard, appreciated, respected, valued and promoted. Everyone has different preferences, values, styles and communication approaches that often contribute to their feeling less than fully valued and accepted. Handling the most challenging, intense, and emotionally charged types of conversations can be stressful.

Consider a mock-up for your communication with someone (a partner, spouse, friend, co-worker, boss, child, sibling etc.) Consider: **where and what's difficult to communicate with this person?** Set your communication space to wellness and see how this changes. Explode that rose.

Ask yourself, "**What takes you out of wellness to yourself?**" **What supports you in wellness to yourself?** If you can put your attention on the energies that support you in having wellness, then you can have it.

Visualize a rose in front of you representing your communication space with others. Imagine owning it and making it your space at a wellness vibration. It doesn't have to be set by your environment.

Listen to your inner voice... ***it's saying something to you!***

Listening to Your Inner Voice

You've heard of Murphy's Law, which says that '**whatever can go wrong will go wrong**'. Well, there's another law, which says that, '**left to themselves, things have a tendency to go from bad to worse.**' When something is making you unhappy, for any reason, the situation will tend to get worse rather than better. So avoid the temptation to engage in denial, or to pretend that nothing is wrong, to wish and hope and pray that, whatever it is, it will go away and you won't have to do anything. The fact is, it probably will get worse before it gets better, and you will ultimately need to face the situation and do something about it.

> *You cannot always hold everything together perfectly, and you cannot be perfectly composed every single day. It's okay to have 'off' days. It's okay to feel weak and overwhelmed and have meltdowns once in awhile. Let yourself have days to be a perfectly imperfect human being.*
>
> *It's okay. YOU are okay. Everything is going to be okay. It is.*
>
> *Bad days will pass, overwhelm will dissolve, and the sun will come up again tomorrow morning, just like it does every day. There will be a brand new sparkling day waiting for your tomorrow."*

Releasing Unresolved External Communication

Some communication can make you feel uncomfortable and it's easy to hold that in the body until it's resolved. Consider how long you hold any unresolved conflict in your body. Give your body permission to release unresolved communication and conflict. If you are holding onto something that was said, begin letting it go down your grounding cord.

Allow the earth and cosmic energy to begin flowing and let it flush any communication that you are ready to let go of. Let go of incidents, blow ups etc. Tuning into yourself, notice how much you have been impacted by external conflict.

Visualize a rose that represents your 5th Chakra where all your telepathy, clairaudience and internal communication occurs. Bring this rose to a wellness color and begin draining any foreign energy that takes the 5th Chakra out of wellness.

One day I will find the right words, and they will be simple."

Jack Kerouac

"I realized why I did certain things and made certain decisions that affected my life not so positively. If I made these choices today, they would produce more positive outcomes. Sessions with Amirah were enlightening and I learned more about myself than ever before. It also made me aware of my full potential and what I can become."

Sophia Simon

Chapter 15 - Practice Guidelines

Practice the following tools this week:

1. Grounding – Quantum Energy Tool #1
2. Center of Head – Quantum Energy Tool #2
3. Replenishing – Quantum Energy Tool #3
4. Run Earth and Cosmic Energy – Quantum Energy Tool #7
5. Acknowledge Your Energy Self
6. Reset Communication to Others
7. Release Unresolved External Communication

GOALS AND HEALING WORKSHEET

WELLNESS COLOR _____

Physical Goal _____

Mental Goal _____

Emotional Goal _____

Spiritual Goal _____

MISSION STATEMENT

_____

WHAT ARE YOU NOTICING DIFFERENT?

_____

_____

WHAT ENERGIES **SUPPORT** YOU? (Colors, memories, beliefs, thoughts)

_____

_____

OTHER

_____

_____

16

5th Chakra Communication Beyond Words

> Wouldn't it be hard if we were assigned to pick each other apart and decide which parts are good and which parts are bad and how someone should be living their life? Or how they should be raising their children? Or how someone should vote? Or what they should be doing for a job? Or how they should wear their hair or how much they should weigh or where they should live or how they should dress or how they should behave?"

Communication!

When we hear this term, we start thinking about the words and language to express ourselves to others. **But...**

Believe it or not words and language are the lowest form of communication there is! With all these spiritual forms of communication, we communicate in pictures, symbols, formulas, vibrations and other spiritual signals.

As spirit we do not use language. Instead, we exist in a world of energy patterns. These energy patterns, or thought forms, are very powerful and can be experienced as pictures, symbols, images and mathematical formulae. All of these convey much more information than words do. A picture is worth a thousand words.

Have you ever had the experience of hearing the phone ring and knowing the phone was about to ring just before it did? It's not some magical sense. It's Pragmatic Intuition.

Pragmatic Intuition

And did you know who was calling you before you answered the call?

If you have had this surprisingly common experience, it may not have been just a lucky guess, but you may well have been using a spiritual ability called *'pragmatic intuition'*.

Pragmatic intuition is a form of intuition that deals with practical affairs, such as knowing who is on the phone before you answer it. Your information on pragmatic intuition is contained in the 5th Chakra energy center in your throat and deals with everything to do with communication.

I use my pragmatic intuition to help with my diet. For example what nutrition my body needs in the moment, what is good to eat or what might not agree with my digestion. It's also very helpful in knowing that you need to take an umbrella when you go out even though it's sunny outside or your sunglasses when it's a rainy day.

In this chapter, you will explore your *'communication space'* with relation to your pragmatic intuition, clairvoyance and communication with your Higher Self and your Spirit Guides. Also, you will release energy from your goals, creating energetic space for your future mockups to have the best chance in manifesting. Clearing foreign energy in your clairaudient channels and resetting your pragmatic intuition raises your goal set point for 5th Chakra wellness.

In manifesting goals, there's *'energy' about creating a goal* before you even start as to whether it's a *'success or failure'* that may block it before even starting. In this chapter, we will also clear *'that'* energy to reset your ability of manifesting goals at an optimum success rate for you.

If this chakra is blocked you may feel insecure, but also weak and not able to word your emotions. Physical problems related to this chakra are: thyroid disorders, sore throats, back aches, ear infections, cold hands and feet, chronic diseases and auto immune disorders.

The voice of a balanced Throat Chakra will be rhythmic and resonant, clear with precise expression, a good communicator, contented, who finds it easy to mediate. Their creativity flows freely in their artistic expression and they find it easy to express their truth. They have the ability to make decisions and once made are able to follow their dreams.

The 5th Chakra, the throat center, serves a function in all aspects of communication. Physically it governs speech, hearing and self-expression, but it is also the container for your spiritual communication. Physical communication lets us know what is going on for us in physical reality and spiritual communication lets us know what is going on in our spiritual reality.

Words and writing can be used to manifest spiritual forces or energy patterns into physical reality.

 Worrying changes NOTHING.

Sometimes our worrying becomes a bigger problem than the problem we are worrying about to begin with.

Please, set your worries aside and step firmly into this very moment. Put your worries inside a rose and explode them. Look yourself in the eye and tell yourself that from this moment forward you will stop filling in the blanks with scary details. Let life surprise you a little."

Communication Center

Your first and biggest spiritual ability of the 5th Chakra is—communication! Consider that only 7% is of what you communicate is actually verbal. We all know that communication is the key to harmonious relationships (personally and professionally), yet how many of us struggle with expressing ourselves openly and honestly, unsure of how the other person might respond?

You get what you want by asking for it, but how many of us have been taught it's better to keep quiet, than to open your mouth and potentially create confrontation or conflict?

Well, communication is not just about exploring the outer world ... it's imperative that you tap into the inner self and communicate effectively.

Communication with Inner Self

Unfortunately, starting in our childhood, we are more often taught to conform than to listen to our own truth and feel safe enough to express it. We are scolded for not wanting to spend time with a certain family member, rather than be honored for our own knowing that this isn't a good person. We are laughed at for speaking to our *'imaginary'* friends instead of being recognized for our connection to spirit. We are told to pick careers that are *'safe and secure'* rather than encouraged to do that which brings us joy.

No matter what, worrying doesn't help anything…it just keeps us from feeling peaceful when we have the power to choose peace all along.

Don't forget that everything has always, always, always worked out somehow. Always. And almost always everything works out beautifully for our growth and our wisdom.

Let yourself go where the peace is. It feels so much better there."

Teachers, parents and society all play their part in quashing our true nature, replacing it with layers of their own misguided beliefs. We usually grow up with no real sense of which part of us is the true us and which part has been influenced by others. Worse, we have been conditioned to accept our conditioning and the true self often remains hidden beneath layers of non-truth.

> Visualize a rose for yourself and that communication part of you.
>
> What sense do you get about your inner voice? What feelings, colors or sound levels does it hold? Is it 'ok' to use or 'not ok' to use?
>
> Ground this rose or symbol to the center of planet, releasing any foreign energy out of it. Own it for yourself and let it vibrate at wellness for you by dropping in your wellness color. Let that symbol dissolve.

Clairaudience

Recently a student shared that at least once a week, her husband would walk into the room where she was sitting and ask, "**What did you say**?" And she'd answer, "**I didn't say anything.**" To which he'd argue, "**Honey, I heard you call me.**"

If this happens to you or if you hear people talking, but no one is around, it's a pretty good indicator that you're **intuitive** and generally speaking a **highly sensitive person** (HSP), both emotionally **and** physically. Because of this, you may be sensitive to noise if you're clairaudient. For example, a loud party or TV may make you feel:

- Tired
- Ungrounded
- Give you a headache
- Jittery

Personally, this is my only complaint about being clairaudient. Too much noise stimulation makes me feel like I am going to crawl out of my skin sometimes, so I actively seek quiet environments.

Communication with Spirit Guides

There are actually two ways that we communicate to our spirit guides—through attention and intention. 'Intention' is when we intentionally use our thoughts and actions to communicate our life's desires to our spirit guides, our soul and the Universe. For instance, we are using the power of intention when we request something in prayer. 'Attention' is what we focus our thoughts, words, time and energy on and is how we most commonly communicate the wrong message to our spirit guides."

Bob Olson

> *Is there some special way you're supposed to talk to your spirit guides, angels, higher self, and/or God?*
> *Do you have to verbalize your wishes or can you talk to them with your thoughts?*

The answer is both. When you think a thought, it creates energy. That energy can be received and understood by guides, angels, higher selves, God, anything with a consciousness.

You can broadcast your thought to a specific energy, like your higher self, or you can cast your thought out to the Universe, like, '*I am ready for love, Universe. Bring it on!*' And hey! **How about hearing from your spirit guides?!**

Hearing Your Spirit Guides

Now hearing back from them, that's another story. They don't communicate using vocal chords and mouths to your ears. They respond energetically, the same way they received your communication. So if you're not able to tune in to their frequency, you won't hear their message.

But there are other ways of receiving their response or communication. For one, you may get an image in your head, a form of clairvoyance. You may hear a thought come back to you like, '**Yes, my child, you are indeed loved**.' That's clairaudience! You may get a warm tingly feeling in your stomach or chills up your back. That's clairsentience.

Alternatively, you may get signs, symbols or synchronicities in your life, which is their way of letting you know they received your message. Interpreting isn't always easy, but do the best you can. That's where consulting an intuitive like myself can also help you interpret your message from the other side. http://www.amirahhall.com/

Spiritual Ability of Clairaudience

Your clairaudience space within you is the space where you communicate with spirit guides.

> **Visualize a rose that represents your spiritual ability of 'clairaudience'. What does that look like? Is that something you are aware of doing? Or are you not aware of it? Ground this space and set it to a tone of wellness (your wellness color) that works for you.**

When your communication space is at wellness you might attract a whole new set of spirit guides at a higher vibration.

Spirit Guides

Connecting with your Spirit Guides is like making a new friend, it requires being consistent, persistence and patient. Clearing this energy space opens the communication channels for you to have more reliable and sacred connections.

> **Visualize a rose that represents your space for** *'communication with your Spirit Guides'.*
>
> **Say** *'hello'* **out to any Spirit Guides you have. You might hear buzzing in your ear(s) as this can be energy from a spirit guide. That's a signal they are trying to communicate with you. Saying** *'hello'* **to them and have them match your energy. Remember your body only hears a certain range of sound.**
>
> **Ask your Spirit Guides to back out of your ear and speak to you through your clairaudience channels. Pay attention to any guide who might be there and any sense that you have about your guide. Set this Spirit Guide rose to your wellness color and explode it.**

Acknowledging Your 5th Chakra Abilities

Uncovering your 5th Chakra abilities can be much like discovering a hidden treasure, that's been underneath a bunch of boxes in the closet. Oh, this old thing? This is my ability?! Identifying what that gift is, whether it is clairaudience, clairvoyance, claircognizance, channeling, or anything else – can be key to developing your abilities to serve you and others in the greatest and best way possible!

> **Visualize a rose that acknowledges each of these abilities:** *separating, validating, setting at wellness and owning these abilities within yourself.*
>
> **There's a lot of energy out there that says this is** *'crazy'* **or that it doesn't exist. Maybe that inner voice doesn't sound like you or maybe you feel that you can't change communication by just resetting the energy.**
>
> **Visualize a rose that represents your 5th Chakra, knowing that within it are these abilities and imagine owning all parts of your 5th Chakra abilities.**

- **Listening To Your Inner voice**
- **Telepathic Communication**
- **Communicating With Spirit Guides and Angels**
- **Intuitive Hearing - Clairaudience**
- **Pragmatic Intuition**

Imagine that wellness color in the 5th Chakra.

Physical Side to the 5th Chakra

The physical side that works in relationship with the 5th Chakra is the thyroid. The thyroid is a butterfly-shaped gland that sits low on the front of the neck and lies below your Adam's apple, along the front of the windpipe.

The thyroid's main role in the endocrine system is to regulate your metabolism, which is your body's ability to break down food and convert it to energy. Food essentially fuels our bodies, and our bodies each "burn" that fuel at different rates. This is why you often hear about some people having *'fast'* metabolism and others having *'slow'* metabolism. The thyroid secretes several hormones, collectively called thyroid hormones that influence metabolism, growth and development, and body temperature.

Parathyroid glands are small glands of the endocrine system that are located in the neck behind the thyroid. These tiny glands, the size of a grain of rice, control the calcium in our bodies--how much calcium is in our bones, and how much calcium is in our blood. Calcium is the most important element in our bodies as it provides electrical energy for our nervous and muscular systems.

Setting Thyroid and Parathyroid to Wellness

> **Visualize a rose in front of you that represents your thyroid and parathyroid gland. Getting a sense of the aura around this gland, acknowledge the aura of the thyroid.** *What kind of energy is vibrating there? What colors or sensations do you notice?*

Ask yourself, *is this set at wellness for your spirit in the body*?

As a spirit you sense things and have awareness through your 5th Chakra that sends information to your thyroid. Based on that communication, your thyroid releases chemicals and hormones into the body that converts them into electro-chemical responses. You get that information from your spirit into the body. Some energy can be present as '*just energy*' and even when nothing spiritual has happened but your body will still produce a reaction.

So, if that process is happening at your wellness vibration without change– then the communication between your spirit and body is humming along. That's the ultimate goal.

> **Visualize grounding a rose representing the thyroid and ask yourself, "***What is the wellness color for the 5th Chakra or the thyroid gland?***"**
>
> **Visualize your wellness color for the 5th Chakra and release any foreign energy, allowing your wellness color to replace and completely fill up the rose.**

Wellness creates the space for this function directly for you and can '*speed up*' the metabolism for some of us.

> **Imagine bringing your wellness rose for your 5th Chakra into your body and notice** '*what is the energy level around that?*'
>
> *What does that feel like as you bring your physical body into 5th Chakra wellness?*
>
> **You know the secret to making your dreams come true, right? It's about being willing to do difficult things, and then to do those things as joyfully as possible.**
>
> **The things that are most worthwhile in life are always difficult to come by...they are rare....they are hard to get and hard to maintain.**
>
> **But they are OH SO WORTH IT.**

Past Successes

 Try not to become a man of success. Rather become a man of value."

Albert Einstein

Success is a wonderful thing but like everything else it is energy. Releasing past successes creates energetic space for '**new successes**'. Bringing the '**past successes**' into '**present time**' let's you have the vibration of '**success**' NOW.

> **Visualize a rose(s) for past successes and collect them up into one rose. Ground that rose and start to bring all those things into present time with you. Let any foreign energy that is not yours in that space fall down your grounding cord.**
>
> **Notice the energy vibration of that success rose. What is the vibration of success you create? What is the vibration of goals you create? Let the rose dissolve.**

 Your time is limited, so don't waste it living someone else's life. Don't be trapped by dogma—which is living with the results of other people's thinking. Don't let the noise of others' opinions drown your own inner voice. And most important, have the courage to follow your heart and intuition. They somehow already know what you truly want to become. Everything else is secondary."

Steve Jobs

Energy and Consciousness

Understanding that energy and consciousness are one and the same, the more conscious and aware we become on any particular topic, the more energy we will have available in that area of life. We do not necessarily see it as the energy. But it is nevertheless present.

Looking at the '**energy on creating goals**' (before you even start, whether it's a success or failure) is what stops 'the starting of the creation'.

Past Failures

> *Are there any failures out there?*
>
> Visualize a rose(s) for past failures and collect them up into one rose. Ground that rose and start to bring all those things into present time with you. Let any foreign energy that is not yours in that space fall down your grounding cord.
>
> Ask yourself, "*Were they 'all your failures'* or *do some of them belong to someone else*? Let the rose dissolve.

There can be a lot of energy on the failures but it is how you grow and learn. It doesn't always mean you failed. Rather it means you tried something new.

Apple's idea is if you don't have a 70% failure rate, then you are not trying enough new stuff. They believe, if you aren't doing it right, you fail only because you haven't failed enough to learn, grow and expand into a broader, more capable you.

We are taking the energy off of your goals by owning them with your own energy so that as you go to make mockups in the future, there's no fear of success or failure. Your goal is something you want, right! Well, first you have to make the goal, then later you can decide if you are a success or failure. And, since failures help us to learn, grow and expand through our mistakes, are they really failures or just training?

Success and Failure

Being able to recognize a failure just means that you'll be able to re-cast it into something more likely to succeed."

Sarah Rapp

It probably won't surprise you if I tell you that thinking about your past successes and failures can influence your performance in present time. There's nothing like a winning season to give a player confidence going into that last game, and nothing like a string of awkward dates to make you nervous about how the next one is going to turn out.

> Visualize roses that represent '*success and failure*' and bring them to your wellness color. It doesn't matter which one is success, as successes can be failures and failures can be successes.
>
> Bring the roses into your aura, and let yourself have both of the roses at wellness.

Goals for 5th Chakra

Visualize another rose that represents a goal that you might want to change. For example, you may have a 1st Chakra goal that might be re-interested in changing or adjusting.

As you re-read your goal, validate yourself for your successes and failures. Maybe you had a recent job interview. You didn't get the job, but the next one you did – thank goodness! You could view that as a failure that turned into a success.

Create a rose or picture for your 5th Chakra goal. Notice its color and vibration. *What is your mock-up for the 5th Chakra? i.e. To clearly hear your inner voice more, be more telepathic, allow pragmatic intuition to work for you?*

Visualize your 5th Chakra goal inside a rose and ground anyone else's energy off of your goal. i.e. *it's not right, too poetic, it's not real, and it's not possible.*

Clear any judgment, *'it's the best goal ever, you are so smart, etc.'*

When you have it at the vibration that works for you right now, bring it inside your aura.

Visualize a new rose for any other goal you want to update for another chakra. Notice how this one got much more serious and begin releasing energy on that goal. Put your past goal into the 5th Chakra rose and explode it.

Visualize another rose for the chakra you are creating a new goal for. Notice how much easier it is now that you got rid of the old goal.

Ground the rose and begin clearing anyone else's attention off of it, good and bad.

When it's set at where you are in present time, release that goal into your aura.

What is your Mission Statement or Vision Statement for the 5th Chakra?

For example, your overall MISSION statement could be:

"I clearly hear my inner voice."

"I trust and allow myself to listen to my inner voice."

"I am open to the guidance of my angels and guides."

"I listen to my heart and willingly follow its guidance."

"I receive clear messages from my Higher Self and take appropriate action."

Add this 5th Chakra Mission Statement to the previous 4 Chakras Personal Mission Statements (Chapter 24).

While others might be standing on the sidelines trying to figure out how to get out of doing the work, how to avoid the most discomfort and how to have a drive-through existence, YOU can be ONE who is willing to do whatever it takes to live an extraordinary life."

"Working with Amirah has been a life-changing experience for me. Her ability to intuitively guide each session for the deeper inner work is unique. I value the Quantum Energy Tools I learned that support me in anchoring my changes while empowering me to love and appreciate my own abilities and gifts to live my life more fully."

Sandra Clawson

Chapter 16 - Practice Guidelines

Practice the following tools this week:

1. Grounding – Quantum Energy Tool #1
2. Center of Head – Quantum Energy Tool #2
3. Replenishing – Quantum Energy Tool #3
4. Run Earth and Cosmic Energy – Quantum Energy Tool #7
5. Reset Communication with Self
6. Reset Communication with Spirit Guides
7. Set Thyroid / Parathyroid to Wellness
8. Set Success and Failure to Wellness
9. Set 5th Chakra Wellness Mission Statement

GOALS AND HEALING WORKSHEET

WELLNESS COLOR _____

Physical Goal _____

Mental Goal _____

Emotional Goal _____

Spiritual Goal _____

MISSION STATEMENT

_____

WHAT ARE YOU NOTICING DIFFERENT?

_____

_____

WHAT ENERGIES **SUPPORT** YOU? (Colors, memories, beliefs, thoughts)

_____

_____

OTHER

_____

_____

Chapter

17

6ᵗʰ Chakra
Sixth Sense

＊————————＊●●＊————————＊

> *You know so much more than you think you know. You ARE SO MUCH MORE than you think you are. You are so much braver than you think you are. You are so much smarter than you think you are. You are so much more wonderful than you think you are. So ... start thinking with the smart parts of you ... you won't go wrong."*

You experience your world through the five senses. Even before you passed through the womb, you heard noises like your mother's voice and heartbeat, and listened to muffled sounds outside. You experienced touch, taste, and even perceived light. Ever since birth, you've attributed your experiences to what you perceive through the 5 senses. You've learned to trust your 5-senses in what you can taste, smell, touch, see, and hear. While sense perception is great in life experience, it's limiting to expanding your conscious awareness.

Through your eyes, you see the physical world and with your 6th Chakra or Third Eye, you perceive the non-physical, spiritual world.

At one time, people counted on their sense of intuition and inner knowing. Before smart phones and other gadgets of modern technology, we had to rely on signals from the environment and primal instincts to guide us. Just like birds can sense when a tsunami might hit, or squirrels know when it's time to gather food for the winter, humans too have an intuitive sense. Most people simply lost touch with it and their ability to trust it.

In this chapter, you will explore your 6th Chakra or the Third-Eye. The sixth of the seven major chakras, the 6ᵗʰ Chakra governs your intellectual and intuitive abilities and your potential for spiritual awareness. This is where imagination, intuition and insight reign supreme and where your **psychic tool of clairvoyance** or clear-seeing originates.

We don't get what we want, we get what we believe. What do you believe is possible for you?"

Kelley Rosano

The 6th Chakra

The Sanskrit name of the sixth chakra is Ajna, meaning '**command'** or '**perception.**' It's located behind the eyes in center of the head. When you see something '**with your mind's eye,**' you are seeing it with the 6th Chakra.

6th Chakra intuition and wisdom are universal and perfect in nature. The 6th Chakra, when highly developed, elevates consciousness, offers deep spiritual insight and perception of non-ordinary reality. It's also a key to ongoing spiritual development.

A c**lear** 6th Chakra is the catalyst that sparks creative genius by uniting the left and right brain hemispheres, thereby merging the intuitive, feeling brain and the rational, thinking brain. It's where the line between dreams and reality becomes blurred as one embraces the concept that we all have the power to create the life of our dreams.

This is also where creative visualization and the formation of one's life visions come into play.

Healthy 6th Chakra

> *Did you know there's a part of you that is even smarter than your brain?*
> *Did you know that the wisdom that comes from this part of you will get*
> *you through all of life's bumpy roads, and the smooth sailing roads, too?*

Someone with a clear, balanced, and developed brow chakra usually has a keen intellect balanced with strong intuitive abilities and relies on their inner voice to show them the way. They often have a good imagination and can visualize things easily. A strong sixth chakra gives a person the ability to **grasp the big picture** or **vision, looking outside the box for solutions to challenges.**

When the 6th Chakra is highly developed, a person will have expanded spiritual awareness and insight, and may be able to perceive and influence non-ordinary planes. Words that might be used to describe a person with a strong, healthy, balanced, clear third eye chakra would include intelligent, intuitive, clear, wise, insightful, and spiritually aware.

Over-Developed 6th Chakra

An over-developed 6th Chakra can be seen in "know-it-all" personality types. They are judgmental, inflexible, and pragmatic. They must see something in order to believe it, and they rarely, if ever, pay attention to or follow their feelings or inner guidance. Their closed minds most likely will prevent them from seeing the "bigger picture" of their lives.

Under-Developed 6th Chakra

People with an underdeveloped 6th Chakra may be fearful of change, of standing out, or of being in the limelight. They may suffer from aimlessness, unclear thinking, or lack of concentration. They may be prone to **follow the crowd** or to go along to get along, even when it is contrary to what they want or believe.

The Third Eye (iii) Formula for Enlightenment

Apply this formula to your life and bask in the glow of *'living in the light'*.

Imagination + Intuition + Insight = Inspired Action

Extraordinary intellect, intuition, wisdom, and spiritual insight are available to everyone, but few of us even begin to tap our profound potential. Clearing and balancing your sixth chakra can help you tap into these vast capacities including:

- Think more clearly.

- Have "vision".

- Develop your imagination.

- Grasp the big picture.

- Expand your consciousness and influence to non-ordinary planes.

- Develop greater spiritual awareness and prepare for the next level of spiritual evolution.

> *May your wisdom serve others.*
> *May your insight bring you new levels of spiritual awareness.*
> *May you understand your true nature.*
> *May you see clearly in every way.*

6th Chakra Wellness

The 6th Chakra is place of clairvoyance where you see colors, energy, visualizations and pictures. It has to do with awareness, seeing with certainty and having clarity of those mental images, pictures and colors.

> Touch the center of your forehead with your forefinger and begin releasing any resistance and anything you are ready to let go of from this space.
>
> Notice how much calmer you feel, the room gets quieter and you feel more centered as you connect with your clairvoyant wellness.
>
> Visualize a rose for the 6th Chakra. Let this come into a wellness vibration that works for your 6th Chakra.

When you see/set things clearly in your mind, and you don't put any energy or limits on your creations, you get what you want. Your needs are met.

Recently, I was nudged to go out shopping but I really had nothing specific that I wanted to buy. I know for many people this might be an everyday occurrence but this particular day wasn't one of those. I really just had a light-hearted feeling of exploring with no specific intention. Suddenly, I found a skirt on sale that was a true '**bargain**' and I had to have it. In my mind, it was if I was being '**directed to my treasure**'.

> *When you are in alignment, things flow and synchronistically fall into place.*

One of my students, who had practiced the **Quantum Energy Tools** (http://bit.ly/29WqnQk) for over 10 years but stopped practicing as she got caught up in the busy-ness of her career. After a recent energy clearing she sat down and within two hours re-wrote and updated her resume. It's as if she had clarity and a renewed sense of self. Her resume reflected back to her all of her past accomplishments. She was shocked not only about her 'channeled flow' but also by her impressive resume. She sent it out to some colleagues and within two weeks she was invited to speak at a prestigious international conference and offered a weekly contributor spot in her industry's leading global magazine.

Manifesting miracles really does happen when you are living in the flow!

Think about your favorite song, your favorite work of art, your favorite piece of clothing. Think about the computer you are reading this from and the chair you are sitting on.

Someone, somewhere, at some time had a crazy idea. It was scary to tell others about it, it was scary to make that idea materialize and then to put it out into the world for others to see, use, enjoy...and judge.

What if the person who wrote your favorite song stayed too afraid to share it?

What if your favorite work of art stayed under the artist's bed and was never seen by another pair of eyes aside from her own?

YOU have a message. YOU have a mission. YOU have a purpose...one that is unique to you and will never be duplicated by another human being, ever.

The world needs you and your beautiful heart. Be brave.....share those parts of yourself.

Clear Visualization

The 6th Chakra is a place of visualization --you visualize throughout every day. Having the ability to '***clearly see***' as well as your own ability to visualize what you want to look at is the 6th Chakra's function. Being able to see your own path, your own truth and seeing what you want to create for yourself happens from the 6th Chakra too.

Throughout this book, you have already been using this ability already. When you use the word '***clairvoyance***' some people automatically think you are reading them or you're a scary psychic trespassing and invading peoples' minds. As you will learn, this common idea is simple a misconception of our innate and under utilized abilities.

As you do the exercises in this book, or meditate -- you are psychically reading yourself.

You are using your clairvoyance and seeing what is right for you. Most clairvoyance is applying this inner information outward rather than bringing outward information from the senses into yourself.

She believed, of course ... because without something to believe in, life would be intolerable."

Rosamunde Pilcher

Physical Side of 6th Chakra

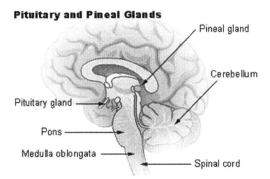

Pituitary and Pineal Glands

- Pineal gland
- Cerebellum
- Pituitary gland
- Pons
- Medulla oblongata
- Spinal cord

You have a spiritual body and a physical body. When these two are connected you have a sense of wellness. Mechanically or physically speaking, your spirit hooks into the 6th Chakra through the endocrine system that consists of the pituitary and pineal glands.

The pineal gland is cone-shaped, located in the middle of the brain behind and just above the pituitary gland. It's the gland that secretes melatonin that boosts the immune system and helps people with jet lag or insomnia.

> **Do not feel bad that you have limitations and cannot do everything you want to do, or if you make mistakes that set you back, or when you sometimes make decisions that don't turn out as you hoped they would be.**
>
> **You are doing enough.**
>
> **YOU ARE ENOUGH.**

Pituitary Gland

The pituitary gland is about the size of a pea and is located behind the center of our forehead, between our eyes. It's known as the master gland because it acts as a main control center that sends messages to all the other glands. The pituitary gland prompts the proper growth of glands and organs and regulates sexual development.

The energetic side of the 6th Chakra is the center of your seeing, your insight, clairvoyance and mental image pictures. That's how the spirit communicates. We see in symbols which are messages from the spirit.

If you want your children to be intelligent, read them fairy tales. If you want them to be more intelligent, read them more fairy tales."

Albert Einstein

The Endocrine Gland Wellness

> **Visualize a rose that represents your endocrine gland. *What does it look like? What does the vibration of melatonin look like?***

Intuition is using a lot of abilities and inputs and we don't have to know where we extract it from. In your day-to-day setting, you do it all the time. You become aware of images and pictures coming to mind.

Seeing and Believing

As we keep saying, if you can't see it, you can't be it. The more you actually see it — real people doing different things — the better off we are."

Gloria Steinem

I didn't really believe psychic surgery. Many years ago, my friend volunteered for some psychic surgery. I stood right next to her, lying on a massage table. The psychic surgeon asked her where she had some problems and then he pulled down her skirt's waistband revealing her belly, and with a flash of hand, I saw his hand go inside her belly and pull out what looked like gooey, yellowish fat. HE PULLED IT OUT! *I darn near passed out!* I couldn't believe what I saw!! And, after that all day I had strong sense of wanting to vomit and was dizzy and unbalanced. To this day, I will NEVER forget the sensations I felt and the mind-bending realization of what happened.

> *I guess you could say that experience shocked my sense of reality and possibilities.*

My friend on the other hand, got up and walked out as if nothing had happened. She was in great energy.

Since that time, I personally had two psychic surgeries. When I was on the table, the surgeon had me pull on something inside me and I pulled it out. I'm not sure I would have believed it except I could feel the tugging of something from inside of myself. I saw it with my own eyes, with my own hands…then I believed it. I was speechless. A part of me got it – seeing, feeling and it was registering on so many levels. Also, part of me didn't believe it, until I felt it. Discernment is good.

Sometimes we have to see it to believe it.

I'm sure you have had some experience in your past where seeing made you a believer.

Clairvoyance – Making It Real

I am enough of an artist to draw freely upon my imagination. Imagination is more important than knowledge. Knowledge is limited. Imagination encircles the world."

Albert Einstein

Clairvoyant space is about seeing and visualizing your own answers and making it more real for you. That's why visualizing what you want to create with mockups makes it more real for you because that's how it works and how you manifest more easily.

Being in clairvoyant space, gives you your answers – Seeing and visualizing makes things more real.

> **Visualization brings life to your goals and answers to your mockups. Having certainty helps you HAVE or make it real.**

6th Chakra

> **Visualize a rose that represents your 6th Chakra. *What does it look like right now? What colors do you see? What emotions do you sense?* (You don't have to assign a meaning to it.)**
>
> **What do you sense about it?**
>
> ***Is it blocked? Is it light and airy?* If you don't see anything – that's ok too!**

> *How much does one imagine, how much observe? One can no more separate those functions than divide light from air, or wetness from water."*
>
> Elspeth Huxley

Wellness Rose

> **Visualize a wellness rose alongside of that 6th Chakra rose. *What are some of the qualities of your wellness vibration in the 6th Chakra?***
>
> **Does it have Neutrality? Certainty? Feel good color?**
>
> **See if you can get 2-3 qualities. It helps to recognize wellness for your self. It's not just a color – it has qualities. Explode the wellness rose.**

The great thing about looking at something clairvoyantly either outward or inward is that by ***having your intention on wellness, things begin to change for the better.***

Visualize a rose for the tone of the 6th Chakra, representing your ability to have insights, interact with your mind's eye and your clairvoyance.

What colors reflect your vibe or tone of the 6th Chakra? You don't have to get any meanings out of it. (Blue white, pink, red, black ... ?)

When you get a sense of it, visualize another rose representing your wellness color next to the 6th Chakra clairvoyance rose. *How much does your 6th Chakra rose easily match that wellness color?*

Notice any blocks, colors or pictures of energy that are not yours that prevents you coming into your wellness. Explode both roses.

Dreams come true. Without that possibility, nature would not incite us to have them."

John Updike.

Reclaiming Your 6th Chakra Certainty

When we get invalidated, we leave our energy at that time period. Reclaiming your energy from times and places where you were invalidated, opens your clairvoyance and certainty.

Visualize a timeline from present time back to birth.

Birth _____ Present Time

Imagine lights appearing on the timeline anywhere *'invalidation'* was put on your 6th Chakra –anywhere your ability to *'see'* got invalidated, you don't see the big picture or you don't see right.

Visualize a wellness rose in present time and begin running that wellness color back to birth. Allow the wellness color to break up any blocks along the timeline and move them off of it.

These might be situations where your certainty was changed or you didn't go along with what you saw.

When you get that wellness energy all the way back to birth, visualize the rose at birth moving forward collecting up your energy along the timeline where you left any energy and bring the rose into present time.

Collect your energy around certainty and clairvoyance, noticing what happens to the rose. It's a good way to gauge how much energy was left on your time line.

As you get the rose into present time, re-own your own energy and set it to your color of wellness. Bring that wellness energy into your 6th Chakra.

You can easily forgive a child who is afraid of the dark, the real tragedy is when men are afraid of the light."

Plato

Pineal Wellness

Visualize a rose for the pineal gland and bring that to your wellness color. *How much of the pineal gland is at 'wellness'?*

Validate whatever change you see. Own that change.

You might see more, differently or have a growth period. You might not see anything.

The point of having this chakra in balance is what it brings to you.

Visualize a rose for *'knowing your own truth, you own insights'.*

How does the world look like when you have your own lens making it real?

From that rose, *imagine what color gives you certainty and clarity?*

What vibration is that for you? Drop that color (vibration of your own information and clarity) on to your crown chakra, at the top of your head.

Trust yourself. You know more than you think you do."

Benjamin Spock

When you have done all that you can do, let yourself BREATHE. And remember that rest, relaxation, and solitude are just as important as all of the other incredible things that you do with your life.

You are such a gift to the world. Take good care of you."

Amirah Hall

"Since I started working with Amirah and Manifesting Miracles 101, amazing things are happening in my life. As a coach, I've just closed the biggest business deal yet. My debt is more manageable and my clients are getting faster results. I am really grateful because I took the risk of working with Amirah when she first arrived in Dubai. The results I'm reaching are happening incredibly fast. I don't have the words to thank her properly. I realized how much I blabber and how sweet and kind she has been. Listening to the Stress Buster Meditation, has helped me close more business. I'm finally able to let go of family resentments and I notice I'm receiving more trust and respect from clients. Thank you so much from the bottom of my heart. These techniques are absolutely amazing."

Manuel P., Dubai, UAE

Chapter 17 - Practice Guidelines

Practice the following tools this week:

1. Grounding – Quantum Energy Tool #1
2. Center of Head – Quantum Energy Tool #2
3. Replenishing – Quantum Energy Tool #3
4. Run Earth and Cosmic Energy – Quantum Energy Tool #7
5. Set 6th Chakra to Wellness
6. Collect 6th Chakra Certainty on Timeline
7. Set Pineal to Wellness

GOALS AND HEALING WORKSHEET

WELLNESS COLOR _____

Physical Goal _____

Mental Goal _____

Emotional Goal _____

Spiritual Goal _____

MISSION STATEMENT

_____

WHAT ARE YOU NOTICING DIFFERENT?

_____

_____

WHAT ENERGIES **SUPPORT** YOU? (Colors, memories, beliefs, thoughts)

_____

_____

OTHER

_____

_____

Chapter

18

6th Chakra
The Spiritual Tool of Amusement

❝ *Starting over one more time is hard...so, so hard.*
You may feel that if you have had to start over again and
again on the same goal or struggle or dream that maybe it is
just not meant to be for you.
Please remember, wonderful human being, that just about
anyone who has done anything amazing or worthwhile
had to get back up and start over again and again...
because those people made mistakes, slipped up, got lazy or
distracted and had to get back on track. Mistakes are how
we learn and grow. Without making mistakes, we would
never learn anything."

When you visualize or see something '**with your mind's eye**,' you are seeing it with the 6th Chakra. This chakra's wellbeing is the key to your ongoing spiritual development and how you perceive the world. Being able to shift your perspective from one viewpoint to another, let's say, from being serious to being '**amused**' is the key to being able to '**shift your energy**' and thus **heal yourself**.

Exploring the 'energy of amusement' works as a **Quantum Energy Tool** (http://bit.ly/29WqnQk), you can begin to use it to affect your overall wellness.

The Energy of Amusement

The topic of healing will quite often invoke a serious vibration of energy. Healing is seen as serious business because the need for healing most often arises from someone experiencing pain or non-wellness whether it's physical, spiritual, mental or emotional.

However, **'serious energy'** is by definition heavy, whereas the energy of laughter or amusement is **'light'**. If we consider physical objects for a moment, it is much more challenging and requires more effort to move something heavy such as a boulder than it does to move something that is as light as a feather.

> **The word amusement is defined as the state or experience of finding something funny.**

> *Your sense of humor is one of the most powerful tools you have to make certain that your daily mood and emotional state support good health."*
>
> Paul E. McGhee, Ph.D.

Serious Energy is More Resistant Than Amusement Energy

> *If you find yourself starting over again, congratulate yourself for being one of the few to have the humble courage it takes to get up and move forward after falling. It really is quite an act of bravery and honor."*

It is harder to move serious energy than the energy of amusement. The **'serious'** energy in pain, is more difficult to release and/or heal, when trying to create change, than if there is some **'amusement'** in that pain.

I was remembering a time many years ago when a sudden acute illness took me to the emergency room. A friend of mine was kind enough to drive me there. While we were waiting for me to be seen by a doctor, we began to find humor in my situation and despite the physical pain I was experiencing, we started to laugh and tell jokes. Even though the act of laughing hurt, I found myself enjoying the experience and my mood was lightening by the minute. Much of the initial fear brought on by the pain was dissipating.

The downside to this was when we realized that the energy of amusement was actually delaying my examination by a doctor. It just didn't appear serious enough in my curtained off area to warrant immediate attention. As soon as we stopped laughing and having fun, a doctor appeared!

Laughter can be a natural diversion. When you laugh, no other distracting thought comes to mind. Laughter induces physical changes in the body. The energy vibration of amusement allowed me to separate enough from the pain so that I could envision healing myself. This is why it is so important to approach healing from a vibration of amusement, regardless of how serious the situation may appear to be. If amusement is initially too much of a stretch, try smiling at the pain or simply breathing deeply in and out and relaxing as much as possible. Just putting your attention on raising the vibration of energy out of fear and seriousness, will help set the space for healing to begin.

A growing body of research supports the theory that laughter may have therapeutic value.

Surgeons used humor to distract patients from pain as early as the 13th century. Later, in the 20th century, came the scientific study of the effect of humor on physical wellness. Many credit this to Norman Cousins. After years of prolonged pain from a serious illness, Cousins claims to have cured himself with a self-invented regimen of laughter and vitamins. In his 1979 book Anatomy of an Illness, Cousins describes how watching comedic movies helped him recover.

Over the years, researchers have conducted studies to explore the impact of laughter on health. After evaluating participants before and after a humorous event (i.e., a comedy video), studies have revealed that episodes of laughter helped to reduce pain, decrease stress-related hormones and boost the immune system in participants.

Laughter truly is the best medicine!! It can help you feel better about yourself and the world around you. After laughing for only a few minutes, you may feel better for hours.

So, *how do you get more laughter in your life?*

We can find laughter in so many ways. Maybe for you it is laughing at films or the TV, laughing with friends, comedy clubs, funny clips on line, joining a laughter workshop, the list is endless. Or if all else fails you could just fake it. Just smile and start to laugh – as with listening to a song and how it changes your mood, so can laughter and amusement.

A sense of humor is the only divine quality of man."
Arthur Schopenhauer

> *It's important to look at the funny side of your life... and try to explore your inner world.*

Looking at the Funny Side of Life

It is too easy to allow life to feel like a weight on our shoulders, but you can learn the tools to see life in a different way. Allow yourself the freedom to let go and just laugh and enjoy the world for what it is, ***powerfully healing!***

> *Try it now - smile, laugh or giggle and feel better about your day.*

Amusement Triggers Healing

Amusement also triggers healthy physical changes in the body. Humor and laughter strengthen your immune system, boost your energy, diminish pain, and protect you from the damaging effects of stress. Best of all, this priceless medicine is fun, free, and easy to use.

Besides being a powerful antidote to stress, pain, and conflict, amusement lightens your burdens, inspires hopes, connects you to others, and keeps you grounded, focused, and alert. With so much power to heal and renew, the ability to laugh easily and frequently is a tremendous resource for surmounting problems, enhancing your relationships, and supporting both physical and emotional health.

Children show me in their playful smiles the divine in everyone."

Michael Jackson

- **Amusement dissolves distressing emotions.** You can't feel anxious, angry, or sad when you're laughing or finding amusement in a situation.

- **Laughter helps you relax and recharge.** It reduces stress and increases energy, enabling you to stay focused and accomplish more.

- **Humor shifts perspective**, allowing you to see situations in a more realistic, less threatening light. A humorous perspective creates psychological distance, which can help you avoid feeling overwhelmed.

- **Incorporating more humor and play into your daily interactions** can improve the quality of your love relationships—as well as your connections with co-workers, family members, and friends. Using humor and laughter in relationships allows you to:

- **Be more spontaneous.** Humor gets you out of your head and away from your troubles.

- **Let go of defensiveness.** Amusement helps you forget judgments, criticisms, and doubts.

- **Release inhibitions.** Your fear of holding back and holding on are set aside.

- **Express your true feelings.** Deeply felt emotions are allowed to rise to the surface.

Take Yourself LESS Serious

 You can be kind, wish everyone the best, and do what you can to be helpful, but that doesn't mean you should ever allow someone to chip away at you. You are way too important. You have the right to protect yourself. You have the right to have some FUN"

One essential characteristic that helps us laugh is not taking ourselves too seriously. We've all known the classic tight-jawed sourpuss who takes everything with deathly seriousness and never laughs at anything. No fun there!

Some events are clearly sad and not occasions for laughter. But most events in life don't carry an overwhelming sense of either sadness *or* delight. They fall into the gray zone of ordinary life – giving you the choice to laugh or not.

Ways to help yourself see the lighter side of life:

- **Laugh at yourself.** Share your embarrassing moments. The best way to take yourself less seriously is to talk about times when you took yourself too seriously.

- **Attempt to laugh at situations rather than bemoan them.** Look for the humor in a bad situation, and uncover the irony and absurdity of life. This will help improve your mood and the mood of those around you.

- **Surround yourself with reminders to lighten up.** Keep a toy on your desk or in your car. Put up a funny poster in your office. Choose a computer screensaver that makes you laugh. Frame photos of you and your family or friends having fun.

- **Keep things in perspective.** Many things in life are beyond your control—particularly the behavior of other people. While you might think taking the weight of the world on your shoulders is admirable, in the long run it's unrealistic, unproductive, unhealthy, and even egotistical.

- **Pay attention to children and emulate them.** They are the experts on playing, taking life lightly, and laughing.

Stress is a major impediment to humor and laughter. Practicing your **Quantum Energy Tools** (http://bit.ly/29WqnQk) is a reliable solution any day.

Checklist For Lightening Up

When you find yourself taken over by what seems to be a horrible problem, ask these questions:

- Is it really worth getting upset over?
- Is it worth upsetting others?
- Is it that important?
- Is it that bad?
- Is the situation irreparable?
- Is it really your problem?

We can often times fall into the trap of seriousness, so remind yourself to keep saying hello to one's amusement.

As laughter, humor, and play become an integrated part of your life, your creativity will flourish and new discoveries for playing with friends, coworkers, acquaintances, and loved ones will occur to you daily. Humor takes you to a higher place where you can view the world from a more relaxed, positive, creative, joyful, and balanced perspective.

Indeed, everyone has their own unique vibration of amusement.

Laughter is the Best Medicine

The added bonus of having an inner smile is that it takes years off your age and will make you appear more attractive. When you are amused and relaxed, you are in a more receptive, effortless and childlike space of wonder. You learn more easily and feel less of a need to make sense of or analyze things. Being '*serious*' is far too heavy and gets in the way of seeing.

Amusement has a powerful centering quality – it helps to put you in touch with your own truth. Truly, amusement is a meditation of the highest order.

Consider having your amusement rose up on the outside of your aura throughout the day. It's like having your own personal comedy show running 24/7. (Using **Quantum Energy Tool** #4 – (http://bit.ly/2aaA0hw) helps you separate your energy from others'.) You get the inside jokes! And the best thing is you don't have to turn on the TV, go some place or even do anything – it comes from an inner place.

Even Growth Periods Are Funny

Life's funny at times. You can always find something that will make you smirk or smile. *Perhaps you read a funny status message on Facebook or Twitter? Or perhaps a friend said something hilarious that kept you smiling through the day?* Looking at the lighter side of things can keep stress at bay and make your growth process pass smoothly, like a well-oiled machine.

Occasionally you meet your shadow and maybe feel a little scared when you do. But eventually you realize it's ultimately a '*lie*' because you are '*light*'.

> *Beauty is the truth. Love and wellness are the truth.*

One of my students shared that as a reminder, he replayed the song in his head from the movie O Brother Where Art Thou, *"Keep on the sunny side, always on the sunny side, Keep on the sunny side of life; It will help us every day, it will brighten all the way, If we keep on the sunny side of life…."*

No matter what you believe you may have done wrong in life, whatever you feel guilty about – you are essentially innocent like a playful child. Imagine life as a kindergarten: *you have permission to play, learn and make mistakes*. So play, learn and make many mistakes. We're not here to be perfect: *we're here to be our own unique selves.* Besides, if you don't learn from your mistakes this time around, there will be other opportunities. There is no rush.

 There is a crack in everything. That's how the light gets in."
Leonard Cohen,

So, whatever comes up – keep your amusement. A good way to become amused that has worked really well for me is putting on fun music that I can dance to in a silly way. You could also watch a comedy show or movie, make up jokes or silly stories, allowing your inner clown out to play, goof around doing nothing or meditating.

Humor can make a serious difference. In the workplace, at home, in all areas of life – looking for a reason to laugh is necessary. A sense of humor helps us to get through the dull times, cope with the difficult times, enjoy the good times and manage the scary times."

Steve Goodier

Serious Energy Vs Amusement Energy

Sometimes it takes the step of finding our amusement or noticing we have lost it so we can find it again. Be amused at being hard on yourself. Using the energy of amusement as a tool can help you tremendously.

> **Visualize a mini-version of yourself out in front of you. Imagine a rainbow out in front of you and observe the rainbow next to mini-you. *What happens to it when you are serious or responsible? Or, when it's your fault or there's a problem?***
>
> **Now, visualize what the rainbow colors look like *when you are in amusement or joy.***
>
> **Imagining your day when you are amused, *how does that look?***
>
> **Visualize the color of amusement and begin running that through your energy channels. Clear out any energy that's not in amusement with you.**

Vision for Yourself

Vision is the art of seeing what is invisible to others."

Jonathan Swift

One of the things about the 6th Chakra is that it's a place where we can create a vision of ourselves for ourselves. Some of what might be **serious** about your vision is other people's ideas about your path or things you imposed on yourself. Replacing them with amusement gives them life and resets them to ease and grace.

> Imagine out in front of yourself your vision for yourself. If it's not clear, just let it appear as a rose and notice the color it's set at.
>
> *How much amusement energy is already set on your path?*
>
> Visualize a percentage or an image of a rose as your gauge. Imagine bringing amusement into your vision of yourself for your future. Have the rose represent your future and infuse it with amusement. Even if it's unclear or uncertain, it can still be light and amusing. You don't have to get too detailed just imagine your future and put amusement into that space.
>
> See yourself walking on your path at the vibration of amusement and as you look at it, let it move back into the future where it belongs.

6th Chakra Wellness

Your vision will become clear only when you can look into your own heart. Who looks outside, dreams; who looks inside, awakes."

Carl Jung

> Visualize a rose for the 6th Chakra set at wellness or amusement for this chakra. Sometimes part of the chakra gets turned off and the way to re-own or reset it is to bring in your own energy.

Sometimes there's a fear of what we might see or there's someone else's fear energy there. When looking from a space of amusement, first you see the magic of the spirit and tend to see things on a lighter side. Re-owning and resetting the 6th Chakra to wellness, you are resetting what you are looking for in your own growth and your own path.

You can just as easily set your 6th Chakra at serious and at problems energy and then find that everything in your life is not working. The choice is yours--you decide where you want to focus.

Gratitude makes sense of our past, brings peace for today, and creates a vision for tomorrow."

Melody Beattie

Reset Your Crown To Wellness Vibration

Write any goals that you received clarity on. One thing I like to do after creating goals is ask myself 'what kind of energy will I need in order to create that goal?" Then, bring that energy or vibration into your energy space with a Golden Sun (Quantum Energy Tool #3 - http://bit.ly/2aaA0hw) that way, you can own and have it RIGHT NOW.

Write down your goals and what you can give yourself at the vibration of amusement.

Refill and renew yourself up with Golden Suns filled with all you want to give yourself. i.e. certainty, neutrality, amusement, inspiration, insight, etc. Fill up your body with these radiant healing golden suns.

What is your Mission Statement or Vision Statement for the 6ᵗʰ Chakra?

For example, your overall Personal Spiritual MISSION statement for could be:

"I am inspired and know my truth."

"My intuition clearly guides me on my path."

"I have clear vision of who I am and where I am going."

Add this 6ᵗʰ Chakra Mission Statement to the previous 5 Chakras Personal Mission Statements (Chapter 24).

Enjoy your new level of certainty, clarity and amusement and congratulations for clearing your space for all kinds of miracles and magic to happen.

We can be kind, but this does not mean that we need to allow everyone near the closest parts of our souls. We must guard the gates to our hearts and recognize that it is a true honor for anyone to ever come close to the deepest parts of us, and this honor should be reserved for a select few who only want the best for us and who love us exactly as we are.

You have a right to stand up for yourself. You have a right to walk away. You have a right to go where the peace is.

"My friends have noticed that I have a different energy about me which I think is quite interesting. I feel more in control of what I'm doing even when it's quite stressful at work. I'm feeling grounded and clear in my mind. The Quantum Energy Tools are NOW my best friends — they are consistent and I rely on them for my sanity."

Helen H, Dublin, Ireland

Chapter 18 - Practice Guidelines

Practice the following tools this week:

1. Grounding – Quantum Energy Tool #1
2. Center of Head – Quantum Energy Tool #2
3. Replenishing – Quantum Energy Tool #3
4. Run Earth and Cosmic Energy – Quantum Energy Tool #7
5. Practice 'Having Amusement'
6. Reset Spiritual Vision for Yourself
7. Bring 6th Chakra Goals to Wellness
8. Add 6th Chakra Peronal Spiritual Mission Statement

GOALS AND HEALING WORKSHEET

WELLNESS COLOR _____

Physical Goal _____

Mental Goal _____

Emotional Goal _____

Spiritual Goal _____

MISSION STATEMENT

_____

WHAT ARE YOU NOTICING DIFFERENT?

_____

_____

WHAT ENERGIES **SUPPORT** YOU? (Colors, memories, beliefs, thoughts)

_____

_____

OTHER

_____

_____

Chapter 19 - 7ᵗʰ Chakra Spiritual Wisdom

> *Jesus the Nazarene taught the Apostles about the importance of activating the pineal gland, which is popularly known in all esoteric traditions as the "Third Eye" or "Single Eye", and is the natural biological channel for Holy Spirit energies: "The light of the body is the eye: if therefore thine eye be single, thy whole body shall be full of light."*
>
> (Matthew 6:22) – Knights Templar Order

The 7th Chakra, or Crown Chakra, is the place where we as spirit are attached to the body. The crown chakra is the center for trust, devotion, inspiration, happiness, and positivity. It's also the center for deeper connection within us and deeper connection with a force of life that is greater than ourselves. For this reason, it can be quite useful to have tools to open the crown chakra.

The 7th Chakra is known as the master chakra of the major seven chakras and is responsible for the following two spiritual abilities:

- **Clear-knowing or Claircognizance**, is when you know something without reading or being told about it. Having *'clear recognition'* is simply knowing something through some gut instinct without any evidence. Maybe you've had a *'flash'*, out of nowhere before allowing you to know or understand something without any previous exposure to that knowledge.

  You may know personal information about someone you just met, or perhaps you're convinced that someone from the past is going to get in touch. This happens to me all the time. Often it's when I'm brushing my teeth or washing dishes or some other mundane task. My brain is relaxed, I'm not overthinking and BAM it's just there--you just know something. Like maybe your friend is pregnant, or your brother just lost his job.

  I recall when my grandfather died. I was camping for the weekend with friends. Out of the blue, I made the comment, "I wonder what I should wear to his funeral?" and my friends looked at me as if I was being negative or plain crazy.

  Some people believe angels, spirit guides, or high-level communications gives this information to them from other forces of the universe. There's a good possibility also that claircognizance may also come from within yourself.

  Whatever the case, the information is received from within the Higher Self from outside of your physical body. The access point for this communication download is through the 7th Chakra. Everyone has an energy access point through the 7th Chakra located on top of the head. Spiritual information and knowledge can come directly to you through this entrance. But in order to receive clear intuitive information, the Crown Chakra must remain open.

- **Trance-Mediumship** is the ability for spirit to leave and enter the physical body. This can be your spirit, God or the spirit of another being. We start this ability as soon as our mother becomes pregnant with us and repeat this ability throughout our lifetime. At night when our body sleeps, when we daydream or when we have "out of body" experiences, we leave our body. We experience trance-mediumship multiple times daily.

If we do not have psychic tools to protect ourselves or remove this energy from our bodies, a couple of things may occur:

1. We leave our body, ultimately not participating much in our physical life. Leaving the body allows us to "get out" of the energy that is in the body that causes us "pain." We may use drugs, alcohol or even food to assist us in leaving the body. Our body may experience depression or apathy.

2. We are such capable spirits that we "manage" all the trance medium energy coming our way. We usually end up in careers managing many people and their lives. We may experience the need to be "responsible", especially for others. We are healers, moms, doctors, nurses, housecleaners, therapists, CEOs, politicians, etc. We may have a hard time taking care of our own needs because when we do, we become overwhelmed by the other energy we have been managing. Our body may experience guilt.

3. Our bodies become ill with "dis-ease" from the foreign energy that inhabits it. If a foreign energy inhabits a body long enough, it disrupts our own energy flow and may manifest into an illness or disease. And yes! These energies run in families. We may inherit our parents trance medium abilities. They were our first teachers!!

I am thankful to all the souls I meet in the journey of life."

Lailah Gifty Akita

Your Connection to Spiritual Wisdom

The 7th Chakra provides a connection to spiritual wisdom, aspirations, and knowledge of the truth. It governs cosmic consciousness and is also the receiver of cosmic energy flowing into and through the energy system.

The physical area that corresponds to the position of the 7th Chakra is also known as the soft spot or fontanelle. The bones in this area of an infant's skull are not fused and are flexible. This allows the child's head to pass through the birth canal and is important for brain development, allowing the child's brain to expand more rapidly than the bones of the skull. The Fontanelle closes as the child develops.

Everyone is a manifestation of the Divine, regardless of their state of consciousness, or form they've chosen to manifest their Light. You are your Higher Self."

Mynzah Osiris

The 7th Chakra Activation

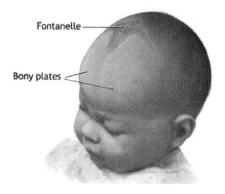

Fontanelle

Bony plates

The 7th Chakra is very active at birth because the new baby needs to start to be more connected with and take greater charge of its new physical body. This sign of physical connection to spirit was so revered by some ancient cultures that they physically cut holes in the skull to keep it open – a practice known as trepanning. The Taoist spiritual masters are said to naturally create a physical opening here as they reach higher levels of enlightenment.

It is not necessary to go to these extremes for you to activate and use the abilities in your crown chakra. All that is required is for you to focus your consciousness on the top of your head and you will start to activate it. Doing this during your meditations is the best way to start as this helps you tune out external influences. Although it is possible to be accessing the abilities in this chakra during your normal everyday activities.

The 7th Chakra Rules the Brain and Nervous System

On a physical level the 7th Chakra rules our brain, top of the head and entire nervous system. It is closely aligned with the pituitary gland, which is the master gland that regulates growth, blood pressure, temperature, pain relief, energy metabolism, urine production, water, sex hormones (testosterone, estrogen) and childbirth. It controls all other glands that are responsible for hormone secretion.

> *Spiritual awakening is an identity shift. You are God!"*
>
> Erin Fall Haskell

Gateway for Spiritual Information

As the master chakra, it regulates all of the other chakras and is the gateway for our spiritual information. It rules the higher self's control of our entire physical incarnation.

The 7th Chakra is also associated with the pineal gland that is a receptacle for the light coming from the higher self. The pineal and pituitary glands work together. The pineal gland '*downloads*' our energy and then the pituitary gland instructs other endocrine glands (and chakras) to assist us in raising the vibrational patterns of our physical form.

Symptoms of a Blocked 7th Chakra

If your crown chakra is blocked then you may experience some of the following symptoms:

- Depression, feeling confined, closed-mindedness, intense worry and anxiety, cerebral tumors, cranial pressure, headaches, migraines, mental disorders, scalp problems, and sleep disorders.

- Fear of religion or spirituality, frustration and unrealized power, little joy in life, fearfulness of things that cannot be understood with the physical senses (even schizophrenia).

Seek to know your sacred soul."

Lailah Gifty Akita

Unblocking Your 7th Chakra

Heaven on Earth Healings can assist greatly if you are ready to let go of whatever is causing your discomfort. If you'd like some help removing blocks to the flow of energy through your 7th Chakra contact me at http://www.amirahhall.com.

Releasing 'Destroy' or 'un-create' Energy

Create a magic wand symbol to collect up any destroy energy in your space or room. Explode roses to shift eh energy in the area.

Collect any gunk, junk, emotions, uncertainty, fears, doubts, worries, insecurities, or any and all other distractors that you are running from and/or carrying forward from yesterday or re-creating now, or carrying for other people, and all of the stuff underneath. Destroy and un-create them now. Let them all go.

You cannot have a positive life and a negative mind."

Joyce Meyer

Snake Energy Destroys Your Creations

The vibration of **'snakes'** is an energy that destroys your creations. Where are the snakes in your space? Are you ready to see them, and ready to clear them? Can you have the healing that comes from removing them from your space and making room for more of your own energy?

I was doing a reading for a friend the other day, and in the process I saw a snake. If there's ever a time to yell "Jackpot!" for me one of those times is when snakes show up. Snakes or snake energy are controls, big lies, fears, representatives of powerful energy that hold us back, energy that isn't ours, energy that we picked up in our travels that interferes with our ability to take a step in our truth.

We all have psychic snakes. We all have little voices that whisper to us that something we want, somewhere we want to go, some choice we want to make is impossible. They're controls that keep us playing small, that keep us **'in our place.' They're deceptive energies.**

And here's the thing: they are not true. They don't belong to you; they are given to you **(gee, thanks, right?).** They're gifts that keep on giving, day in and day out, and often we don't even know that they're there. When they show themselves, it indicates that we're ready to see them, to say hello to them, and to let them go.

I can't get caught up in the negative because that destroys you."

Jenni River

Once you have cleared them out, you have more space to fill with more of your own unique vibration, more of the energy you bring into the world. There is actually more space in your space, and you can choose how to fill it. It's the ultimate de-cluttering move.

> *Can you imagine what your life would be like if you could remove the energies that keep you playing small? Where would you be in your career? What would your relationships look like? How would your daily life change for the better if you were working from a space that contained more you and fewer snakes?*

Amirah Hall

> *Ask yourself what snakes you are ready to release. Visualize a rose for 'snake energy' and let it absorb any/all snake energy from your aura into it. And notice what happens.*

Delete the negative; accentuate the positive!"

Donna Karan

Releasing Resistance Energy

The Universe will always give you what you have asked for. The question is how soon will you allow it? How many things will you use as your excuse to have RESISTANCE that does not allow it? That is the only question...**How long are you going to hang on to these habits of thought that don't let it in?**

And the good news is, if ever you are not letting it in -- you've got a signal that's telling you. Having a negative emotion means basically that where you are vibrating at will not allow it in. It is not more difficult to create a castle than a button. Most of you have more buttons than castles, however, because they're easier to expect.

When you are looking at the problem, you're resistant to the solution."

Abraham Hicks

The solution can't come to you because you are vibrating at the energy of the problem, resisting the solution. Releasing the problem or energy that created the problem creates space for the solution to appear.

> Visualize a rose for the energy level of *'resistance'* and collect up any/all resistance energy in your space. Explode roses inside your space.

Spiritual Seniority

The human spirit needs to accomplish, to achieve, to triumph to be happy."

Ben Stein

The 7th Chakra has to do with knowingness and spiritual seniority. Visualize a rose and set it to a wellness vibration or color that works for your 7th chakra. Bring the wellness rose into your 7th Chakra space.

You know about seniority-- someone has been on the job longer than you or when
you're growing up, your parents had the final word. You get trained to get approval outside of yourself. If you moved forward or made a decision without permission, it was likely you'd be yelled at or punished in some way.

Giving Up Your Seniority

Being an adult, you would expect that it should be different now. In many ways it is. Except for =how much of a residual '*giving up your seniority*' do you carry? And how do you get your seniority back?

> Off the top of your head, from 0-100%, *how much do you look outside of yourself for permission when you go make money? Have a relationship? Design your career?*
>
> **Are you unconsciously or consciously asking for Mom or Dad's approval or validation?**

You do this because you are sensitive to the energy you took on in the past. You really try to avoid triggering that old pain – maybe you find reasons not to move forward (procrastinate) or take an indirect route (I need more education or time to study).

Getting Back Your Seniority

Getting your seniority back is as simple as releasing the old energy that gets triggered when you move forward – not over-riding or protecting the old pain. You want to release it, so you can regain that part of your creativity.

Using the **Quantum Energy Tools** (http://bit.ly/29WqnQk) helps you get your seniority back and having energy clearings helps get your life back on track.

Considering that your crown chakra has to do with knowingness, seniority and contains your own spiritual information and inspiration, focus is on the '**seniority**' vibration.

Say **YES** to '*being senior in your own universe*'!

> Visualizing a rose that represents your seniority, *what color do you see?*
>
> Begin to vibrate your crown at that seniority color. As you vibrate at that color, create an image or a chakra person or a stick person in your mind. Visualize tossing some neutral purple energy at the image and allow it to

stick to any pictures or programming where you cannot be senior in your own space.

Where on the image do you see the purple energy sticks?

Begin deprogramming those places by collecting all the purple energy into a magic wand rose. Blow it up. Notice if you can see what those programs are or how they affected your ability to be senior in your own universe.

What happens to your space as you are deprogramming?

What changes are occurring in your space?

With the vibration of seniority on your crown chakra, begin running that energy through your energy channels, letting it run throughout the body.

Visualize a rose for the vibration for your knowingness. *What is the color?* Reset your color/vibration of knowingness by letting it vibrate in your crown chakra.

Visualize a chakra person for yourself and toss a ball of neutral purple energy at it to ignite any energy that would invalidate your own 'knowingness'. Begin deprogramming that energy by collecting all the purple energy into a magic wand rose and explode it.

Releasing Competition Energy

Visualize a rose for the ***vibration of competition. How much energy of competition is affecting your space?*** Begin deprogramming that energy by collecting all the purple energy into a magic wand rose and explode it.

The only things in my life that compatibly exists with this grand universe are the creative works of the human spirit."

Ansel Adams

Your Spiritual Information

Visualize a rose for the **vibration for your spiritual information. What is the color and vibration?** (It's not usually just one color, but all colors) Reset your color/vibration of your **'spiritual information'** by letting it vibrate in your crown chakra. Deprogram by exploding roses with any pictures/energy that prevents you from having your own spiritual information.

No pessimist ever discovered the secret of the stars, or sailed to an uncharted land, or opened a new doorway for the human spirit."

Helen Keller

"I've changed a lot since I started working with Manifesting Miracles 101 training and Quantum Energy Tools. I am able to control my emotions and people see me for who I am. I have set clear boundaries with others and realize for the first time in my life, I now have true friends. I feel happy—it's as if I'm a totally different person! People at work are noticing too that I have changed and appear to be more open. Every day there are new miracles—I couldn't be happier. Thank you with all my heart for this practice. I would be lost without it."

Reema A, Dubai, UAE

Chapter 19 - Practice Guidelines

Practice the following tools this week:

1. Grounding – Quantum Energy Tool #1
2. Center of Head – Quantum Energy Tool #2
3. Replenishing – Quantum Energy Tool #3
4. Run Earth and Cosmic Energy – Quantum Energy Tool #7
5. Set 7th Chakra to Inspiration
6. Set 7th Chakra Goals to Inspiration
7. Release Old Goals

GOALS AND HEALING WORKSHEET

WELLNESS COLOR _____

Physical Goal _____

Mental Goal _____

Emotional Goal _____

Spiritual Goal _____

MISSION STATEMENT

_____

WHAT ARE YOU NOTICING DIFFERENT?

_____

_____

WHAT ENERGIES **SUPPORT** YOU? (Colors, memories, beliefs, thoughts)

_____

_____

OTHER

_____

_____

19

Wellness
Creative Inspiration

C laircognizance, sometimes called knowingness or inner knowing, is the ability to be still and instantly know your spiritual information. It refers to the ability to simply know something to be true without any supporting external information, logic or reason. **You just know it**.

> *Everyone can 'know' what they need to know, when they need to know it.*

This aspect of **'knowing information'** is accessed through the 7th Chakra, otherwise known as the crown chakra. This information is not stored there but rather has information on **'how to access'** this wisdom and knowledge.

Here are some examples of claircognizance to help you get more familiar with it:

> Have you ever had the experience where you became strangely certain about something?
>
> - "I just knew I shouldn't take that flight. I knew there would be an accident. I don't know how I knew, I just knew."
> - "I just knew the pharmacy would not have everything I needed to buy and I should have instead gone to another location. I went anyways to the first location only to discover – I was right! Then, I went to the second location to buy what I needed."
>
> Or have you instantly received clear and accurate information that you say aloud or act upon before you can analyze it?
>
> - "By all appearances he looked like a nice guy, but I just knew he was a crook and so I didn't do business with him."

> • "Although the new tenant seemed to look like a perfect match, I just knew she was going to be high maintenance and demanding.

There may be no rhyme or reason for it, no logic, no information you can point to-- just pure unquestionable knowledge. No interpretation is required and there's no room for misunderstanding. This ability helps us bypass the intellect and have a spiritual perspective on life.

Focus your attention on the things that make life worth living"

Tommy Rosen

Developing Inner Knowing

You can access your inner knowing by focusing your conscious awareness on the 7th Chakra, meditation and by sitting in stillness. From this vantage point, as you tune out the outer world and connect with the inner world, you will raise your awareness and be able to simply '*know*'.

It's helpful to record your experiences in your **Miracle Journal** and develop an awareness of when you are experiencing your inner knowing. Over time you will begin to trust and act upon this information, rather than passing it through your analyzer and discounting it. Like any spiritual ability it will improve and develop the more you practice and use it and don't give in to your doubts.

Before enlightenment – chop wood, carry water. After enlightenment – chop wood, carry water."

Zen Proverb

Access to Any Information

Each of us has access to any and all information we need to meet all of our life challenges and create a happy, healthy, fulfilled and enjoyable life. Claircognizance helps us focus at a '*soul level*' on understanding human consciousness. We are not our physical bodies but rather multi-dimensional, eternal spiritual beings. Most of us have had thousands of physical bodies and millennia of learning experiences relevant to life on earth. All this wisdom can be accessed via the crown chakra using claircognizance.

So we each have an enormous amount of wisdom to draw from. The 7ᵗʰ Chakra, through the psychic sense of inner knowing allows us to access the knowledge, which is most useful to us during the current set of life circumstances.

If you want to find the secrets of the universe, think in terms of energy, frequency and vibration."

Nikola Tesla

Benefits of Claircognizance

Other benefits of activating your claircognizance include:

- Helps cultivate a sense of wellness and faith in yourself and your higher purpose
- Increases open-mindedness as we have a wide scope of experience to draw from
- Develops an understanding of the unity of all life as we are one with ALL
- Improves peace of mind the more you listen to your Higher Self
- Re-programs your mind, integrating your divinity.

Challenges of Mastering Claircognizance

Instantly knowing information truly is a great power, once you start to develop it. However, once you realize how much you really do know, you may experience some challenges to your spiritual growth.

There is little sense in attempting to change external conditions. You must first change inner beliefs, then outer constitutions will change accordingly."

Brian Adams

Temptation to Control Others

When you share your information, others may become impressed at your ability. They may believe you have more power and knowledge than they do and you may be tempted to play God. It can be tempting to manipulate others in ways of your choice.

This may sound outlandish, but the most important part of developing spiritual awareness is to heal and know yourself first. Truly, that is what knowing yourself means and as well as having a strong clear connection to God.

Examples of people who have struggled in this way include military dictators, politicians and cult leaders such as Jim Jones of the Peoples Temple, who encouraged a mass suicide of his followers in Jonestown, Guyana by getting them to drink poisoned '*Kool-Aid*.' David Koresh, of the Branch Davidians and the siege in Waco Texas is another example. As is Hitler in World War II and Idi Amin in Uganda.

All spiritual leaders must watch that the ego does not usurp this powerful aspect of spiritual consciousness, even church ministers, catholic priests, rabbis, motivational speakers and self-help gurus like James Arthur Ray, who had a follower die in a heat lodge because they were encouraged to stay longer than was comfortable.

Share Everything

Another challenge that can be encountered as you open your knowingness is the belief that you know it all including what is right for the world and what is best for others. Remember your information may not be appropriate or meaningful for others. We are all unique individuals and have our own information to support our path.

You may be familiar with 'The Long Island Medium' on TV. She has no control of when she receives spiritual information and believes she has an obligation to share everything that comes through her, whether a person has asked her to or not. The show follows her as she approaches people in the street and in the supermarket and delivers spiritual messages.

Such individuals mean well and want to help people, but they do not know how to control their gift and believe they have an obligation to share everything that comes to them. In many cases it is their ego that is running the show.

Other examples of claircognizance gone wild include conspiracy theorists. David Icke was an example of this in the early days of his spiritual awakening. He was so excited about everything he knew he blurted it out to everyone, including the newspapers and press who made fun of him. Now he is still outspoken, but tells people to take away only what feels right for them. He believes that politicians and the royal family are reptilians and the Illuminati are controlling the planet. This may be great information for some, but it is not appropriate for everyone.

The trick is to offer your information as an option or a choice for people and to ask if they would like to hear about it first.

Losing Touch With Reality

Some people have experienced their spiritual abilities opening without having any conscious awareness that of what is happening to them. Because the crown chakra is a channel to multiple other spiritual realities, activating the 7th Chakra without knowledge of how to stay grounded and focused in this reality can lead to some disturbing experiences.

I have experienced this directly with some of my clients, who have had a history of being diagnosed with various mental disorders, even to the extent of being hospitalized. Mostly they are relieved to meet someone who doesn't think they are mad. Then they are grateful when I teach them how to control their experiences using a few very simple spiritual techniques that put then in a more grounded state and enable them to control their crown chakra.

I am not a medical doctor, psychologist or psychiatrist but I do believe that some forms of mental illness are related to an imbalance or damage of the 7th Chakra and to people opening the abilities in their crown chakra without a teacher or mentor to help explain their experiences and guide their growth.

I don't blame the doctors. ***How could they know any different?*** This information is not generally accepted in the mainstream. Most people when faced with a person who hears voices that no one else can hear, or sees and talks to people who aren't there, or who is sensitive to energies that everyone else has learned to ignore, would come to the typical mainstream diagnoses of physical mental disorders. Our medical professionals are only just beginning to seek healing from spiritual/energetic sources.

We are all connected. To each other, biologically. To the earth, chemically. To the rest of the universe atomically."

Neil deGrasse Tyson

Know Thyself

Claircognizance allows us to learn to control our own energies and creations. An activated 7th Chakra leads to great power and does it's best healing when used in one's own space rather than to control another.

The future is not there waiting for us. We create it by the power of our imagination."

Pir Vilayat Khan

Energy of Creation

As spiritual beings, we have incarnated on earth to come from wholeness, infinity, and interconnectedness.

...the word inspiration as meaning 'being in-Spirit.' When we're in-Spirit, we're inspired...and when we're inspired, it's because we're back in-Spirit, fully awake to Spirit within us."

Dr. Wayne Dyer

Visualize a rose that represents the *'energy of creation'*, your inspiration as a spirit. Notice its color and qualities. Own that vibration, bring it into your aura and make note of the qualities.

Reset your 7ᵗʰ Chakra at your wellness color for goals.

The secrets of the universe aren't really secrets. It's just that humanity is too subjugated by their blissful ignorance to ask the right questions. When you have all of the answers, but are unable to ask any questions to them, then all you have are secrets."

Lionel Suggs

Energy of Inspiration

Motivation is ego-driven. But inspiration is spirit-driven--a force that takes hold of us, not the reverse."

Dr. Wayne Dyer

Visualize a rose that represents the *'energy of creation – inspiration'*. Visualize a rose for your *'inspiration as a spirit'*. Is it still at the same color?

Going To The Edge of The Universe

Re-establishing your aura around your body and be aware of your body and your grounding cord.

Bring your awareness to stepping outside of your body and 'be' at the corner of the room. Let yourself, your spirit, step outside of the room

and be outside of your house. Notice the distance between you and your body as you step away of it.

Then step out to the edge of the atmosphere. Stepping outside the atmosphere up to the moon. Then step farther to the edge of the solar system and have awareness of the distance from your body to where you are as a spirit.

Step outside the solar system to as far out as you can imagine in space at the edge of our galaxy. Notice how much space you have as a spirit and be at the Edge of the Universe.

However you define that for yourself as a spirit, say 'hello' to that space of the edge of the Universe. Make note of how you see or experience this space.

From this space say 'hello' to the *'energy of creation'*. Visualize a rose for your *'inspiration as a spirit'*. Notice the color and quality of that rose. Own that vibration.

As you see that 'inspiration as a spirit', make note of those qualities and explode the rose.

Inspiration Into The 7th Chakra

Match the energy of *'inspiration'* with your 7th Chakra and notice how it feels to match it. Explode roses.

Allow your 7th Chakra to be set to your *'highest havingness'* for this vibration of *'inspiration'*.

Bringing this rose with you, begin to return to your body and step in through your crown chakra allowing this energy to fill the rest of the body to the highest havingness that the 7th Chakra can have. Any remaining energy will stay up in the 8th chakra or the creative rings until your body is ready to receive it.

Set 7th Chakra Goals to Inspiration

Visualize a rose for your 7th Chakra goals. Alongside, visualize another rose for the 'inspiration energy' that you brought in from the edge of the Universe and let it fill up your goal rose.

Act on Inspiration

Visualize a rose for your body to be able to use and act upon inspiration.

Visualize a Havingness Gauge and ask it, *"how much of that energy am I able to act on?"* If you like where it's at, that's great. If not, imagine a magic wand rose and collect up any foreign energy and then explode the rose.

Consider: *Where can you see yourself acting on inspiration?*

Visualize a rose for a specific goal you have. Set it to the *'vibration of inspiration'*. What happens if you bring the goal right now into the body? Ask yourself, *"What fuel do you need to get that goal? (Foods, rest, exercise, etc.?)*

Bring that goal rose into the 7th Chakra and allow that image to go through your whole aura. Notice how your body reacts. Explode rose for any resistance energy in the body.

Releasing Old Goals

Having the energy of *'old goals'* take up energetic space in your aura and can block the creation of new goals. Releasing them, you reclaim energy that has been going into them trying to create them.

Create a rose for any goals that are no longer in affinity with you. Begin releasing any old goals that are no longer in affinity with you. Fill up a rose and explode it. Continue exploding roses until you are certain you have released all your old goals.

If there is anywhere that your body is resisting any of those past time goals, explode roses and release whatever is resisting them.

Acknowledge inspiration energy in the 7th Chakra again and set your present time wellness color into the 7th Chakra.

Visualize a rose for your goals and bring that into present time where they can be in affinity with you. Replenish yourself with Golden Suns.

Enjoy the enthusiasm and excitement around this energetic space of 'inspiration'.

What is your Mission Statement or Vision Statement for the 7th Chakra?

For example, your statement could be:

> *"I am creatively, inspired!"*
>
> *"I am aligned with my highest inspiration!"*
>
> *"I am divinely connected with my soul's goals and gifts."*

Add this 7th Chakra Mission Statement to your Personal Mission Statement in Chapter 24.

"I'm feeling more worthy and it's as if my whole life is 'accelerating'. People are starting to tell me, 'Is there something different about you?' and that makes me really happy that people are seeing the changes in me. I feel more open to new things even as fears are bubbling up I am hopeful and excited about the future. I'm excited about LIFE everyday!"

Karen Higgins

Chapter 20 - Practice Guidelines

Practice the following tools this week:

1. Grounding – Quantum Energy Tool #1
2. Center of Head – Quantum Energy Tool #2
3. Replenishing – Quantum Energy Tool #3
4. Run Earth and Cosmic Energy – Quantum Energy Tool #7
5. Set 7th Chakra to Inspiration
6. Set 7th Chakra Goals to Inspiration
7. Release Old Goals
8. Create 7th Chakra Personal Spiritual Mission Statement

GOALS AND HEALING WORKSHEET

WELLNESS COLOR _____

Physical Goal _____

Mental Goal _____

Emotional Goal _____

Spiritual Goal _____

MISSION STATEMENT

_____

WHAT ARE YOU NOTICING DIFFERENT?

_____

_____

WHAT ENERGIES **SUPPORT** YOU? (Colors, memories, beliefs, thoughts)

_____

_____

OTHER

_____

_____

21

8ᵗʰ Chakra
Your Life Purpose

Most people are aware of the 7 major chakras but did you also know that there are more than a dozen more chakras beyond these first seven? These higher chakras are the links between your personality and your higher self. When they are balanced, open and activated they allow you to access an expanded universe, increasing your spiritual awareness and to free yourself from karma.

 Man is free at the moment he wishes to be".

Voltaire

The 8ᵗʰ Chakra also known as the soul star chakra or seat of the soul, is located approximately 6"-2' above your head and is not a set location like the previous 7 chakras we discussed. If you've ever seen paintings depicting holy figures with circles of golden light around their heads, you've seen a visual representation of the love and light that flows from activated higher energy centers.

That 8th Chakra is the part of you that never comes into an incarnation and it's more esoteric than the previous 7 chakras we have explored. It's a constant from lifetime to lifetime and although it's not the Higher Self, it's where the higher self might sit.

For example, if you go to a movie theater, the part of you that is sitting on the seat is like the 8th Chakra. You don't go into the screen. You never go into the movie. It can impact you but it doesn't change you. It is the constant. The 8th Chakra is your connection to the astral plane, the Supreme Being (The Source, God) and that Higher Self part of you.

Every man is a divinity in disguise, a god playing the fool."
Ralph Waldo Emerson

Sets Your Life Plan

It's a little abstract for people to understand but it's something we really explore in my 1-2-1 mentoring program. It really has your original essence of a spirit or the DNA of the body. The 8th Chakra sets the plan for you taking your incarnations each lifetime. It's a silent part of you that you have to listen to. In essence, you have to '**ask it**' as it won't force something on you.

You can ask your 8th Chakra questions like:

What's my answer?

What is my true path?

It is beautiful to discover our wings and learn how to fly; flight is a beautiful process. But then to rest on the wings of God as He flies: this is divine."

C. JoyBell C.

Your Original Spark

This spiritual notion is based on the theory that when one first incarnates as a new spirit, for the first-time ever, there is an **original frequency or vibration to the beginning of your existence.**

This energy level and your ability to vibrate in your 8th Chakra can get lost, obscured or otherwise dimmed as we travel from one life to the next on our spiritual journey.

We will process this energy and help you reconnect with this vibration and reclaim your '**true spirit.**'

It's much like the crown or 7th Chakra, in that it's part of your knowingness, your spiritual information. Your spiritual knowingness actually originates from the 8th Chakra but comes through your 7th Chakra in a form that your body can interpret and integrate the information.

Each of us has a memory and an identity that starts from birth until now. That's your conscious memory. The 8th Chakra memory starts from that original spark of the divine and continues through all of your incarnations right up to present time. All of your awareness is stored there, past and future lives. It's all in the 8th Chakra where there is NO TIME – NO SPACE.

 Many times a crisis may arise in our lives when we have ignored our soul's calling and presence in our lives. It often stops us long enough to go more deeply into those things that truly matter."

Christie Pennington

Access Your Life Purpose

The 8th Chakra is like the data room for your soul's contract or your life purpose. Your soul enters this world with a goal of learning lessons with the purpose to evolve. Although it may not be clear to you at the human level, your soul's purpose is always clear to your Higher Self.

Activating the 8th Chakra allows you access to your Higher Self enough to enter your data room or the Akasha (etheric field in which a record of past events is imprinted) for a glimpse at your soul contract. Once that happens, don't be surprised if you begin to feel like you need to shift your focus, especially if you have spent years ignoring your true passion.

That nagging voice that tells you to follow your true path is really your Higher Self offering guidance, nudging you to get to work on whatever your soul is meant to do while in this body at this time.

Opening your 8th Chakra and stepping through the veil that separates your earthly self from your eternal soul will open your eyes to the vast space beyond physical plane boundaries.

 We come here to experience, to express as individuals, as ideas in the mind of God."

Christie Pennington

Connection With The Supreme Being

Your 8th Chakra is where the higher self can connect with the Supreme Being and isn't really something that should be brought into the body. If you have seen anyone who has done that you might notice they have very little ability to connect to this earth reality.

Describing the 8th Chakra is a little like interpreting art, there are lots of ideas and in the end you have to explore it to discover your own answers. My answers explain how it works for me and using your clairvoyance helps you to see how it works or relates for you. You have to really get your sense of it for its deeper meaning.

Since the 8th Chakra is rather nebulous or vague in this reality, your **Quantum Energy Tools** (http://bit.ly/29WqnQk) will help you get more connected to the body and access this information for yourself.

Because you're a creation of God, you reflect the Divine qualities of creativity, wisdom, and love."

Doreen Virtue

Clear Karmic Leftovers

Karmic leftovers and patterns build up after lifetimes and they are what keep you rooted to this planet and keep you separated from your divine connection. We forget how to bring that Source in, what is true and what isn't.

With your 8th Chakra being the gateway to the Divine, it's the last chakra that holds the human information that's not needed in the expanded universe of an open and activated 8th Chakra. The residual karmic patterns are waiting for you to clear them out once and for all before you move on and connect with your Higher Self. Activating the 8th Chakra clears unwanted patterns that are not useful anymore and connects you with the greater, expansive universe, starting with your Higher Self.

The chain of awakening within the chakra system doesn't always activate in an orderly or logically based manner. You cannot open this chakra until significant clearing and opening has been done in the lower seven chakras."

Insight State

Discover Spiritual Gifts

With an activated 8th Chakra and expanding spiritual awareness, you may find that you develop new spiritual abilities. Perhaps you've always been intuitive, but with an open 8th Chakra, you'll discover your powers of intuition increasing. Other latent talents may reveal themselves as you continue to widen your 8th Chakra, including astral travel, telepathy, clairvoyance, and even energy healing. At first, these new capabilities may seem overwhelming, but please don't worry! Your higher self would never bestow these gifts upon you unless you were ready. Working with an energy healer or other type of spiritual teacher can help you control, manage, and develop your newfound abilities.

> *Wellness within is where we bring the body and spirit together in harmony and in communication with each other.*

Bringing Body and Spirit Into Harmony

> **Visualize a rose and ask what vibration for the 7th Chakra will validate your body and spirit in harmony?** *What is your wellness color? What color brings those two together? What color allows spirit into the body and to consciously interact with the world?* **Set your 7th Chakra to that color.**

Discovering Your Original Spark

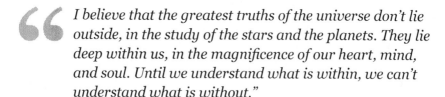

I believe that the greatest truths of the universe don't lie outside, in the study of the stars and the planets. They lie deep within us, in the magnificence of our heart, mind, and soul. Until we understand what is within, we can't understand what is without."

Anita Moorjani

In some ways the 8th Chakra is indefinable because as soon as you define it, it loses all the rest of what it is.

There's a Quote:

The birth of the organization is the death of the idea. Once you make it solid, you lose the idea or inspiration."

Unknown

Therefore, when looking at our 8th Chakra concept, it's better to just imagine it and how you perceive it, rather than define it logically.

Original Essence

A part of your spiritual being is timeless. It has awareness and information about all of your lifetimes and the bigger picture of who you are.

> **Visualize a rose in front of you that can represent your 8th Chakra.**
>
> **Ask yourself, "*how far is it above my head*?" Just get a sense of where it's located.**
>
> **Acknowledge that bigger part of yourself. Wake yourself up to it.**
>
> ***What is your original essence color?* Notice if you get any sense of energy movement. *Is this something that you connect with frequently? Do you go here a lot or just walk around in it?***
>
> **Ask yourself, "*what is this for you? Is it a source of answers? Are you in alignment with this part of yourself?*" Get an intuitive feeling for it, as it might not show itself visually for you.**
>
> **If you were to dialogue with this part of yourself, '*what would it tell you*?'**
>
> **Does it have a message for you?**

Ask that question. Let an answer come to you. It might be a color, an image or something else. ***Is there anything you would want to say to this part of you?*** If you think it as a part of you, how do you open a dialogue? Talk to it and listen to it.

> **Be aware of yourself in the middle of your head, imagine letting your attention of self go up into that 8th Chakra.**
> **One way to do that is if you consider anything that would motivate you, move you, or pull you in any direction. Consider moving away from these emotions, judgments or issues and look at yourself from a spiritual viewpoint.**

A spiritual viewpoint from the 8th Chakra is not moved or pulled from anything in the world. **You become a neutral observer.** You start to look at yourself without judgment – just observation.

> Without any need to change anything about yourself, move into that place, that energy level, look at yourself. Look down at your body from pure neutrality.
>
> Say hello to all that you have created and all the things you are learning about and growth you are creating. From this perspective, turn your attention upward to the cosmos and consider saying *'hello to the cosmic consciousness'*, the Supreme Being, the SOURCE of ALL.
>
> Imagine creating a connection to that source and opening that communication up.

Really it's always been there – you are just remembering it.

> Imagine that connection starts coming down into the middle of your head and into your body. As you come into awareness of the larger part of you, you will get an awareness of a connection to the greater Source.
>
> As you come in, visualize a rose for the life you are creating.
>
> *How might it be different for you if you let your 8th Chakra be your guide as the source of creating your life?*

Some say that the ultimate goal for all of us is to reflect that Divine Self, that true self of the 8th Chakra into the world.

Others say it's really about how to have fun. And to start getting everything you desire in this life. You've heard the expression, **'He who dies with the most toys wins'.**

> *It's power-- it's about all kinds of things.*

As you start to connect with the 8th Chakra, you can find out what it is all about for you. You can explore what that means for you.

If you go 'unconscious' going there – that's ok. I have spent many hours of going unconscious myself. This subject is sometimes hard to broach. That's part of opening that door. You are stepping into a place that is unconscious to you yet, so that's why you experience unconscious. Just not knowing where you are. But you have to step through it first. As you move forward, your experience with your 8th Chakra will expand.

As long as there isn't a lot of drooling you are ok. Don't feel bad if you went unconscious. You went there as a spirit and started to open the dialogue.

It is not enough that one surrenders oneself. Surrender is to give oneself up to the original cause of one's being. Do not delude yourself by imagining such a source to be some God outside you. One's source is within oneself. Give yourself up to it. That means that you should seek the source and merge in it."

Sri Ramana Maharshi

Your Birth As A Spirit

It might take a little imagination expansion to consider all the way back to where you can find a rose that is your 'original essence', or what is called **'your birth as a spirit'**.

Visualize a timeline from present time all the way back to your *'birth as a spirit'* that is your original essence.

Original Essence_____Present Time

Visualize bringing that Original Essence rose forward through the timeline and anywhere where your energy got stuck on the timeline. Collect up any dark spots, marks and light into the rose. You are bringing forward the energy of YOU through the timeline anywhere it got stuck on the time line. Explode roses along the timeline.

You are bringing back to your present self any of your spiritual energy that got scattered throughout time. Sometimes it means finding forgiveness, amusement, getting angry or what ever it takes to *'get your energy back'*. Let that rose grow to reflect how much energy you are bringing back to yourself.

Don't burden yourself with details. Just imagine getting the bulk of your energy. Once you get that in front of you, explode the rose to release the energy back into you wherever it belongs.

It is the imagination that argues for the Divine Spark within human beings. It is literally a descent of the World's Soul into all of us."

Terence McKenna

Reset Wellness for Chakras

Visualize a rose out in front of you for your 1st Chakra. Ask yourself, *what is your wellness color for the 1st chakra?* Let the rose go into the 1st Chakra.

Visualize a rose out in front of you for your 2nd Chakra. Ask yourself, *what is your wellness color for the 2nd Chakra?* Let the rose go into the 2nd Chakra.

Visualize a rose out in front of you for your 3rd Chakra. Ask yourself, *what is your wellness color for the 3rd Chakra?* Let the rose go into the 3rd Chakra.

Visualize a rose out in front of you for your 4th Chakra. Ask yourself, *what is your wellness color for the 4th Chakra?* Let the rose go into the 4th Chakra.

Visualize a rose out in front of you for your 5th Chakra. Ask yourself, *what is your wellness color for the 5th Chakra?* Let the rose go into the 5th Chakra.

Visualize a rose out in front of you for your 6th Chakra. Ask yourself, *what is your wellness color for the 6th Chakra?* Let the rose go into the 6th Chakra.

Visualize a rose out in front of you for your 7th Chakra. Ask yourself, *what is your wellness color for the 7th Chakra?* Let the rose go into the 7th Chakra.

Visualize a rose for your original essence for the 8th Chakra. Allow it to vibrate at that the original essence color. Imagine stepping away from the body and up to the 8th Chakra and into the neutral observer.

From this point, say hello to the body and all those chakras and the alignment of wellness.

Visualize an image of yourself in the alignment of wellness for each chakra and visualize yourself vibrating there. Validate the concept from your 8th Chakra that all chakras are in alignment with the 8th Chakra.

That energy that you create as you vibrate in wellness at the 8th Chakra is that expression of your *'true self'* and where you can start to bring that vibration into the body.

Say hello to the Supreme Being again and align yourself to the source or the Cosmic Consciousness.

Re-center yourself in the middle of your head at the 6th Chakra and acknowledge your creation of being incarnated in this lifetime for your own reasons and growth on your own path. Acknowledge this for yourself.

> **Visualize a rose and ask yourself, *"what is that for you? What is your own true expression itself?"***
>
> **Allow any considerations that pull you away from that to fall away. You can imagine that as little roses that light up in your aura, lights, anything that would pull you away – let them come to awareness in your aura and send them down your grounding cord.**

> **Visualize a pure Golden Sun filled with your own energy and fill your body with it, replenishing wherever you are releasing energy. Be sure to give yourself extra Golden Suns over the next few days.**

" *The Infinite Being, God, is with me, and vibrates in every molecule and cell of my being."*

"It's so great to be in the flow. I would have never imagined this feeling before (I'm feeling tingles as I say this) but every day is 'inspiring' to me. A lot of people promise the moon and it comes across as New Age hype, but Amirah truly holds your hand and guides you along what can feel like a rocky path of reinventing yourself--from the inside out. I truly understand that this type of work requires a master to guide, inspire and monitor your progress while you take your steps in Miracle Mastery. Everyday I feel 'new and improved'; what a powerful journey this is of self-discovery, expansion and manifestation."

Marla Dillingham

Chapter 21 - Practice Guidelines

Practice the following tools this week:

1. Grounding – Quantum Energy Tool #1
2. Center of Head – Quantum Energy Tool #2
3. Replenishing – Quantum Energy Tool #3
4. Run Earth and Cosmic Energy – Quantum Energy Tool #7
5. Reset Original Essence
6. Reset Chakras for Wellness

GOALS AND HEALING WORKSHEET

WELLNESS COLOR _____

Physical Goal _____

Mental Goal _____

Emotional Goal _____

Spiritual Goal _____

MISSION STATEMENT

_____

WHAT ARE YOU NOTICING DIFFERENT?

_____

_____

WHAT ENERGIES **SUPPORT** YOU? (Colors, memories, beliefs, thoughts)

_____

_____

OTHER

_____

_____

Chapter

22

8th Chakra Wellness Dare To Be You

Go forward and never look back. Because if you look back, you may see how many people are gaining on you! When you see an obstacle, EMBRACE it. Conquer it. Destroy it."

Following your heart creates heaven on earth for you.

One of the most important questions to explore for yourself is, '**Who or What is God to YOU?**' especially considering you're in search of wellness.

Whether we realize it or not, we're all looking for a way to feel connected with our core happiness, our Source, God, Higher Power, etc. **You already know 'who God is'!** Intuitively that is.

We know that our Creator is the Source of our life force, wellbeing, joy and love. Whether or not you are conscious of it, I also believe deep down inside we know that we are never separate from God. It's only because of our false sense of guilt, shame or un-worthiness that we create an illusion where we are separated from the ALL.

God is already within us and we are already within God. That is what gives us life.

In her book **The Dynamic Laws of Healing**, Catherine Ponder reminded us that there is an infinite amount of healing energy available to us at all times through the Creator and regardless of your religion or spiritual practices, you can tap into this healing source at any time.

> *You've undoubtedly heard the phrase, "Let Go and Let God."*

Believing that the universe will rise up to support you when you can't figure out the answer is incredibly reassuring—plus it works!

What do you need to do it? Just welcome the Divine!

Welcoming the Divine

For thousands and thousands of years, people have called on the name of the Creator to bring the Divine into their presence. This is one of the reasons we pray, and also why prayer is so powerful. The sound of prayer, either spoken or sung, as it resonates in our bodies is also healing. According to the Kabbalah, an ancient Jewish text, the Hebrew letters have specific healing properties when spoken aloud. The same is true for the Quran, which is the Word of God made text. At a minimum, speaking words or prayers out loud can change the vibrational patterns around you, which just might help you manifest your dream or desire with the help of the Law of Attraction.

The ancients believed that the phrase '*I AM*' was a synonym for '**the God within you**.'

Consider how many times you say '*I am*' in a day. ***Are you affirming what you want to bring into your life? Is it possible that your words are unknowingly cutting off your connection to healing energy?***

Restoring Balance

No matter who you are, there are times when you will feel stress, ill health, or low energy. All of us argue with our boss, partner or family members every now and then. Imbalance of any kind often arises when you lose your connection to the Divine—when you cut off the circulation of healing energy.

What's important is you can regain your health, prosperity, and equilibrium by connecting to the Creator.

> *The root of happiness is actually the core essence of who we are. To be happy we just need to align with our Self!*

That sounds easy, doesn't it! Actually it is.

The Root of Happiness

When we experience ourselves as formless Spirit, we know ourselves as an ocean of love, wellness, truth, compassion, peace and joy. This is where you and I are One Being within our Creator, where we meet and occupy the same space at the same time. **This is the root of happiness!**

Your path has its own simple beauty and mystery. It is never what you think it is, yet it is never beyond your ability to intuit the next step."

Paul Ferrini

Miracles Happen!

As we align ourselves more and more with our core or Source (by choosing a positive direction of thought), amazing things come into our lives which we couldn't have planned or anticipated. I call these '**miracles**'. For instance, if you've been dealing with an illness, the perfect practitioner will cross paths with you at just the right time. Or just the right piece of information you need about an herb or nutritional supplement will come your way. Or if money has been an issue, some new avenue of income will open up for you in some unexpected way.

Following Your Heart

When we violate our own hearts, we go against our own conscience and cannot live freely, happily, openly, with others or with God. It's when we follow the laws of love written in our hearts, that we feel connected to all and full of life.

> **When we satisfy ourselves, we satisfy all -- including God. So, be true to yourself.**

Being untrue to your heart destroys your creations, dreams and goals only to create your own personal hell. But if you follow your heart, it will create heaven on earth for you. Each moment in life, each choice, is a fork in the road. Which way will you go? Where will we end up? It depends on how well we obey our hearts.

A '**following your heart**' example for instance is when you live according to what you know and feel is right. You avoid things that you know and feel are wrong which reflects, '**I am a good person**.' Feeling good about yourself, you are open to being loved. You want to be seen and known and have open communication. The message you give to others is that, '**I am happy to be** *loved by you. You are welcome into my life—let's talk*!' Ultimately, the effect this creates on relationships happens because you feel good about yourself. You are open to being loved. Others will love you, talk to you and spend time with you while you end up feeling nourished and understood. Because you are receptive to love, people are willing to love you.

Ignoring Your Heart

An '*ignoring your heart*' example for instance is when you didn't do something that you knew you should do or you did something you shouldn't have. You feel bad about it and begin thinking that you are '*not good*'. You translate that into '*I don't deserve to be loved*'. Love becomes harder and harder to get because deep down inside you believe you are not a good person or worthy of love, and hide from others and the world. You minimize yourself in your career and relationships sending the message to the world, '*I don't want to be seen or known. Just leave me alone*'. Others on the other hand, perceive you as being unreceptive or rejecting them. Then you feel unnourished and misunderstood. Seeing the way people respond to your withdraw, you believe, "*People don't love me because I am no good!*" The real interpretation would be, '*People don't love me because I don't let them.*'

> *"To thine own self be true" ends the destructive cycle that is put in motion when we ignore our heart's own feelings.*

Many people think that to '*follow your heart*' means to be whimsical, inconsiderate, selfish, and non-committal. And tell me, just how do you feel about whimsical, flakey and selfish people?

Following your heart has been given a bad rap. In truth, no human heart would ever approve of selfish, whimsical living. Since your heart is also the Heart of God, there is no conflict. Being in alignment with your own heart, you will do right by God and all others.

 To thine own self be true, and it must follow, as the night follows day, thou canst not then be false to any man."

William Shakespeare

Spiritual Freedom

Freedom means the opportunity to be what we never thought we would be."

Daniel J. Boorstin

Spiritual freedom might have different meanings for different people. For me – It is my freedom to **Be, Do and Have**. That is, whatever one decides for themselves as a spirit.

One of the qualities of a spirit is that you are always *'being something'*.

And by having spiritual freedom, you can choose and be whatever you want.

When we lose our *'spiritual freedom'* it's because we get stuck being something *'we are not'* or *'don't want to be'*. Consider a time when you went along with someone's idea of the best way to be. Or when you did something because you thought it would make someone else happy, not because you wanted it for yourself.

> **Visualize a rose that represents your Higher Self and the wellness color for spiritual freedom for you. What does that mean to you to have spiritual freedom? What qualities does it have?**

Freedom consists not in doing what we like, but in having the right to do what we ought."

Pope John Paul II

> **Faith wavers...it just does. That is why it is called faith!**
>
> **Some days we have all the faith in the world and we just know for sure that everything is going to be okay; that our life is exactly where it is supposed to be and that we are on track. Other days our faith is tiny, and we are not sure how we are going to make it through, if at all.**
>
> **Your faith is enough today! No matter how tiny; no matter how small. Today it is enough. Your faith will grow where it needs to grow. It will!**

Going To The Edge of The Universe

Part of your spiritual freedom is for you to go to the edge of the universe.

Acknowledging your 8th Chakra, bring your attention be up to the top corner of the room behind you and wave to your body from there.

Let your attention be above the building, step up above the planet to the edge of the atmosphere. Step out near the moon and get a sense of that further and further distance. Let yourself be at the edge of the solar system, then at the edge of the galaxy and finally, spiritually be at the edge of the universe.

Notice what this feels like for you right now. Notice the space you have as a spirit at the edge of the universe.

Visualize a rose out at the edge of the universe that represents your spiritual freedom. *What is your energy level like (color) at the edge of the Universe*? (It might be a little different from this different perspective.)

Begin matching that color and vibrating at your spiritual freedom color.

Own your spiritual freedom. Take it, have it, be it! Being at your spiritual freedom vibration let's you take your steps on your path, at that vibration.

Now begin moving back towards your body from the edge of the universe, to the edge of the galaxy, to the edge of the solar system, near the moon, to the edge of the atmosphere – still vibrating at your own spiritual freedom.

Be above the building, be at the corner of the room and from there say hello to your body once again.

Ask yourself, *"what it would look like to bring that into the body"*

Can you bring that *'spiritual freedom'* with you to your body? If so, as you step back into the body, bring with you whatever level of spiritual freedom body is ready to accept.

Send a *'golden hello'* right down into the middle of your head from the corner of the room, saying *'hello'* until you get a sense there is a clear connection and follow one of those *'hellos'* right into the center of your head.

Notice what it's like to come into your body on a *'hello'*. Often we come into the body on a demand or an expectation.

Amirah Hall

Ground yourself as your re-center into your body. Notice your crown chakra and let it start to vibrate at whatever sense of spiritual freedom you brought with you from the edge of the universe.

I hope for nothing. I fear nothing. I am free."

Nikos Kazantzakis

Life Goals

What are the most important goals that you have for your life? To enjoy living your life? Being happy, healthy and able to pursue ideals and passions?

Being at your *'spiritual freedom'* vibration, visualize a rose for your life goals. What would be the effect on the pursuit of those goals if you were vibrating at your own *'spiritual freedom'*?

Would that change anything about your pursuit of your goals? Notice if there are any changes in your rose. *Does it open, close, grow etc.?* Explode your rose.

The word 'enlightenment' conjures up the idea of some superhuman accomplishment, and the ego likes to keep it that way, but it is simply your natural state of felt oneness with Being. It is a state of connectedness with something immeasurable and indestructible, something that, almost paradoxically, is essentially you and yet is much greater than you. It is finding your true nature beyond name and form."

Eckhart Tolle

Higher Self

Your Higher Self is you -- the real you. Because it's YOU, it knows you intimately more than even the angels or your spirit guides. It encompasses your soul consciousness. The part of you that is living with a body is just a projection of the consciousness of your Higher Self. It's a more complete version of you and is aware of the plan you made for yourself before you incarnated into this life. Your instruction manual for your life is stored here therefore connecting to it gives you key information about why you're here and where you should be going next, and with whom you should be going there.

> Imagine stepping up and being in your 8th Chakra and allow your attention to be with that Higher Self part of you.
>
> From there say 'hello' (connect or acknowledge) to the Supreme Being, the Source of ALL. Connect with God!
>
> Imagine opening up a dialogue with yourself and the Supreme Being and start to dialogue about *'what are you here for in this lifetime?'* What are you here to *'be, do or have'*?
>
> You may have thoughts come into your mind. If hearing isn't your thing, imagine yourself sitting on a bench inside a beautiful park and invite the Creator to sit down next to you. Notice any feelings or thoughts that come to your mind.

What light is to the eyes - what air is to the lungs - what love is to the heart, liberty is to the soul of man."

Robert Green Ingersoll

Spiritual Goals

> It's easy to forget that there are parts of your life where faith has turned to certainty, where you don't have to cling to faith anymore. There are things you just know. All through your life you'll have times where it is easy to remember your faith, and all the things you know deep in your soul. You'll also have times when you forget your faith and the things you know for sure.
>
> Whichever place you're in today. Know that the faith you have right now is enough. It will grow.
>
> Hold onto it, take care of it, and believe it!

You probably have tons of goals that quickly come to mind. You probably have career goals perhaps with your eye on that raise or promotion you may have or educational goals such as going back to school or earning a degree. No doubt you have relationship goals, maybe to find a relationship, to avoid them all together or to strengthen the one you have. You probably even have mundane goals like clearing clutter in your bedroom closet or scouring the oven.

Have you ever thought about 'spiritual goals'? They might include taking a spiritual retreat or spending a week in silence. Perhaps experiencing complete bliss or finding inner peace! Or, developing extraordinary spiritual abilities and/ or living in alignment with spiritual values including forgiveness, compassion, love and gratitude. They could even include healing your past or learning to live in the *'now'*.

> *What are some of your 'spiritual goals'?*
>
> Visualize a rose that represents your *'spiritual goals'*. It's ok if you can't articulate them all. Consider what colors you see or sensations you receive.

There are no right or wrong answers. The idea is just for you to open up to and communicate with the Higher Self part of you and the Supreme Being. Whatever that is for you is perfectly fine. You might consider what you would like to tell either your Higher Self or the Supreme Being.

> *Ask your Higher Self or the Supreme Being if there is a message for you.* Listen for either an answer or dialogue. You might consider it in the form of a rose or a symbol so you can see it. Come back into the center of your head and bring that answer into the 7th Chakra. Bring that rose with the answers into your body. Replenish your aura with Golden Suns.
>
> Another way to communicate with the Supreme Being or your Higher Self is to write a letter about what you want to communicate. This is totally private and just for you. It could be a wish list for you or anything that you want to communicate to yourself or bring into your life. You are here to express whatever occurs to you. A big part of your *'spiritual freedom'* includes being able to communicate to the Supreme Being with no intermediaries.
>
> Visualize a rose for what you just wrote. Creating communication with the Supreme Being, notice what that looks like to you in that rose.
>
> *Was there any energy on that for you? Were you unsure of what to say? Is it hard to do? What did you want/expect from this communication?*
>
> Begin draining any energy off the communication space by grounding the rose.
>
> Imagine any energy concerning the writing of your communication being released from the rose.

> Bring the color of your *'spiritual freedom'* into the rose. Own that rose and that communication with yourself. You can express and pursue it any way you desire. Own that communication and the freedom to express, bringing the rose into your space once it is clear and let yourself have that internally.

Freedom is from within."

Frank Lloyd Wright

Connecting to Source Raises Your Vibration

If all existence is energy and energy is inherently vibrational, it's logical that everything in existence is vibrating at one rate or another. In the case of human beings, it's our emotions that tell us how we are vibrating.

When we feel good, we vibrate at a high rate as we are in the flow of life, aligned with Source Energy. When we experience emotions that make us feel stuck, limited, fearful etc., we are vibrating at a low rate or outside the natural flow of Source. Therefore, raising and aligning our vibration to the Creator / Source of All is the way by which we can restore our balance and wellbeing. And, according to the Universal Law of Attraction and The Law of Vibration, we attract and manifest what is matching our current frequency.

If we are vibrating in a place of **fear, anger or guilt**, we will attract and manifest like individuals and circumstances that are vibrating in fear, anger or guilt. Similarly, if we are vibrating in a place of **joy, love and freedom**, we will also manifest our vibrational match.

> Acknowledging yourself and God within you, allow your 7th Chakra to vibrate at *'spiritual freedom'* allowing your communication with Higher Self and the Supreme Being to be open and accessible. Visualize that *'spiritual freedom'* color at the 7th Chakra.
>
> Visualize a rose that represents your goals for this lifetime.
>
> Grounding this energetic space of your *'spiritual freedom and communication'* with the Supreme Being, drain any obstacles that might prevent you from having that. Imagine bringing that rose into your aura and 'have' that in the body in the PRESENT time.
>
> Acknowledge yourself in that *'freedom and spiritual wellness'* vibration. Replenish yourself with a Golden Sun, giving yourself validation for your wellness and your spiritual communication with yourself and the Universe.

Congratulations in taking this BIG step in owning your space for spiritual wellness.

The most important kind of freedom is to be what you really are. You trade in your reality for a role. You give up your ability to feel, and in exchange, put on a mask."

Jim Morrison

Spiritual Mission Statement

What is your Mission Statement or Vision Statement for the 8th Chakra?

For example, your statement could be:

> *"I am divinely connected!"*
> *"I have spiritual freedom and claim my life goals!"*
> *"I am aligned with Source and have open, clear guidance always."*

Add this 8th Chakra Mission Statement to the previous 7 Chakras Personal Mission Statements in Chapter 24.

CONGRATULATIONS!!!
YOU HAVE NOW COMPLETED PERSONAL MISSION STATEMENT FOR LIVING IN ALIGNMENT.

Your work is to discover your work and then, with all your heart, to give it to yourself."

Buddha

"I completed Amirah's Miracle Mastery Mentoring program and learned to apply the Quantum Energy Tools everyday in my life. All I can say is that, I don't recognize myself as I'm really very different now. Life has become much easier; things manifest much quicker for me. My clairvoyance is stronger and I trust my intuition. I recently returned from a trip from Katmandu, Nepal where I met another healer who 'clairvoyantly' saw Amirah's energy in my aura. He said to me, "This blonde lady you are working with, she is doing very well with you. All your chakras are balanced. They are nice and clean and you are very aligned." I didn't say anything about her and was shocked that he saw her work yet didn't know anything about her.

So many changes have occurred for me including closing a floundering business I struggled with for five years as I'm moving onto bigger and better things. That's all because of her. I manifested many, many things that I want to happen and the Universe is surely bringing them closer into reality. Amirah guided me every step of the way – it's as if she opened the lock to my self-imposed prison cell. That was definitely validated by the Nepalese healer who said, "I was in the forest and the blonde lady was guiding me out of the forest."

Annie, Dubai, UAE

Chapter 22 - Practice Guidelines

Practice the following tools this week:

1. Grounding – Quantum Energy Tool #1
2. Center of Head – Quantum Energy Tool #2
3. Replenishing – Quantum Energy Tool #3
4. Run Earth and Cosmic Energy – Quantum Energy Tool #7
5. Set 8th Chakra to Spiritual Freedom
6. Match Spiritual Freedom Vibration at the Edge of The Universe
7. Align With Spiritual Goals
8. Connecting To Source of All
9. Set 8th Chakra Spiritual Mission Statement

GOALS AND HEALING WORKSHEET

WELLNESS COLOR _____

Physical Goal _____

Mental Goal _____

Emotional Goal _____

Spiritual Goal _____

MISSION STATEMENT

_____

WHAT ARE YOU NOTICING DIFFERENT?

_____

_____

WHAT ENERGIES **SUPPORT** YOU? (Colors, memories, beliefs, thoughts)

_____

_____

OTHER

_____

_____

Chapter

23

Conclusion

Now what?

Consciously creating your desires is the ultimate goal of this book. Manifesting Miracles 101, The Art of Being in The Flow, is your guidebook for continuing practice, expanding self-expression and manifesting more than you can comprehend today. Honestly speaking, there's never an ending.

Applying the principles, lessons and practices learned within these chapters, brings you to a new level of awareness of yourself and the world around you. This work continues ... even with stop and start practices you will realize that there's no going back to the old you. In each chapter, you've read some of the many testimonials shared by students over the years of how their lives have changed by diligently applying the techniques and tools outlined in this book. Here's more **Testimonials** (http://bit.ly/29XgUvw) on what you can expect in working with these powerful **Quantum Energy Tools** (http://bit.ly/29WqnQk).

You have set in motion new patterns of energy that are creating something new for you. *How deep do you want to go down the rabbit hole?* Certainly if taking your manifesting abilities to the next level, it's can be expedited through practice, practice and more practice of being aware of your energy and influences upon it.

'*Consciously creating*' is our goal here together. To support you on your path, additional Resources offer you ongoing support you on your journey of Manifesting Miracles as you explore and excel in The Art of Being in the Flow.

I invite you to explore a complimentary, thirty-minute Energy Evaluation Session (http://bit.ly/2ais7ZQ) and opportunity to discuss any of your '*life concerns*' and/or '*energy imbalances*'.

GET YOUR FREE SESSION

http://bit.ly/2ais7ZQ

I sincerely thank you for visiting www.Amazon.com and kindly leave your book review as it greatly improves this books exposure and increases Amazon ranking.

To your many, magical miracle moments! And, many blessings of abundant creations.

24

Personal Mission Statement

What is your OVERALL goal for <u>Manifesting Miracles 101</u>*?*

_____

_____

1ST CHAKRA MISSION STATEMENT

_____

2ND CHAKRA MISSION STATEMENT

_____

3RD CHAKRA MISSION STATEMENT

_____

4TH CHAKRA MISSION STATEMENT

_____

5TH CHAKRA MISSION STATEMENT

_____

6TH CHAKRA MISSION STATEMENT

_____

7TH CHAKRA MISSION STATEMENT

_____

8TH CHAKRA MISSION STATEMENT

_____

Resources

Here are some videos to support you on your journey of Manifesting Miracles as you explore and excel in The Art of Being in the Flow.

Quantum Energy Tools

Grounding Guided Meditation - Quantum Energy Tool #1
http://bit.ly/29QepYP

Creating Clarity Guided Meditation - Quantum Energy Tool #2
http://bit.ly/2ab0oc6

Replenishing Guided Meditation - Quantum Energy Tool #3
http://bit.ly/2a0NtJZ

Setting Healthy Boundaries - Quantum Energy Tool #4
http://bit.ly/2ae7H1b

Healing Magic Wand - Quantum Energy Tool #5
http://bit.ly/2anilA6

Healing With Color - Quantum Energy Tool #6
http://bit.ly/2aqzQDm

Stress Buster Guided Meditation - Quantum Energy Tool #7
http://bit.ly/2awq1lf

Mockups Guided Meditation - http://bit.ly/29Vd5FG

Having And Receiving Gauge - http://bit.ly/29VpKN0

Video List

Clearing Chaos Making Miracles Guided Meditation - http://bit.ly/2ak1uQV

Chakra Clearing Guided Meditation - http://bit.ly/2aFlvDA

Chakra Cleansing Guided Meditation - http://bit.ly/2aqyOr3

Manifesting Money Miracles - https://youtu.be/xd2ahM72I04

Clarity Guided Meditation - https://youtu.be/3l44QU6dj_k

Powerful Nano Frequency DNA & Light Activation - http://bit.ly/2aJnPb0

Activating Miracles Guided Meditation - http://bit.ly/2a22ZVp

Foreign Energies, Beings and Entities Affecting Your Energy
http://bit.ly/2a0RnCT

How To Clear Competition Energy & Enhance Authenticity
http://bit.ly/29QfPmo

How to Collect Your Energy and Be More Present - http://bit.ly/2awqXq2

How to Protect Yourself & Stop Absorbing Other People's Energy
http://bit.ly/2aitl7r

Law of Attraction SECRET ENERGY TOOL - http://bit.ly/2aitFDa

What I Learned From My Near-Death Experience - http://bit.ly/2arppgC

Other Transformational Programs

Live With Your Light On Mentoring - http://bit.ly/2ab1CEa

LOVE UP Your Life - http://bit.ly/2ae8dfJ

Miracle Mastery Mentoring - http://bit.ly/2aitwiO

Contact Amirah - http://bit.ly/29QfKPl

Subscribe to our Community Mailing List – Receive Special Offers, Book Discounts, Updates and New (http://www.amirahhall.com/blog)

About The Author

Amirah Hall, MSc, BA, is a globally recognized mind body health and wellness expert, Reiki Master, Quantum Energy expert, peak performance trainer, meditation teacher and author of <u>WAKE UP Shift Happens</u>, <u>LOVE UP Your Life: 10 Secret Quick & Easy Steps Using The Science of Attraction Principles</u> and <u>Manifesting Miracles 101: The Art of Being in The Flow</u>. She is often referred to as the Miracle Mentor and a SoulMystic and can be heard on many guided meditations, available on YouTube.com/amirahhall1 and on amirahhall.com.

Amirah Hall has also been a featured expert on Dubai One TV, NBC 7, San Diego Business Journal, Sharjah University, UAE and Ritz Carlton Wellness Week, UAE. Amirah Hall has also been a featured writer for various publications including Gulf News, The Light Connection and Vision Magazine.

She helps renew your life while experiencing more love, healing, happiness and success. Amirah Hall teaches you the practical, effortless and proven ways to experience healing and success as you create the life that you want.

Regardless of what you do as a living, Amirah Hall provides you with techniques that you can use to improve all areas of your life.

In her profession, Amirah Hall has touched the lives of many thousands of people worldwide including members of the Royal Family while living in Dubai for five years. When she is not mentoring and teaching about manifesting miracles, she travels, dances, meditates and enjoys healthy living. She will soothe your soul, mind and body into the perfect state of relaxation thereby uplifting your consciousness. She will indeed clear your negativity and fears while freeing you from impure and unhealthy energies.

SCHEDULE YOUR FREE SESSION

http://bit.ly/2ais7ZQ

60807506R00173

Made in the USA
Charleston, SC
06 September 2016